296.082
Ai 4   Aiken, Lisa.
            To be a Jewish woman.

296.082
Ai 4   Aiken, Lisa.
            To be a Jewish woman.

Temple Israel Library
Minneapolis, Minn.

———

Please sign your full name on the above card.

Return books promptly to the Library or Temple Office.

Fines will be charged for overdue books or for damage or loss of same.

TO BE A JEWISH WOMAN

Lisa Aiken

JASON ARONSON INC.
Northvale, New Jersey
London

Production Editor: Muriel Jorgensen

This book is set in 11-point Schneidler by Lind Graphics.

It was printed and bound by Haddon Craftsmen in Scranton, Pennsylvania.

Library of Congress Cataloging-in-Publication Data

Aiken, Lisa.
    To be a Jewish woman / by Lisa Aiken,
      p. cm.
    Includes bibliographical references and index.
    ISBN 0-87668-609-9
    1. Women in Judaism. 2. Women, Jewish – Religious life.
    3. Judaism – Essence, genius, nature. I. Title.
    BM729.W6A35 1992
    296′.082 – dc20
                                   91-31680

Manufactured in the United States of America. Jason Aronson Inc. offers books and cassettes. For information and catalog write to Jason Aronson Inc., 230 Livingston Street, Northvale, New Jersey 07647.

This book is dedicated to my parents,
Janet and Sidney Aiken—
May they be blessed with long and healthy lives—
and in memory of their parents,
Rose and Phillip Segall and Anna and Louis Aiken—
Peace be upon them

Contents

PART II RELATING TO PRAYER

Foreword

The general topic of Judaism and women is one to which I've dedicated considerable time in my lectures and writings. My grandfather, Rabbi Moshe Feinstein, זצ"ל, had believed that this would be a crucial issue of potential divisiveness between Jews, and I was thus instructed to dedicate considerable time to various facets of it.

The present book, which Dr. Aiken has written, is most engrossing and contains a wealth of information. I have reviewed the book thoroughly with her, and I recommend it to anyone who is searching for a greater understanding of the role women actually play, and theoretically should play, in Judaism. Even Torah scholars who have not devoted much time to researching these issues will find much of the information most illuminating and will be fascinated by this almost encyclopedic book.

Dr. Aiken is to be commended for having the courage and determination to author and publish this work. May God grant her both professional and personal success and happiness.

Rabbi Mordecai Tendler
Bais Knesses of New Hempstead
19 Tamuz 5751

Preface

In March 1988, I was presented with a wonderful opportunity. I was invited by the Union of Orthodox Jewish Congregations of America (O.U.) to be a scholar-in-residence at a synagogue in Sacramento, California. As such, I was asked to speak about topics relating to Jewish women and how they can find meaning in life through Judaism. Although I had spoken at various college campuses in 1980 about similar issues, the O.U. invitation was the first to come from a national, large-scale organization. After witnessing the audience's enthusiasm for the presentations, I felt that I had a mission to accomplish. That mission was to convey these ideas to audiences on a larger scale. I decided that the best way to do this was to write a book that addressed Jewish women's issues from a traditional perspective.

This book began as a compilation of many lectures I gave throughout the United States from 1988 to 1990, most of which were given to people with limited knowledge about Judaism. Ultimately, Arthur Kurzweil convinced me that a comprehensive book on women's issues was necessary. Therefore, the original manuscript was expanded to include a wide range of topics and included input from many Jewish women.

On my lecture tours, the audiences whom I address are usually curious about my Jewish background. They typically assume that I was the beneficiary of an extensive formal Jewish education and that I came from an Orthodox Jewish home. In fact, neither is true. Due to the efforts of my parents, I attended a Jewish day school for six years, where one of my teachers was a Torah-observant Jew. My exposure there to Mrs. Rivka Shapiro was the catalyst for my beginning the process of becoming an observant Jewess at the age of 8.

I attended public schools from the age of 12. By the time I entered college in the early seventies, my interest in feminism was quite strong. The more I studied world history and sexual politics, the more I was distressed by how various religions and secular societies have treated women. At the same time, I struggled to find a niche for myself within an Orthodox community. This struggle included my engaging in many unorthodox practices, such as leading women's *minyans,* performing what are traditionally men's rituals in group settings, and trying to encourage observant Jews to become more open to feminist ideas.

After searching for an authentic expression of Judaism for many years, I discovered that observant Judaism was a complete and satisfying system in its own right. However, it required years of intensive study, investigation, introspection, and honesty to appreciate how fulfilling it could be intellectually, emotionally, and spiritually. My search involved tremendous effort as I looked for, and discovered, role models who lived and practiced authentic Judaism. In the process, I learned that the status, prestige, and power that Jews often seek from the world at large are paralleled by or exceeded by what observant Jewish women have obtained. These women derive their self-esteem from having been created in the image of God and knowing that they have a vital role to fulfill in this world.

During the past 15 years, I have tried unsuccessfully to find more than a handful of books written by knowledgeable, observant Jewish women about topics relevant to women. Precious little has been written about how a modern Jewish woman can find a place for herself in traditional Judaism, especially if she is not married or does not have children. Almost all of the books that address women's issues in Judaism have been written by men or by nonobservant women. Most of the books written by men are written from a male perspective, with an analytical style that is more appropriate for talmudic study than for dealing with the dilemmas and emotions concerning observant Jewish women.

The overwhelming majority of the other books that address Jewish women's issues have been written by women who have axes to grind about what they perceive are antifeminine biases in a male-dominated religion. These authors have rarely researched primary sources, and they have little appreciation for the concept of divine revelation of the Torah, its inviolability, and the integrity of traditional textual and legal interpretation. These books tend to be emotional diatribes against traditional Judaism, with recommendations for reform.

Over my two-decade-long quest for an authentic expression of Jewish femininity, I have been privileged to have met a number of remarkable women who excel in every aspect of Jewish womanhood. They exemplify scholarship, self-development, true femininity, charity in every sense of the word, and excellence in raising children; they are true "women of valor." They have greatly inspired women like myself to learn more about Judaism and to live it in an authentic way.

It is impossible to appreciate traditional Judaism by merely studying it intellectually. It must be experienced from within and appreciated as a total way of life in order for it to feel gratifying. It is difficult to experience the self-esteem that Judaism instills in women when one only reads about Judaism in books or views Judaism from a distance.

It is my hope that this book will fill a gap in the lack of traditionally oriented books about issues that interest Jewish women. I hope that women and men alike will be inspired by the ideas that will be presented and that the ideas will help them better appreciate the richness and complexity of traditional Judaism. Perhaps it will also serve as an impetus for some readers to experience the treasures of traditional Judaism from within a community.

Many readers may hope that this book will address certain emotional voids. Bringing this book to fruition addressed a certain emotional void for me and is the culmination of a dream. That dream was to be able to learn Torah and to teach it to others who wish to know more about it. I am very grateful to all who made this dream a reality.

Tammuz 5751

Acknowledgments

This book is drawn from traditional Jewish sources and is rarely original. In some cases the contents are largely contributed by others. Several chapters contain ideas formulated by and conveyed most clearly to me by Mrs. Tzippora Heller. She has served as my primary role model of the ideal Jewish woman and has had a profound influence on my thinking about Judaism. I am indebted to her for her graciousness in sharing her knowledge with me, as well as for her exemplification of what a Jewish woman *par excellence* can be.

I am thankful to Mrs. Feige Twerski for supplying me with the ideas for the chapter on the blessing, "Who Has Not Made Me a Woman," and for her assistance in serving as an outside reader. Mrs. Leah Kohn provided much of the material for "Contributions of Sarah to the Jewish People." Both of these women, along with Mrs. Heller, are examples of "Women as Redeemers of the Jewish People."

I would like to thank Rabbi Yitzchok Kirzner for his contributions to the chapters on prayer. His ongoing personal influence and assistance have greatly influenced my synthesis of Judaism with the rest of my life. He, Rabbi Yehoshua Leiman, and Sholly Fisch have given generously of their time as outside readers for this book.

I am especially thankful to Dr. Henry Azrikan, without whose efforts this book would never have been written. He, along with Rabbis Yitzchok Rosenberg and Pinchas Stolper, have given me their unwavering support in promoting my public speaking, which served as the basis for this book.

Finally, I cannot adequately express my gratitude to Rabbi Mordecai Tendler for his involvement in reviewing and improving the original manuscript of this book. His conscientiousness in scrutinizing every line, locating obscure references, clarifying and correcting ideas, and lending his support to this project has been extraordinary. He devoted more hours of his precious time to this endeavor than either of us initially thought would be necessary, let alone possible. I thank him from the bottom of my heart.

Introduction

We live in a society of instant gratification, where hard work and waiting often seem anachronistic. FAX machines, electronics, and computer networks allow people to communicate in seconds that which formerly required weeks or months to convey. Microwave ovens, instant replays, and express mail reinforce the mentality that if anything is worth having, it should be attainable immediately. When life feels painful or distressing, having a drink, taking drugs, or paying money to remove the discomfort are often preferred methods of reinstating one's equilibrium. In contemporary times, if people have the opportunity to take the fast, painless track in life, they often opt for it at the expense of their personal development.

Secular democratic societies promote the importance of having rights. Everybody is entitled to various rights, including the right to pursue instant happiness however one wishes, as long as no one gets terribly hurt in the process.

In many ways, it is hard for Torah-observant Judaism to compete with the secular world on the secular world's terms. Traditional Judaism is based on the belief that some 3,300 years ago, God revealed His will to the world when He gave the Torah to the Jewish people. The Jews pledged that they would faithfully observe the structured and restrictive life-style that God commanded them to keep forever. This code of law was designed to bring holiness into the world and to teach us how to channel our animalistic and egotistical drives in ways that will serve spiritual goals. Rather than encouraging us to be slaves to our drives, it teaches us how to elevate them by being servants of God.

Observant Judaism promises no instant gratification, no easy highs, no guaranteed emotional or financial outcomes. Nor does it teach that we are entitled to rights simply by virtue of being alive. We have rights because we were created in the image of God and have accepted His moral obligations upon ourselves.

Authentic Judaism challenges us to direct our material, psychological, and sensual drives in ways that allow us to grow spiritually in the process. This involves applying moral limits to our desires in ways that we would not ordinarily choose to be restricted. Because spiritual growth is a process that is intended to occur over a lifetime, integrating Judaism into our lives does not result in instantaneously feeling gratified or fulfilled. Appreciating true spirituality requires a great deal of effort and hard work, because it necessitates our giving up what comes most naturally to us and applying tremendous discipline to all areas of our lives. Therefore, in order for us to appreciate what Judaism offers, we can't gauge it by how it makes us feel in the short run.

WHAT IS TORAH-OBSERVANT JUDAISM?

Torah-observant Judaism is predicated on the belief that God created the world in order to give of His goodness to people. He wanted us to derive maximal pleasure from the world but without our feeling like freeloaders who only take from a world where everything is provided for us. People who only take, and who serve no useful purpose, do not feel very good about themselves. Therefore, God taught us how we can earn our keep and thereby maintain our self-esteem. We accomplish both of these objectives by observing His will as it is expressed in the Torah. The Torah commands us how to act in order to do what our Creator wants, thereby bringing His goals for the world to fruition.

If we were naturally attuned to wanting to do exactly what God asks of us, He would not have needed to command us to do various things—we would naturally fulfill His desires. Obviously, we are commanded to engage in behaviors that initially feel foreign to us, or to refrain from engaging in certain acts that we would otherwise wish to pursue. The tension that this creates exemplifies how spiritual and religious refinement necessarily makes us uncomfortable as we make what is foreign feel familiar. We engage in a lifetime process of spiritual growth by over-coming challenges that entail many falls and failures, discomforts and frustrations. Yet in the end, we hopefully evolve as people who have self-esteem and are competent and mature.

We Jews must be suspicious of any quick spiritual fixes. We must also be wary of trading in the difficult process of spiritual growth for the ease of comfort and familiarity. Most people resist change. We automatically seek comfort in what is familiar and emotionally reassuring to us. Unfortunately, if we primarily emphasize feeling comfortable above all else, we can undermine our ability to realize our true spiritual potentials.

If we are willing to accept these challenges, instead of feeling overwhelmed by our discomfort, we can reach tremendous spiritual heights along the journey.

Many Jews want to express their Judaism only in ways that feel good or comfortable. By equating "religious" with "emotionally gratifying," people define "religious experiences" very subjectively. For one person, watching a beautiful sunset is a "religious" experience. For another, being under the influence of mind-altering drugs is "religious." For yet a third person, being in the company of family or friends feels "religious."

For Jews, a truly religious experience is one in which we connect ourselves to God, based on how He wants us to relate to Him. A truly spiritual experience for us can only be in the context of doing His will as He revealed it to us in the Torah.

One of the major challenges that modern Jewish women face is how to feel good about ourselves as Jews while we are surrounded by secular influences that are at odds with Jewish values. The secular world primarily values us according to how visible we are, how much money or possessions we have, how much power we wield, and how many educational degrees we possess.

This challenge was highlighted to me when I had the following experience several years ago: I frequently hosted Sabbath guests in my home, few of whom I had met before they appeared at my door. When we would sit down to eat, the guests typically asked me about my various endeavors, and we had lively discussions about a wide range of topics. One week I was especially exhausted and had no energy to be a talkative hostess. I had spent so many hours treating patients, writing books, lecturing, and cooking for fourteen Sabbath guests that I was understandably fatigued. At dinner Friday night, my guests asked me what kind of work I did. I replied that I was a housewife. Consequently, no one spoke to me for the rest of the meal, except to ask me for a recipe for the dessert

I had made. At subsequent Sabbath meals, I would tell guests the same thing whenever I was too tired to verbally entertain them. The results were uniformly the same. The guests invariably directed their attention to others at the table.

Another example of how accustomed secular people are to relating to others according to their profession or formal education is as follows: When I lecture about topics of Jewish interest, my arrival is normally announced by brochures that emphasize my professional accomplishments, even though they are largely irrelevant to my lectures. Unfortunately, if the advertisements were to emphasize my own personal endeavors to advance my spiritual growth, it is questionable if anyone would show up to hear me.

In general, secular values are at odds with Jewish ones. Judaism values humility, which in secular terms is akin to being a "wimp." Judaism values modesty, which is erroneously viewed as lacking self-esteem. It also values family development and spiritual nurturing over material acquisitions, and self-control more than ostentation. Yet, it is difficult to find these Jewish values fulfilling when we are raised on American dreams. Today's Jewish woman may feel that functioning in a domestic role is akin to sacrificing her identity. Other women sacrifice their femininity so that they can achieve success by internalizing the standards of a male-dominated professional or business world.

Once women have internalized this stress on "equality," meaning that women should take on male responsibilities (as well as their own), authentic Jewish perspectives seem anachronistic. Torah-observant Judaism does not believe that men and women should be equally visible in public, identically educated, or fill identical roles. Women who value having male "rights" often feel that traditional Judaism strips them of their validity, recognition, self-esteem, and power.

Some women believe that they can only get spiritual fulfillment from experiences that are in public view and publicly demonstrate that they are on par with men. When women observe a law here and a ritual there, rather than immersing themselves in a totally observant way of life, certain laws also seem to disenfranchise them. It must be stressed that women's roles and obligations were never meant to be observed in a piecemeal way, and they cannot be appreciated in bits and pieces. Doing so is akin to taking a small patch from a huge mosaic and questioning why those specific pieces were included.

Judaism is, and was always meant to be, a total way of life. It can only be truly appreciated when it is experienced within the totality of its system. Reacting emotionally to women's commandments as seen individually, or to women's exclusion from certain commandments that pertain to men, is not a useful way of appraising the validity of observant Judaism. People should not identify "problematic" parts of Judaism divorced from the whole, question their relevance for women, and dismiss them because they are not emotionally appealing.

It would be reasonable to assume that women who limit their religious expression primarily to synagogue worship will feel like second-class Jews unless they participate in those services' rituals. On the other hand, traditional Judaism pervades every aspect of life, only a small part of which pertains to the synagogue. As such an all-encompassing system, it recognizes women's importance and has means built into it that develop their self-esteem. One of the primary ways that it does this is by emphasizing the essential and unique contributions that women make and by highlighting their efforts, which the world requires in order to achieve perfection.

People often expect observant Judaism to provide the emotional nurturing to make up for deprivations in other parts of their lives. Since women in the secular world have long been devalued, they often want Judaism to make up for the happiness and secular status that they have been denied for so long. Judaism can enable people to feel self-worth and happiness, but not necessarily by providing what secular society values. It takes patience and study to discover how Judaism validates our identities, feelings, and self-worth. We must also be willing to abandon our need for Judaism to validate us on our terms; rather, we must find validation in Judaism's terms.

To be intellectually honest, we must pursue the truth, even when continuing along familiar paths might feel more comfortable. We should ask if traditional Judaism can help us develop our spiritual potentials and not concern ourselves with whether it feels easy.

No one would expect to appreciate the genius of people like Beethoven, Michelangelo, or Einstein without intensively studying their works. Similarly, it takes years of studying, performing Jewish rituals, being part of an observant community, and struggling in order to appreciate how authentic Judaism provides women with a vehicle for true spiritual development and expression.

THE JEWISH CONCEPT OF FREEDOM

How can a modern woman find a place for herself within the framework of observant Judaism? A major component of secular freedom is the

ability to make personal, social, political, and financial choices. These
choices are determined by one's emotions and intellect, social norms,
and cultural factors. Frequently, this means that fulfilling one's personal desires becomes a primary goal in life.

Judaism views freedom differently. Our first experience with
freedom was when God liberated the Israelites from the slavery of
Egyptian overlords. As slaves, we were not the masters of our bodies,
possessions (objects), or time.

When we were freed at the time of the Exodus, God brought us
through four stages of redemption: our physical departure from the
land of Egypt; our salvation from Egyptian oppression outside of the
land of Egypt; our redemption from the physical deprivation and
material poverty of slavery, which also allowed us to make free
choices; and God's taking us as His special nation when He gave us,
and we accepted, the Torah.[1]

Our sages tell us that if God had only liberated us from the prison
conditions of Egypt, allowing us to have physical well-being, this
would have been valuable in and of itself. Had we only been rescued
from the mental and emotional persecution by the Egyptians, this
would have been valuable in its own right. By contrast, the third stage
of redemption gave us the ability to make free choices, but this was not
valuable in its own right.

Freedom of choice is only worthwhile when it is followed by the
fourth stage – our willingness to act according to God's will, as it is
expressed in the Torah. Exercising free will for its own sake has no
value to the Jew.

Freedom from subjugation by mortals is only important if it is
replaced by something greater. The "something greater" is gaining
freedom from human beings in order to be servants of God. Gaining
freedom from people only in order to serve ourselves, to be slaves to our
sensual, material, and egotistical drives, is not freedom. Achieving
freedom from a human master in order to have the opportunity to
achieve greater worldly pleasure is not valuable as an end in itself. It is
simply exchanging the limitations set by others for those dictated by
our inner drives.

There is no true freedom from either of these masters unless we
accept the Torah. The Torah teaches us how to take our physical,
intellectual, spiritual, and emotional drives, and channel them in a way
that we can uplift ourselves beyond the confines of our physical beings.
Unless we exchange the servitude of mortal limitations for connection
to the infinity of God, we are not liberated.

All physical endeavors are doomed to be relegated to oblivion when we die or over the course of history. The only way that we can transcend the finitude of the physical and mortal world is by attaching ourselves to God, who is infinite and immortal. When we infuse our actions and possessions with holiness, we invest them with infinite meaning and immortality. We make our lives holy by bringing God into our daily actions and thoughts.

A totally free world is full of confusion and illusions. A world that is free of constraints does not necessarily pave the way for our discovering our true selves or for finding true meaning in life. By limiting some of our freedoms, Judaism gives us the benefits of structure, clarity, and goal direction.

For a Jew, freedom is not the ultimate goal in life. A person whose life is unbound by the structure and constraints of Torah can be analogized to a violin. When the strings of the violin are not yet bound, they are free. However, it is only after the strings are bound that they can make beautiful music. Similarly, it is only when we bind ourselves to Torah that our souls are free to sing their songs.

When we accept the structure and constraints of a Torah way of life, we have a framework within which we can choose meaningful lives.

THE MODERN JEWISH WOMAN

Can a modern woman find satisfaction in observant Judaism? If her goal is to make unencumbered choices about her body, her material wants, and how she spends her time and energies, then she will not find satisfaction in observant Judaism. For observant Jews, our bodies and possessions are gifts loaned to us by God, and we are supposed to use them according to the owner's manual that is set down in the Torah.

On the other hand, if a woman chooses to live a way of life that is governed by Torah, she will be able to actualize herself. She can develop the physical, emotional, intellectual, and spiritual wherewithal to transcend the material and physical world. She can find ultimate meaning in life, along with an inner sense of satisfaction, dynamism, and self-esteem.

I

The Sources

1

Traditional Biblical Interpretation

In order to embark on our journey of understanding Jewish perspectives about women, we need to understand biblical verses that are relevant to the topics at hand. Jewish belief and practice is largely based on the Five Books of Moses (also known as the *Chumash,* or the Written Law), and their elucidation through homiletical explanations *(Midrash)* and the Oral Law (known as the Talmud). The *Midrash* and Oral Law were conveyed by God to Moses when He explained the Torah to him on Mount Sinai some 3,300 years ago.

The *Chumash* is the word of God, given as an instruction to humanity as to how He wants people to live. It was written in Hebrew and cannot be understood without the Oral Law and the *Midrash.* This is because God wanted the *Chumash* to be a "shorthand" expression of His will, which would require interaction with a spiritual mentor in order to understand it. Our spiritual mentors learned the Talmud and *Midrash* from their teachers, who ultimately traced their connections back to Moses himself. In this way, the oral traditions were faithfully transmitted from one generation to the next from the time the Torah was given.

The Torah was never intended to be a mere history or legal textbook. It was meant to teach us how to live. What better way to insure this than by writing it in a manner that requires explanation by religious

3

mentors and teachers who live what they have learned, and who transmit a moral life-style along with imparting technical knowledge.

Not only was the *Chumash* generally written in a style that required explanation via the Talmud and *Midrash,* but the meanings of the words and the verses themselves cannot be understood from the written text alone. Biblical Hebrew is a very precise language, with every letter and word in the *Chumash* deliberately chosen by God to convey certain meanings. No word or letter is superfluous or written by mistake. Therefore, when a given word appears in the text instead of its synonym, or when a phrase uses more words than are absolutely necessary to convey an idea, their significance requires explanation.

Since biblical Hebrew is so precise, appellations of people and things are neither accidental nor haphazard. When the *Chumash* gives someone or something a name, it is not simply supplying us with a conventional way of referring to it. A name denotes the exact essence of that thing or person. Not only do Hebrew *words* give us information about the person or object in question, but so do the very structures of every Hebrew letter.

In part due to this precision, certain Hebrew terms have no English equivalents. This means that any translations will necessarily be inaccurate. For this reason, a proper understanding of biblical texts requires reading them in the original Hebrew with attention to their nuances.

Every word in the Torah is subject to analysis in order to understand its deeper meanings. However, we are not allowed to interpret these meanings willy-nilly. Rather, we have traditions and exegetical principles that guide us in understanding them. We also have commentators who have elaborated on many of these verses according to our traditions. Their ideas will frequently be presented throughout this book.

This book will present both facts and theories about men and women. Many of these theories are interpretations of Jewish laws or Torah verses that certain individuals have advanced, and are not necessarily undisputed. Rather, they are simply avenues by which some people attempt to understand the meanings of certain concepts or reasons for God's laws.

Some readers may find these theories disagreeable, and they should feel free to reject them. When this happens, they should not be deterred from appreciating the value of the factual presentations of Judaism, which are the major thrust of this book.

2

All about Eve — What Really Happened in the Garden of Eden

Most feminist literature views the biblical accounts of Creation as demonstrating Judaism's sexist views about women. In order to lay to rest the distorted ideas that have appeared in various books, this chapter will examine the biblical accounts of the creation of First Man and First Woman, how they came to sin in the Garden of Eden, and what ramifications these events have for us. By presenting the original text with traditional commentaries, this chapter will illustrate the tremendous potentials that Judaism believes women possess, while recognizing that both men and women can misdirect these potentials.

The traditional Jewish views of men and women are derived from the Creation narrative in the Book of Genesis.[1] Interpretations of this narrative were transmitted to us through oral traditions and by our sages. The creation of Adam and Eve is detailed in the Torah as follows:

> God created the man in His image, in the image of God He created him; male and female He created them. And God blessed them.[2]

When God created the world, He did so in order to give of His goodness to humanity. He wanted people to be partners with Him in creating and perfecting the world. That man was created "in the image of God" has been interpreted to mean that Adam was endowed with the

5

Godly potential of giving. One of God's distinctive qualities is that He is a total Giver. Being perfect, He gives, but never takes. Another Godly quality is the ability to exercise free will, which He also imparted to Adam. When Adam would choose to act in ways that were consistent with God's will, he would thereby express the divine image within himself.

Adam was the progenitor of all humans. He was created as a person who had within him all of the qualities and souls of every person who would ever exist. As such, God's plan for Adam was also His plan for all people who would ever live.

When the Torah refers to Adam in the above verse as "them," instead of as "him," some of our sages explain this to mean that Adam was a singular being who was dual-faceted *(du partzufeem)*.[3] He consisted of both a man and a woman joined together.[4]

Apart from his physical duality, he also had a passive side and an active side. In this state, Adam was totally self-sufficient and wanted to be the source of everything that he needed. (In keeping with this interpretation that the first person was originally created as a being with both male and female characteristics, Adam will be referred to in the neuter form here.)

> The Lord God formed the person (from) the dust of the ground, and He breathed into its nose a soul of life, and the person was a living creature.[5]
>
> And the Lord God took the person, and He placed it in the Garden of Eden, in order to work it and to guard it. And the Lord God commanded the person saying, "From every tree in the garden you may surely eat. And from the tree of knowledge of good and evil you should not eat from it, for in the day you eat of it you shall surely die."[6]

At this point in time, the first person is referred to by the Hebrew term *adam*. This is why, after it was divided into its male and female parts, the first man is called Adam in English. Adam derives from the Hebrew word *adamah*, which means earth.[7]

THE NATURE OF THE FIRST PERSON

The earth and everything in it were created to fit into a plan that God had for all of creation.[8] He wanted to give of His goodness to humanity because His nature is to give, but He did not want people to feel like freeloaders by having them take without doing anything to earn what they received.

This is one reason why God gave the first person a commandment to observe. By doing God's will, s/he would have earned the many gifts God had already bestowed on him/her. It would also have had a feeling of self-esteem resulting from having made an effort that fulfilled God's desire for him/her.

The Name "Adam"

It has been suggested that Adam's body was created from the earth to teach us that just as the earth is passive, the earth within each of us should teach us to be passive enough to accept God's plan for creation.

A second interpretation as to why Adam was created from earth is because s/he was supposed to strive to fit into the plan which God had for the earth overall. That plan required people to observe His commandments.

The Hebrew name *Adam* can also be broken down into two parts — the letter *alef* and the word *dom*. This can be translated to mean, "the one (*alef*) who is silent (*dom*)." This alludes to the fact that Adam was created to accept God's plan for how the world was supposed to operate and for how people were supposed to act within it. In order to accept God's will, people would need to have a certain passivity to them.[9] The name Adam alludes to the fact that the first person had a side that was passive, receptive, and silent. This facet was necessary to allow human beings to subjugate their egos enough to accept God's plan for how they should best live.

God created Adam as a person whose every physical need was provided. In this state, s/he wanted to be the source of everything s/he needed. However, no one can realize his or her divine image if they devote themselves to supplying all of their daily needs on their own.[10]

MAN'S SELF-SUFFICIENCY IS NOT GOOD

Although Adam was physically self-sufficient, s/he had a deep emotional void. Since s/he was so unique, there was no one else in the world with whom s/he could have an equal relationship. God created Adam this way so that s/he would feel an existential loneliness. In this state of physical self-sufficiency, with no one to whom s/he could give, the Torah says:

The Lord God said, "It is not good, a person's being alone. I will make for the person a helper against itself."[11]

This verse has been interpreted to mean that as long as Adam was physically self-sufficient without having to work, God termed him/her "not good." This was because as long as Adam had everything provided, s/he was essentially a taker. In order to be able to imitate God, which is the greatest calling of a person, Adam would have to be a giver. In a state of self-sufficiency, s/he had no one to whom s/he could give. God did not want people to take from the world without contributing to its upkeep.[12]

And the Lord God had formed from the earth all of the animals of the field, and every fowl in the heavens. And He brought them to the person to see what s/he would call each (one). And whatever the person called each living being, that is its name. And the person gave names to every animal, and to every bird of the heavens, and to every animal of the field. And the person found no helper against itself.[13]

God showed Adam all of the animals so that s/he would see that all of the animals primarily related to their mates only out of sexual need.[14] S/he had to see that no animal could be a physical or spiritual partner nor an intellectual equal to it.[15] At this point, s/he realized that the kinds of relationships that animals had with their mates were not what s/he was seeking. S/he wanted a relationship of intimacy and caring. At this point, Adam felt terribly lonely because s/he lacked a soul-mate. It was only after Adam realized what was missing, and expressed this need to God, that He put Adam to sleep and created an appropriate partner for the first person.[16] This mate was designed to be an equal partner—someone to whom he could subsequently give and from whom he could receive.

At this point, the reader might be wondering how God could have created the first person in a manner that seemed to be flawed. He created Adam such that s/he needed to be improved upon later by being divided into male and female halves.

A possible explanation for this is that God deliberately created Adam in an imperfect state so that s/he would later recognize his/her shortcomings. Before having a partner, s/he felt deep loneliness and was unable to relate to or give to another person. S/he was unable to imitate God as long as s/he had no one to whom s/he could give.

God did not create people so that He could abandon them and leave them to their own devices. He wanted people to yearn for a relationship with Him. Since the human soul once experienced familiarity with God, it always yearns to reconnect with Him. However, we may not be aware of this yearning, or inner lack, until we discover that we need things that only God can provide. When Adam recognized that s/he was not truly self-sufficient, s/he was more motivated to seek out God as s/he strove to develop and grow.

God wanted the first person to realize that the presence of another person should not distract one from the mission of serving Him; rather, God wanted the first person to realize that a man and a woman should combine forces in a total union of body and soul in their emulation of Him.

This helps explain why God created humanity as sexual beings, not merely as emotional, social, or spiritual ones. He wanted humans to be able to combine together in a physical union as a poignant reminder that a total combination of physical and spiritual forces is necessary to truly serve God.

THE CREATION OF WOMAN

Once the Torah explains why it was necessary for woman to be created, it proceeds to tell us how this was accomplished:

> And the Lord God caused a deep sleep to fall on the person, and s/he slept. And God took one of the ribs and closed the flesh underneath.[17]

God created the woman by separating the first person into two component parts—a feminine side and a masculine side. By separating Adam into two facets, neither of which was totally self-sufficient, He created the opportunity for the man to contribute to the woman what she lacked and vice versa. In so doing, God formed a "helper against him." This means that the woman was created to be of equal value to the man being helped.[18]

> And God built the rib which He had taken from the man into a woman. And He brought her to the man.[19]

The Torah says that God created woman by "building" her from Adam's rib (*vayiven*). Some interpret this to mean that God endowed women with greater understanding and comprehension (*binah*) of people's emotions and of relationships than He gave men.[20] Both *binah* and *vayiven* come from the same root, meaning "within." Building is the act of taking something from within and expanding on it. Comprehension is gaining an understanding of something from within.

The fact that woman was "built" from an internal part of a person predisposes her to comprehending the entirety of situations from the "inside." That is, women can generally see a forest without first having to see all of the trees.

> And the man said, "This time it is bone of my bones, and flesh of my flesh. This (one) shall be called woman *(ishah)* because she was taken from man *(ish)*." Therefore, a man should leave his father and his mother and cleave unto his wife, and they shall be one flesh.[21]

When a man and his wife join with each other in the service of God, and in a sexual union, they can re-create the original state of the first person as a dual-faceted entity. Moreover, now that the first man and woman were separate beings, they could join in an act where each was a giver, instead of a taker.

This story teaches us that God intended men and women to be different from each other, and their differences are desirable. He created woman because there was something unique and essential about her, without which the world would be incomplete. The *Midrash* underscores this by saying that a man who has no wife lives without good, without help, without joy, without blessing, without atonement, without peace, without life, and is incomplete.[22]

Since women and men each need to contribute something essential to the world, erasing their differences is not good. A unisex world reinstates the very same self-sufficiency and emphasis on taking that God originally termed "not good."

Once the first woman was separated from her mate, they could form a complete human being only in partnership with each other.[23] Yet, as separate entities who can unite, men and women can create something that is greater than the sum of their parts, including the creation of a child.[24]

The existence of women also allows men to mature. Until a man marries, he directs his love to his parents.[25] This means that when he leaves his role as a child, he must also leave behind the type of relationship a child has with his parents.

Children are primarily takers, but this hopefully changes as they grow up. They must therefore leave behind their unique relationship with their parents in order to pursue a mature relationship that will develop their emotional and spiritual potentials. The ultimate relationship is when a man joins with his wife as a giver, not as a taker. At such a time, a man and woman can form a unit that is truly divine in nature.

The Critical Importance of Women

Since the first person was created in order to perfect the world by giving, its original state of self-sufficiency was not desirable. Therefore, it was necessary for God to separate the female from the male part in order for Adam to have an equal partner to whom he could give. Until woman was created, Adam was termed "not good."

Another reason why God created woman was so that Adam would not think himself a demigod by virtue of the fact that he was created qualitatively superior to all other creatures and was the sole creature on earth who had no mate. By recognizing that a woman can provide him with the love, companionship, and nurturing that he is unable to supply himself, man realizes that he has limitations. This is not the case with God, who has no limitations. He needs no one to supply Him with His emotional needs, since He has none.

FIRST WOMAN AS A HELPER

Woman was created to be man's equal partner.[26] Women possess their own intrinsic godliness, which they are supposed to use to help men recognize their strengths, as well as to overcome their limitations in spirituality, power, and control.

The fact that the first woman was created as a "helper against him" has various interpretations. One interpretation is that God will cause the following to occur: When a wife and husband strive toward spiritual growth, they will work in tandem. They will be in an antagonistic relationship, however, when they strive to accomplish goals that do not foster spiritual growth.[27] The fact that women were created to help men overcome their spiritual limitations implies that women can sometimes pick up shortcomings in their mates and can help them overcome them. The same is true for men being able to act as spiritual advisors to their wives.

God did not want man or any creatures to think that man was the ruler on earth the way that God is the ruler in Heaven.[28] This partly implies that a woman will want to help her mate overcome his spiritual limitations. In particular, her existence helps him conquer his arrogance and hubris by motivating him to channel his greatness toward the service of God, rather than serving his ego and personal desires. By creating the woman as a "helper against him," God endowed her with the ability to evaluate the correctness of her husband's actions and be a spiritual advisor to him. As long as he was alone, he couldn't objectively evaluate himself. His wife could, however, by being removed enough to criticize him in a constructive and loving way.

When the Torah says that women were created to be "helpers," one might think that this is an unimportant role. In fact, just the opposite is true. This role is critically important and is one means by which women imitate God.

Helping relationships are often between two people who are of unequal status. For instance, a homemaker and her maid, a king and his servants, an employer and his office workers all have relationships where the "helpers" are of lesser status than the person being helped. In other relationships, the "helper" is of higher status than the one being helped. When God helps us, when a mother helps her child, and when a doctor helps a patient, the helper has greater status than the one being helped.

In general, how much power a helper has in a relationship determines whether the helper has more or less status than the one being helped. When a woman helps her husband, her role often has greater status than his.

Christian English books refer to the first woman as "Eve." It is noteworthy that the Torah refers to the first woman by different appellations at different times. When she is created as a "helper" to Adam, she is referred to simply as *ha-ishah*—literally, "the woman" *par excellence*.

Biblical Hebrew uses many words to denote a female. To name a few: *almah* (a woman of marriageable age), *betulah* (a virgin), *bachurah* (an adolescent), *naarah* (a woman between 12 and 12½), *nikeivah* (female), *yaldah* (girl), and so on. The term *ishah* denotes a woman who has achieved spiritual greatness. *Ha-ishah,* the term used to refer to the first female, denotes a woman *par excellence.* Such a woman was deemed an appropriate partner for Adam, who was created with enormous spiritual potentials. He was described as being "just a little lower than the angels" when he was created. Presumably, his wife was of equal spiritual stature.

The Torah's description of the first woman as a helper has little in common with current conceptions of helping. The Torah's perspective is that a helper is someone who acts like God. It is noteworthy that the Torah refers to both women and God as helpers. Whereas the woman is referred to as a "helper" here, the primary instances where the Torah refers to helpers are with respect to God.[29]

When God acts as a helper to human beings, He allows us to play a role in our accomplishments. We are not supposed to passively receive

His help; rather, we are supposed to actively participate in contributing to the world as He requires us to do. The ultimate way that He acts as a "helper," or asks us to do the same, is by assisting others in their own growth.

Since God created the first woman to be like Him in this endeavor, she was also termed a helper *(ezer)*. This is interpreted to mean that an integral desire for a married woman is to want to help her husband. Part of his nature is that he will want to be helped.

This relationship becomes oppositional *(kenegdo)* when men do not want to be helped, or when women do not want to help. Under normal circumstances, it will be part of a woman's nature to want to help her husband. When he rejects her desire to do so, or if she refuses to do so, it can create tension and opposition.

Theories about Men's and Women's Natures

Once God formed woman as an entity separate from man, the masculine part was termed *ish* (man) and the feminine part was termed *ishah* (woman). In Hebrew, both of these words share the two letters *alef* and *shin*. Together, these letters form the word *aish,* which means "fire." In addition, the man's name contains the letter *yud,* whereas the woman's name contains the letter *heh.*

Our bodies were created from earth, share many of the earth's properties, and return to it when we die. The fact that the names for "man" and "woman" contain the word "fire" teaches us that once the feminine and masculine facets of the first person were separated into discrete beings, it gave them and their descendants the ability to be like fire. Fire is extremely active, it always rises, and it can alter things quickly. The soul is analogized to fire, insofar as it always strives to rise to its Source (i.e., God), and can change a person's physical nature.

Adam was created with a soul, which endowed him with the potential to be like fire. He was able to elevate his physical being, and the world, to great spiritual heights. However, as long as he was physically self-sufficient, he had no motivation to channel this "fire" to perfect the world.

Once Adam was separated into *ish* and *ishah,* he and his wife gained the capacity to perfect themselves by acting on the world and by giving of themselves. This was because as discrete beings, "fire" was now a dominant force in each of them. They could use this fire to actively do God's will.

DIFFERENCES BETWEEN MEN AND WOMEN

It has been suggested that men's natures are generally more predisposed than are women's to expressing their spirituality in terms of strength. Men's natures predispose them to ridding the world of negativity, such as eradicating people who do evil by fighting them, uprooting injustice, and so on. Women, on the other hand, are more predisposed to nurturing and to creating a home. Women help men develop their connections and rootedness with the world around them. Whereas men may want to rid the world of what is negative, women's primary desire is to nurture and contribute that which is positive.

God is characterized by His attributes of power as well as nurturing. God wanted men and women to develop their respective attributes of power/control and nurturing and to mutually give to each other in marriage that which each individual lacks. In this way, when a couple lives together harmoniously, they can bring God's Holy Presence (*Shechinah*) into their lives. They can allow their relationship to be dominated by their separate and disunified desires, or they can channel these desires to form a Godly partnership.[30]

THEORIES REGARDING HOW PARADISE WAS LOST

Once the Torah discusses how and why man and woman were created, it then explains how they damaged their spiritual greatness by sinning in the Garden of Eden.

When God created Adam, He commanded him not to eat of the fruit of the tree of knowledge of good and evil. It has been theorized that God wanted Adam to limit himself in certain ways for his own benefit. Had Adam followed God's command, he would have demonstrated that he could subjugate to God's will his need to know and be in control of everything.

How was it possible that Adam allowed his personal desires to supersede God's will?

The serpent in the Garden of Eden represented evil and used its influence to encourage Adam's and Eve's infamous rebellion to occur. The serpent took it upon himself to try to corrupt them and make them violate God's command.

The snake operated by making the woman question why God wanted her not to eat fruit from the tree of knowledge of good and evil. Eve should have refuted the snake's questioning of God's will and should have recognized that the benefits of contravening God's will were mere illusions. In other words, she should have demonstrated that the Almighty put limits on people for their own benefit.

God created the apparent temptations and sensual benefits of the world so that we would enjoy them in a state of spiritual elevation, or reject them when this is impossible. By rejecting the illusory benefits, we demonstrate that following our Creator's will is more important than the benefits of any sin.

Had they acted appropriately, Adam and Eve would have reinforced God's role as the ultimate Master of the Universe and Director of the World. The snake was in the Garden only so that Adam and Eve would reject its temptations, thereby ratifying the fact that everything in the world – the illusions and temptations included – come from the same Godly source.

With this in mind, we may now proceed to the snake's encounter with Eve in the Garden of Eden, including some interpretations by our sages of the events that transpired.

THE SIN IN THE GARDEN OF EDEN

Shortly after the woman was formed, the serpent approached her in the Garden of Eden. It asked her, "Didn't God tell you not to eat from every tree of the garden?"[31]

In fact, God had only prohibited Adam from eating the fruit of one tree. The snake used this provocative remark as a pretext to engage her in conversation.[32]

She replied that she was allowed to eat from every tree in the Garden with the exception of the one in the middle. Were she to eat from or touch that tree, God had warned that she would surely die.

Although the woman indicated that touching the tree was prohibited, God had only forbidden eating its fruit, not touching it.

The serpent replied, "You shall not surely die."[33] It then pushed her into the tree, and she saw that nothing happened by touching it.[34] Through a variety of personal reasonings that are too complicated to elucidate here, Eve began to doubt the veracity of God's word. She then began to convince herself that sinning would have no negative consequences.

This is paradigmatic of how temptation operates. It tells us that if we do something wrong, a threatened punishment will never occur.[35]

The serpent continued enticing Eve by telling her that God's real reason for prohibiting her from eating the forbidden fruit was because "on the day you eat of it, your eyes will be opened, and you will be like God, knowing good and evil."[36] It suggested to her that God had eaten of the forbidden fruit, which then endowed Him with His ability to create the world. She could do the same if she would only eat of this same fruit.[37]

In this argument, the snake appealed to the woman's desire to acquire knowledge, power, creativity, and to be independent of God.[38]

Eve viewed the forbidden fruit as "a desire for the eyes" *(taavah láeinaim)*.[39] She believed that the fruit would make her Godlike in her omniscience.[40]

Eve's desire for knowledge, creativity, and physical pleasure, which no fruit could possibly provide, led to her initial downfall. Once she ate the forbidden fruit, it internalized within her an impulse to go against God's will, as well as feelings of jealousy, lust, and a desire for honor.[41]

Once she sinned, she realized that she was destined to die and that Adam would remain alive and remarry. Her fear that she would die, while Adam would love a second wife who would supplant her in receiving his affection, led her to encourage him to fall with her. She decided to give her husband the fruit, thinking, "If we die, we will both die. If we live, we will both live."[42]

Adam listened to her because he wanted to maintain his attachment to her, instead of obeying God's command to refrain from eating the forbidden fruit.

(A different interpretation suggests that he sinned because he imagined that by eating the fruit, and thereby internalizing a negative inclination within himself, he could subsequently achieve more spiritual greatness by eventually overcoming it. As long as the negative inclination was not a part of him, his spiritual development did not feel like much of an accomplishment.[43])

According to either explanation, Adam substituted his judgment and made emotionally based decisions instead of following God's will for him.

Our sages suggest several fruits that could have been the forbidden fruit, none of which is an apple.[44] Each symbolizes a certain quality that Adam and Eve hoped to attain by eating it. For example, some say that the fruit was wheat, which symbolizes knowledge. This suggests that the primary quality Adam and Eve hoped to attain by eating the forbidden fruit was knowledge.[45]

Figs are also suggested. This symbolizes that Adam and Eve sought physical pleasure. Figs are a food that people eat only for its taste (as opposed to wheat, which we primarily eat for its nourishment). Therefore, figs symbolize a desire for physical gratification.[46]

THE FIRST WOMAN AFTER HER SIN

When the first woman ate the forbidden fruit, she let her physical desire rule her spiritual, immortal side, thereby making it inevitable that she would die. Had people used their physical desires only to serve God, they would have remained immortal.[47] Once they used their physical drives to achieve ends that were independent of serving their immortal souls, the man and woman attached themselves to their bodies' limitations. Once they disconnected their bodies from totally serving their souls, their bodies became subject to the limitations of the physical world. This meant that they would inevitably die, as does anything that is physical.

Eve recognized that Adam's weak point was his desire to stay attached to her.[48] At this point, instead of interacting with Adam to perfect the world, she used her potentials to convince him to share her fate. She told her husband, "I will die. You won't get a new mate, nor will you remain single (i.e., you will eventually die anyway). Let us stay together and share a common fate."[49]

Adam very much wanted to retain his attachment to his wife, and he could not imagine living eternally without her. There were no other women for him to marry, and he could not fathom how God would create another mate for him *ex nihilo*. Therefore, he agreed to eat the fruit that his wife gave him.

It should be noted that the Christian idea of original sin has nothing in common with the Jewish view of what happened in the Garden of Eden. The Torah says that Adam and Eve had had sexual relations prior to their sin with the forbidden fruit.[50] Sexual relations between them were considered desirable and good. It was only after eating the forbidden fruit that sex could be used for lust and sin, and only under such circumstances was it considered negative.

Prior to sinning, Eve did not experience nine months of pregnancy. Every time that she had sexual relations with Adam, she was destined to give birth to a child immediately afterward. Her sons Cain and Abel were both born this way, prior to the eating of the forbidden fruit.[51] It was only after she sinned that childbirth and child-rearing took their present form.

GOD'S REACTION TO DISOBEYING HIS
COMMANDMENT

After the man and woman sinned and assigned the blame for their behavior to others, God "cursed" them, as well as the serpent, with ten "curses" each. These "curses" were not intended to be expressions of vengeance. Although people may punish others out of revenge, this is not how God operates. Whenever God punishes, His goal is to educate the person, as well as to provide a vehicle through which he or she can rectify whatever it is they did wrong.

This was the case with the first woman as well. When the Torah says that God "cursed" her, it really means that her physical existence was changed. The ten changes that affected her were intended to help her rectify what she had damaged by sinning. Given her state after sinning, these changes were the best way to help her live productively and repair the damage that she had caused.

Since the woman was originally created to be Adam's partner in perfecting the world and since she misdirected her potentials, she had to learn how to correct this part of herself. Her punishments were considered curses because they felt bad and they could allow her to mischannel or neglect her spirituality if she did not use them properly. All of her changes directly or indirectly interfered with her attachment to her husband, since it was her inappropriate manipulation of this attachment that led her to encourage him to sin.

Eve's changes affect all of her female descendants because it is up to them to fulfill the mission that she did not actualize. All human beings are delegated the task of perfecting the world because the first couple did not accomplish this.

Just as women have taken over Eve's role (and men Adam's), they are also subject to the limitations and changes that Eve (and Adam) brought into the world. At the same time, Jewish women have been given specific commandments whose observance allows them to bring back into the world the spirituality that was lost when Eve sinned.

THE TEN CHANGES THAT GOD BROUGHT
TO WOMAN

When God changed the first woman, He altered her physical being, and pain became part of many sexual, pregnancy, and birth experiences.

God told her: "I will greatly increase your pain and your travail (of childbirth). In pain you shall bear children, and your passion shall be to your husband, and he shall dominate you."[52]

The ten changes that were brought to Eve (and to her female descendants) were:[53]

1. Women would have menstrual cycles, which would be uncomfortable. Prior to this time, Eve had no menstrual cycle.
2. The first time a virgin would have intercourse, it would be painful.
3. Raising children would cause anguish, including the need to nurse, dress, clean, and carry them around until they are independent. Mothers would worry that their children would not grow up the way they would like.
4. A woman would be overly shy about her body.
5. A woman would feel discomfort during her nine months of pregnancy. Prior to this time, a child emerged after every act of intercourse.
6. Childbirth would be painful.
7. A woman would be forbidden to marry two husbands.
8. A woman would have a sense of sexual longing when her husband was away on a trip.
9. A woman would desire her husband sexually, but would find it emotionally difficult to openly ask him to have intercourse with her. Women would sexually desire their husbands even when it would result in the pain of pregnancy and birth.[54]
10. A woman would desire to stay home.

These changes were not meant to be prescriptions about what women *should* seek; rather, they were meant to be starting points in helping women correct and perfect their abilities to nurture properly. Thus, although a menstrual cycle, pregnancy, childbirth, and the like may be uncomfortable, it doesn't mean that women shouldn't try to alleviate their pain. Their awareness of these discomforts and pains should heighten their sensitivity to use their life-creating abilities as vehicles for spiritual growth for themselves and others.

In general, the changes heighten women's awareness of their potentials for nurturing and how they can be misused. For example, Eve used her persuasive abilities to induce Adam to sin. Since Eve was the embodiment of all female souls that would ever exist, her female descendants would have the role of correcting the errors that she had made. The changes would help ensure that women would rectify Eve's failing, and thereby bring the world back to Paradise. To this end, the changes encourage women to use their persuasive powers and creative capacities for nurturing, rather than for the opposite.

Explanation of the Changes

These changes have been elaborated upon by our sages. For example, they interpret the idea that parents will find it painful to raise children beyond the obvious physical and emotional difficulties of child-rearing. They suggest that parents will find child-rearing painful because children reflect their parents' shortcomings, and whatever contradictions and character flaws parents express, children pick up and mimic with impunity. One of the most painful things that parents see is when their children do what the parents model, rather than what they say. This pushes parents to overcome their own negative traits in order to better their children's lives, as well as their own.

Another facet of women feeling anxious about raising children is that their children will not turn out exactly as the mothers hope they will. Mothers must recognize that they can't control their children's lives. This forces them to realize the centrality of God's protection and intervention, and how, without His help, children can't possibly thrive.

When Eve ate the forbidden fruit, she wanted to develop herself and help Adam without including God. The anxiety over raising children can encourage women to draw closer to God and include Him in all of their endeavors.

Woman's Sexuality

Our sages interpret the woman's subservience to the man as meaning that women will sexually desire their husbands but will not be able to ask them for sexual intimacy.[55]

This idea reflects God's awareness, based on Eve's actions, that a sexually outgoing personality would not be conducive for a woman's spiritual growth. Therefore, He made these changes so that the new woman would be more perfect than Eve was initially. A woman must make her husband desire her sexually by properly directing her nurturing. Metaphysically, this corrects Eve's mistake.

THE MAN'S TEN CHANGES

Just as the first woman was changed in ten ways, so was the first man. His changes were:

1. He was originally created taller than normal as a physical reflection of his spiritual greatness. His physical stature was reduced to reflect his spiritual decline.
2. He would feel weak whenever he would ejaculate.
3. The earth would grow thorns and brambles.
4. Man would have anguish in earning a livelihood.
5. Man was to eat the grass of the field. (When Adam heard that he and his cattle would eat the same food, he pleaded to God, and the next curse was substituted for this one.)
6. Man would eat bread by the sweat of his brow.
7. Adam lost the initial extraordinary beauty that God gave him. (This original beauty was a physical manifestation of his spiritual beauty.)
8. The snake lost his hands and feet and could no longer serve his intended role as an effective servant for man.
9. Adam was banished from the Garden of Eden and lost his status as lord and master of the world.
10. Men, being dust, would return to dust. He was destined to die and be buried.[56]

All of Adam's changes interfered with his ability to maintain a constant attachment to his wife. For example, his need to toil in order to earn a living, as opposed to having God provide food for him without any human effort, takes a man away from his wife. It also physically tires him so that he can't have marital relations as frequently as she might want.[57]

When men use their changes properly, they can elevate themselves so that they appreciate God's rule over them. For example, when they work for a living, they should recognize that their financial success depends on God's granting it.

FIRST WOMAN'S APPELLATION AS "CHAVAH"

Only after God delineated all of these changes to the first woman was her name changed to *Chavah* (Eve). Adam named her Chavah because "she is the mother of all life."[58] Until this point, she was always referred to as "the woman at the pinnacle of her spirituality"—*ha-ishah*.

Before she brought death into the world, the woman's primary focus and nature was not to be a mother. It was to be a partner with Adam in perfecting the world. After the sin, mothering became a primary role for her. Instead of bringing death, she could nurture people to gain physical and spiritual life.[59] After sinning, her new role was to be a "mother of all living" because humanity's mission shifted to future generations.[60]

Chavah also means "conversation."[61] Chavah was created to be a helper to her husband. She misdirected her helping energies, as well as her use of speech, by enticing her husband to sin. Our sages tell us that women were granted greater linguistic potentials than men in order to create connections with people that can nurture and correct the world. Thus, it made sense that after her sin, woman was renamed to reflect the new potentials by which she could rectify the world.

IMPLICATIONS FOR FIRST MAN'S AND FIRST WOMAN'S DESCENDANTS

The first man and woman possessed within them the souls of every person who would ever exist. Just as they each had a unique soul, so do each of their descendants. The nature of every soul is that it wants to do God's will.

God gave us bodies as physical vehicles to perform His commandments. When we do a commandment *(mitzvah)*, which represents God's will, it draws His Holy Presence into us. Thus, we can actively connect ourselves to God by doing His *mitzvot*. We bring spiritual values and Godliness into the world through our actions. Our thoughts alone are not sufficient to do this because we need to concretize reality in the tangible world in which we live. We do this through action, not only via thoughts or feelings.

Subsequent to Adam's and Eve's sins, each of their descendants inherited the task of rectifying the sin done by their progenitors in Paradise. As generations went by and this was not accomplished, the mission of rectifying their sin was eventually transferred to the Jewish people at the time they accepted the Torah. It is our task to draw down God's presence into the material world as much as possible. Men behaving appropriately corrects Adam's mistake, and women exercising their free will properly does the same for Eve's error. The Torah teaches us how to do both.

Since the nature of Adam's and Eve's sins were slightly different, men and women have somewhat different roles in bringing greater holiness into the world. These roles and behaviors will be explored further throughout this book.

LILLITH

Feminist literature often speaks about Lillith as the counterpart of Eve. Lillith is a woman who is described in a text known as the Book of Jubilees. Reference to Lillith again appears in a text known as the Alphabet of Ben Sira. The story says that God created Adam and Lillith at the same time, from the dust of the earth. Lillith did not want to be Adam's helper, so she escaped from him. God then made Adam a second wife, Eve, who was content to be his helper.

The legend about Lillith does not reflect mainstream Jewish thinking. The sources where it primarily appears reflect sectarian ideas and are almost never used to derive Jewish law. The sects who wrote these texts died out long ago, and their ideas were rejected by mainstream Judaism.

The story about Lillith is not found in the Talmud and is therefore not a theme that was prominently discussed by the rabbis. Thus, the sources of stories about Lillith are not considered to derive from traditional Jewish sources.

There is only one scriptural reference to Lillith, and it appears in Isaiah.[62] It refers to Lillith as being among the beasts of prey and spirits that will lay waste to the land on the day of vengeance.

On the other hand, the Talmud makes several references to a *lillith*.[63] A *lillith* is a female demon of the night who has a human face, long hair, and wings. (There are also many varieties of male and animalistic demons.) These talmudic references do not describe the origins of the Lillith concept.

God's Attributes – Kabbalistic Concepts

Since we are mortal and limited in our perceptions, we cannot understand God's essence. To the extent that we can know and understand who and what God is, we do so based on how He acts in our world. The ways He "acts" are categorized as various divine "emanations" (*sefirot*) or positive attributes He manifests in our world.

There are seven such emanations: lovingkindness, strength, beauty (truth), triumph, glory, foundation, and royalty. Just as God has these attributes, He has endowed us with some measure of comparable potentials, which we can develop. When we wish to emulate God's attribute of lovingkindness, we may do so by visiting the sick, giving charity to the poor, dowering poor brides, comforting mourners, and so forth. We may emulate His attribute of strength by exercising moral fortitude, restraining ourselves from sinning, and by conquering our negative inclinations. We display the attribute of beauty when we integrate the physical and the spiritual worlds.

We can display foundation (*yesod*) by channeling our sexual energies constructively. This can include creating and sustaining a positive relationship with a spouse and by being loyal.

Just as God created positive energies that He lets flow into the world, He also created negative ones. These parallel the positive attributes. *Lillith* is the negative sexual energy that parallels the positive sexual energy. For example, when someone is disloyal to a friend or corrupts the loving relationship of marriage and friendship, he or she misdirects sexual energy and *lillith* results.

This is a metaphysical explanation of what *lillith* is. A more philosophical explanation follows:

The stories that describe Lillith's creation can be understood to mean that God created people with the freedom to choose to properly channel, or to misdirect, their sexual potentials. When Lillith refused to channel her sexuality in a way that could elevate the union of a man and a woman, God's plan for the world was frustrated.

In this context, *lillith* is a characterization of a woman's refusal to channel her sexual energies in a way that complements those of her husband. When these energies are misdirected, a couple cannot express the metaphysical unification of their divine attributes. Philosophically, *lillith* is the expression of a person's ego desires fighting against God's master plan for the world.

This is why *lillith* should not be viewed as a role model for the Jewish woman. Lillith's rebellion was not merely a personal striving for independence from man or a quest to develop an egalitarian relationship with him. Rather, she rejected God's plan for how she needed to help bring the world to its intended goal. She rebelled against the Creator who put her here for a critical purpose.

The Masculine and Feminine Aspects of God

The union of a husband and wife is supposed to reflect God's divine image. In kabbalistic literature, God is described as having a feminine as well as a masculine aspect. The masculine aspect of God is an anthropomorphism that describes how God presents Himself as being near to us (immanent), even though His essence transcends anything that we can fully comprehend. This aspect of God is known as the "Holy One, blessed be He."

The feminine aspect of God is what allows us to receive the experience of the Divine Presence. This aspect is known as the *Shechinah*.

Our life task is to make ourselves receptive to God's manifesting His presence in our world. This means that we must act in ways that allow Him to give to us, and allow us to experience Him, as well as our making ourselves receptacles (vessels) for the Divine Presence. In this sense, the male force of providence is the aspect of God that acts upon the world. The female force is that which allows us to be receptive to His power.

We should not learn from the Lillith story that women must be helpless and powerless in order for Judaism to give us credence. Rather, a woman must be receptive to God's immanence and her husband's giving in order to create a Divine Image within their marital relationship. When she is prepared to emulate the Divine Presence, she can complement man's purpose for existing. Only when they each appropriate their respective roles can they fulfill God's purpose in creating them.

3

Men and Women in Traditional Judaism

With the Creation story in mind, we may better understand traditional Jewish perspectives about men and women.

MAINTAINING DIFFERENCES

God found it necessary to create the first man and woman with different characteristics. The Torah underscores the importance of maintaining these differences through laws that apply differentially to men and women. For example, it is prohibited for a man to wear women's clothing or to engage in feminine behavior (e.g., wearing make-up), and vice versa. In general, Judaism emphasizes maintaining the differences that God created, rather than diminishing them.

For instance, the Torah prohibits erasing differences between species. It forbids us to graft plant species together, to weave flax and wool together, to mate two species together, to mix dairy with meat, and so forth. If God had wanted us to eradicate certain differences, He would not have deliberately created and blessed them.[1]

Judaism has a premise that every physical creation has a spiritual message to teach us. It cannot convey that message when its distinctiveness is undermined and obliterated.

27

God deliberately constructed the human body such that we can observe how He intended for us to use it. Rather than evolving as a biological accident, our anatomy reflects our spiritual challenges and endowments. It has been suggested that we have two ears and two eyes but only one mouth so that we can observe and listen more than we speak. Our minds are higher than our hearts (which is not true of many animals), to reflect the idea that our intellect (based in our heads) is supposed to rule our feelings (based in our hearts), rather than the other way around.

When God created the first woman, the Torah tells us that she was created from Adam's rib. This was so that her influences on him, and her primary mode of development, would be internal.[2] The fact that women's reproductive organs and genitalia are internal also suggests that the optimal way for women to function is to develop themselves internally. Men's corresponding externality suggests that they should develop themselves more in their external functioning in the world.

With the above as background, we can now examine the Jewish roles for women and contrast them with modern secular values.

POWER

One criticism often leveled against Judaism is that it renders women powerless. In American society, many of the ways in which women differ from men are seen to reflect women's lesser importance, rather than demonstrating separateness with equality. This is exemplified by how societies reward the ways in which men, but not women, traditionally exercise power.

We can define power as the ability to effect change. In American society, visible and external power is valued. Political power, positions of authority and status, military power, and money are all examples of external power, because they have the capacity to effect visible changes in how people live or in the way society functions. However, there are many ways of effecting change in society without using visible or external means.

One type of power is the ability to influence people to change in ways that are neither visible nor readily apparent. This can occur through personally influencing others. This type of change may not be readily visible, even though it may be every bit as potent as more obvious means of causing change. For example, psychotherapy can be a very powerful tool in causing people to change. It does not use external or visible means, nor is it a process that is typically regarded as an exercise in power. Similarly, a parent's, teacher's, or mentor's personal influence can be a very powerful tool in molding others' character and behavior, yet it is much more subtle than political, financial, or physical power. It also tends to be less overtly rewarded by society than are other forms of power. How often are there ticker tape parades for teachers or clergy? How do their salaries compare with those of politicians or sports figures?

If you were asked to think of the three most powerful people that you know, you might think of the President of the United States, the leader of Russia, and the political or military leader of a third country. These are people (probably men) who represent externalized power. Now think about the person, or people, who changed or influenced your life the most. Chances are excellent that one of the first people who comes to mind is your mother. Mothers have a tremendous amount of power by virtue of their personal influence on their children, but this power is not externally visible.

Judaism believes that men and women should have equal rights to influence others, but that women generally should not exercise this from positions of authority. The positions of legal and external authority are generally reserved for men, whereas the power that is exercised from the home and in personal domains is primarily wielded by women.

ROLE DIVISIONS IN JUDAISM

Secular society frequently encourages its members to compete for its prized goals – externalized power, material acquisition, and a visible place in society. This contrasts strongly with the Torah's perspective, which promotes a society that has multiple goals, each of which is attainable by, and designated for, different groups.

The Jewish people originally consisted of people who were assigned various roles, each of which was valued for its unique contribution to the Jewish nation. For example, the priests served God in the Temple and taught Torah. The Levites (tribe of Levi) sang praises to God and played musical instruments in the Temple. Other tribes engaged more intensively in commerce and agriculture. After a certain point in history, all Jewish kings emerged only from one family, and so on.

The distinctions between many of these roles were absolute, and no group was allowed to usurp the mandated role of another group. For instance, priests and Levites were not granted an equal portion with the other tribes when the land of Israel was divided among them, whereas nonpriests were forbidden to serve as priests in the Temple. Every group had a unique role within the Jewish nation's collective service to God.

The importance of this type of pluralism is also reflected by the fact that Jews are required to observe 613 commandments. No single individual can personally observe all of them. It requires the collective input of all Jews observing the commandments to fulfill them.

In a similar manner, multiple goals in Judaism allow women to be valued in their own right, not only when they are like men. This stands in contrast with recent innovations by Jewish groups to make women "equal" to men by minimizing the importance of their feminine roles, while encouraging the women to be more like men. For example, "egalitarian" *minyans* tend to stress women's imitating men by performing male rituals in public, rather than by having men pray in more internal and less visible ways.

Each sex has its unique gifts and contributions to make to the Jewish people. A plurality of roles allows each group of Jews to make its special contribution that will allow the Jewish nation to properly serve God.

REQUIREMENT TO IMITATE GOD

In secular society, many people measure their importance and the value of their lives by what they acquire, rather than by what they give. One of our fundamental obligations as Jews is to imitate God. We were not commanded to become millionaires, professionals, or politicians. We *were* commanded to imitate God. One of the primary ways that we do this is by imitating His deeds of lovingkindness. It is only by giving that we can truly exercise the divine image inside of us.

God wanted people to become interdependent and unified through giving. In addition, by giving, we also expand our influence over others and our importance to them.

On the other hand, we reinforce our finitude when we take. This is because the more we take, the more we tie ourselves to the limited, finite world. Furthermore, whenever we take from the material world, it deprives someone else of that same thing. Therefore, taking from the finite world creates separations and barriers between people. When we take, our goals necessarily exclude others, rather than including them in our consciousness and viewing them as extensions of ourselves.

Women were created with the potential of imitating God in the two greatest ways possible—by creating new life and by giving of themselves in the development and nurturing of others. As is well known, Judaism values women's ability to bear, nurture, and raise children. It also stresses how important it is for them to be stabilizing forces in their husbands' and children's development. Yet, despite Judaism's preference that women marry and have children, men are the ones who are commanded to marry and to procreate, not women.[3] The preferred role for women is to marry and have children, but Jewish law does not require this of them. Should a woman not be able to, or not wish to develop her potentials as a mother, she still has many other ways of imitating God and actualizing herself as a Jewess.

Whereas the most desirable goal in secular society may be for women to imitate men, the highest goal for both Jewish men and women is to imitate God. As long as a woman's goal is ultimately to develop herself in order to serve God, not herself, many paths are open to her. This is not the case for a man, for whom Judaism proposes that he can never fully actualize himself without being married and having children.

From a Jewish perspective, should a woman choose to take on the challenge of having children, her job is not simply to be a "baby machine." Rather, it is to create and mold a Jewish body and soul who will carry on the mandate of perfecting the world in accordance with God's will.

SELF-ACTUALIZATION THROUGH *MITZVOT*

Judaism encourages men and women to actualize their respective strengths by taking what God has granted them and using it to further the spiritual growth of themselves and others. The Torah teaches that there are different paths by which men and women can best do this.

Before we can develop what is positive in ourselves, we must first avoid doing things that harm or destroy ourselves or others.[4] Then we must do what helps us actualize ourselves and develop the world. We accomplish both of these goals by observing the commandments of the Torah, which legislate what we should and should not do.

The Torah contains 613 commandments, or *mitzvot*. Of these, 365 *mitzvot* tell us what not to do, and 248 tell us what we should do. These are known, respectively, as negative and positive *mitzvot*. There are also innumerable behaviors that Jewish law doesn't specifically permit or forbid. No code of law could possibly legislate every conceivable action.

In order for us to be observant Jews, we must do more than simply perform what the *mitzvot* require. We must also behave appropriately in situations that are not specifically legislated. We deduce how to act in these situations based on how we should act in legislated ones. This is known as the "realm of permissible things" or *divrei reshut.*

The negative *mitzvot* are designed to prevent us from harming ourselves or others. These apply equally to men and women (with only three exceptions)[5] because both sexes have similar ways of not harming themselves. The positive commandments are specific means by which we actualize ourselves. These apply differentially to men and women, as we shall see.

THEORIZED DIFFERENCES IN PRIMARY INTELLECTS

Just as women were created physically different from men, some Jewish sages say that they were also created with a primary way of thinking that is different from that of men. Women and men are presumed to be equally endowed with the intellectual faculty of *chochmah* – innate knowledge. However, intellectual development in other spheres is presumed to be different for most men than for most women.

As was mentioned previously, the creation story is interpreted by some to suggest that God created women with a primary intellect of *binah*[6] and that they have more of it than do men.[7] *Binah* is typically mistranslated as "intuition." Intuition requires no intellectual functioning. It is simply an innate capacity. *Binah* actually refers to our ability to enter another person's emotions and thoughts and draw conclusions from the knowledge we obtain through this process. This might be better translated as "inner reasoning."

Men are considered to be more innately endowed with *daat* – the ability to tie themselves into facts, figures, and details. *Daat* might be translated as "analytical reasoning." This does not mean that all men or all women think only in one realm to the exclusion of the other. It means that, in general, most women tend to have more *binah* than do most men, whereas most men tend to have more *daat* than do most women. There are nonetheless some women who have better analytical reasoning than do some men, and some men who have better inner reasoning abilities than do some women.

All three of these intellectual faculties are important. The Torah says that God created the world by using the faculties of *chochmah, binah,* and *daat.* Some 2,000 years later, He commanded the Jews who left Egypt to build Him a sanctuary *(mishkan)* in the desert. This *mishkan* represented a world in miniature where God could dwell among the Jewish people. He told the Jews to create this mini-world using the faculties of *chochmah, binah,* and *daat.*[8]

If God did not believe that the faculties of *daat* and *binah* were equally important and equally valid, He could have created the world with only one of them. The fact that He created the world with both, and required the Jews to use both in building the *mishkan,* reflects the fact that the world cannot flourish without making use of both of these complementary faculties. Men and women are supposed to value their respective intellectual capabilities and use them in their daily functioning.

There are numerous ways in which women can develop and enjoy their *binah*. One way is by studying Torah in a manner that nurtures their particular intellectual strengths: women can study the Torah by analyzing and understanding the emotional and religious characteristics of our forebears, the significance of various symbols and objects, and the motivations that fueled the behavior of biblical characters. Attending to the whys and overall pictures of biblical narratives, as opposed to the academic study of legal details, are some ways by which women can nourish their *binah*.

Binah can also be nurtured by relating to people and doing deeds of lovingkindness. The processes of being wives and mothers, of hosting guests, visiting the sick, and working for charitable causes allow women to use and develop their *binah*.

Vocationally, women can also nurture their *binah*. When women have sought employment outside their homes, they have traditionally gone into the helping professions and teaching. Although secular society may have its own reasons for relegating women to "helping" types of jobs, many women choose to go into professions that require them to be sensitive to the nuances of human relationships. When they find these jobs satisfying, it is frequently because such jobs tend to fulfill their *binah* and nurturing abilities.

Apart from the physical and intellectual differences between men and women, there are also emotional differences that are valued. Since we process emotions through our minds, men and women perceive experiences differently, according to whether their experiences are filtered through *daat* or *binah*. Thus, emotional awareness tends to be different for women than it is for men. Women are frequently more emotionally aware than are men, and men are frequently more tied to the details of their experiences than are women.

Psychotherapists often find that women tend to be more emotional than men, and men tend to intellectualize and obsess about details more than women. It is quite interesting to note that male patients frequently focus on the details of their experiences, whereas women may more readily describe how they felt about what happened. When these characteristics are manifested in an extreme way, they result in people being histrionic (overly tied to their emotions) or obsessive-compulsive (overly tied to details). Women are more frequently histrionic than men, whereas obsessive-compulsive males outnumber females.

Keeping the above differences in mind, we can now examine how, and perhaps why, Jewish laws apply differently to each sex.

WOMEN'S EXEMPTION FROM CERTAIN *MITZVOT*

Of the 613 *mitzvot* in the Torah, women are only exempt from keeping seven that apply to all men.[9] (There are other commandments that apply only to certain individuals or groups, such as priests, first-born males, Levites, kings, married men, and so forth.) These seven are referred to as "time-bound positive *mitzvot*" and require Jews to say the *Shema* prayer, wear *tefillin,* wear a fringed garment *(tzitzit),* count the *Omer* (the days between the Passover and Shavuot holidays), hear the blowing of the *shofar* (ram's horn) on Rosh Hashanah (Jewish New Year's), sit in the *succah* during the holiday of Succot (Tabernacles), and take a *lulav* (a palm branch bound with willow and myrtle) and *etrog* (citron) on the first day of the holiday of Succot. With the exception of wearing *tefillin,* women are not prohibited from doing any of these commandments. In fact, they frequently take it upon themselves to observe the remaining five, with the exception of not wearing fringed garments.

One reason that has been suggested as to why men are required to observe more time-bound *mitzvot* than women is that men need more external reminders of the preciousness of time, and they require extra reinforcement to use it to serve spiritual goals. Certain external reminders of time are superfluous for women since they have internal, biological clocks that run according to days, months, and years.[10]

The Torah teaches us that time is potentially holy. Each moment has its own unique meaning, and each moment of every day is endowed with the possibility of serving a spiritual purpose. The time-bound *mitzvot* serve to keep Jews constantly aware of the potential sanctity of time, which can be brought to fruition through our actions. Since men are not tied to biological clocks, one way of becoming conscious of time is to surround themselves with *mitzvot* at the start of every day. They put on *tzitzit* (a fringed, four-cornered undershirt), pray the morning service, put on a *tallit* (prayer shawl) and *tefillin* (phylacteries). On a monthly basis, they reinforce their awareness of time by sanctifying the new month and set spiritual goals for it. On a yearly basis, they commit themselves to keeping their spirituality alive during the intervals between one holiday and the next.

Since men have more *daat,* they tend to be more attuned to the details of the secular, external world. They therefore need external reminders of the importance of sanctifying time. Women have internal biological rhythms that serve this same purpose. Jews do not consider a woman's menstrual cycle to be an accident of nature. It was deliberately created by God to teach a certain spiritual lesson.

One way that women reinforce the message of their menstrual cycle is by observing the laws of family purity, which heighten their awareness of the sanctity of time. Through men's extra time-bound commandments and attention to sanctifying the external world, and women's observance of family purity and attention to inner worlds, both men and women can imitate God and sanctify life. However, both arrive at the same goal using different means, which are best suited to each sex.

DIFFERENTIAL PRIORITIES

Another reason that has been advanced as to why women are absolved from doing certain time-bound *mitzvot* is that this requirement would create tension for them. Although women are not obligated to marry or have children, Judaism recognizes the likelihood that they will probably choose to do both. In order to facilitate these choices, the Torah does not obligate them to observe certain time-bound commandments. This is because married women's primary responsibilities, especially if they have children, are to their families and to their homes. Were they to have other responsibilities hanging over their heads, it would unfairly stress them. What women are required to do is so critically important in guaranteeing the eternity of the Jewish people that it overrides the requirement to do certain time-bound commandments.

Since men are supposed to refine themselves vis-à-vis the external world, Judaism presumes that they are likely to be drawn away from their true spiritual goals through their interactions with the external world. Therefore, the time-bound commandments that govern men's time and behavior every morning teach them that their first priority upon awakening is to consecrate their hearts and minds to serving God for the rest of the day. This helps prevent men from getting caught up in eating, working, self-absorption, and focusing on the secular world as ends in themselves.

Since women are supposed to actualize themselves by developing in internal ways, women do not have to be legislated away from the external distractions that men have in order to focus on their relationships with God. There is a presumption that women are more innately focused on their internal states than are men and that women are more aware of the needs of others. Thus, their realm of self-actualization allows them to observe somewhat fewer rituals. This is because the Torah assumes that women will use their *binah* to appropriately give of themselves to others, rather than being distracted by the external world.

As an example, when a woman with a family awakens every morning, she must immediately make judgments about what each person needs. If she has young children, the first order of the day may be for her to feed the baby, make breakfast for the other children, and send them off to school. If she were required to attend *minyan,* say the morning prayers by an early hour, and sequester herself away from the distractions of her children, it would be counterproductive to raising a family. Her first priority is to imitate God by helping take care of her children. Once they are taken care of, if she can reasonably make time for it, she can then focus her attention on directly relating to God. Were she required to observe time-bound *mitzvot,* they would often interfere with her ability to tend to the family's needs, which are primary.[11]

Women are not obligated to attend prayer services in the synagogue. However, women who do not have conflicting responsibilities to their families are encouraged to develop their connections to God through daily prayer, including attendance at a synagogue, if they so desire. They should also strive to give of their time, caring about and giving charity to others. For instance, if they have an income, they can give 10 percent of it to charity. They can similarly volunteer professional or free time to those who need such help or demonstrations of concern and comfort. In addition, they are encouraged to learn Torah in a way that is relevant to them.

THEORY ABOUT WHY WOMEN NEEDN'T STUDY TORAH FOR ITS OWN SAKE

Many people erroneously believe that women are not required to study Torah. There are actually two aspects to Torah study. One may learn

Torah in order to properly live a Jewish life, or one may learn it for its own sake, that is, purely in order to study it. Women are required to learn Torah in order to properly fulfill their religious obligations. They are exempt from the obligation of studying Torah for its own sake, which applies to men.

One explanation for this exemption is that women do not need to study Torah for its own sake in order to develop themselves intellectually or spiritually. Since women have more *binah,* it is unusual for them to feel spiritually nurtured by the analysis of details which characterizes Talmud study. Men's study of Torah tends to delve into the details of events and the commandments. It includes questions like "How much is required?" and "What are the various opinions about how one must perform this act?" Women are often more interested in the deeper meanings of the commandments and scriptural narratives and the ethical lessons that can be gleaned from them.

Women's *binah* is as much an intellectual gift to be appreciated as is *daat* for men. Women have historically nurtured their *binah* via family and personal interactions, such as teaching their daughters about Judaism, rather than their learning it through books. Nowadays, it is rare for women to get this type of spiritual nourishment from their environments. This is why most Torah sages recommend that women nurture themselves by studying Torah, but in a different way than do men.

If a woman wishes to learn Talmud in order to understand Torah better, she is rewarded for so doing. However, it is inappropriate for anyone to insist that women be spiritually and intellectually nurtured through the same means that men find most gratifying. Men are required to study Talmud and to learn it for the sake of learning. Due to men's *daat,* such learning can nurture them spiritually and intellectually.

One of the Jewish commentators says that men have psychological traits and aggressive tendencies that are incompatible with the peace and tranquility of the World-to-Come. Their constitutions can only be rectified through constant immersion in Torah study. Since women are innately predisposed to serenity, they do not require constant Torah study in order to merit the World-to-Come.[12]

Women are required to learn all of the things they are required to perform or are forbidden to do. They are also required to familiarize themselves with the Five Books of Moses, the Prophets, and the Holy Writings. They must additionally study Jewish ethical works that teach how to develop proper ways of relating to God and other Jews.[13]

Women (or men) who excuse themselves from learning Torah tend to starve themselves spiritually. Without formally studying Torah, most Jewish women (and men) will not be able to develop themselves religiously. Moreover, when they neglect their spiritual development, women also tend to feel disenfranchised as Jews. Whereas men may identify as Jews through certain daily or weekly rituals, such as prayer in the synagogue, or putting on a *tallit* and *tefillin,* a woman who does not nurture herself through Torah study will find it much more difficult to identify with Judaism.

WOMEN'S EMOTIONAL AND SPIRITUAL NURTURING THROUGH PRAYER

Some people mistakenly think that because women are not commanded to pray in the same way that men are, they do not have to connect themselves to God through prayer. Women should strive to pray the *Shemoneh Esrai* (18 benedictions) every morning and afternoon. When they cannot do this, they should at least pray in some form every day.

Women who neglect prayer deprive themselves spiritually, since our current life-styles do not allow us to sufficiently nurture our relationships with God without prayer. Therefore, a fundamental aspect of women's self-actualization is through Torah study and prayer.

WOMEN'S SPIRITUAL GROWTH THROUGH WOMEN'S *MITZVOT*

Feminist literature often stresses how women are excluded from doing various rituals that are required of men. What is discussed less often are the specific laws that women are required to observe in a more intense manner than are men. The specific commandments that men and women differentially observe are all necessary to achieve the ultimate goal of sanctifying the world.

One of the Torah's goals for men and women is to elevate the spheres of time, place (which includes objects), and person to a higher, spiritual level. To this end, women are exempt from seven time-bound commandments, but they also have three special commandments that are custom-made for them. These are the *mitzvot* of keeping the laws of sexual holiness (*taharat hamishpachah*), the separation of a piece of dough when they bake bread (*challah*), and the lighting of the Sabbath candles.[14] It has been suggested that each of these *mitzvot* taps into something special that women can uniquely contribute to the world. The Torah designates these *mitzvot* to women so that they will bring their spiritual influences into the material world.

Women have the ability and mission to bring Godliness into their bodies and homes by observing their special *mitzvot* and by using their *binah* to discern how to elevate the details of daily life to an overall, holy way of life.

The Contribution of Laws of Family Purity

When Adam and Eve were created, the sole function of their reproductive organs was to serve God. After they sinned in the Garden of Eden, this function could be misdirected to serve their own lusts and desires. A husband and wife can return to the sexual primeval state of Adam and Eve in Paradise when they observe the laws of family purity. Under such circumstances, sexual intimacy allows a husband and wife to join with God in the creation of a new life. Through sanctifying this intensely physical act, Jews can bring to fruition part of God's plan in creating the universe, while fulfilling women's needs for meaningful sex.

In general, women search for a spiritual dimension in a physical relationship with men more than men do with women. One way that women experience this is by feeling exploited when a physical relationship with a man is devoid of emotional or spiritual dimensions. Men may also feel this same pain; however, they generally tend to do so less intensely and less frequently than do women. Women in a strictly physical relationship feel their souls' pain when they search for true intimacy and fail to find it.

The laws of family purity stress the importance of almost every day in a woman's monthly cycle and require her to relate to her husband accordingly. Only after her period has stopped, she has waited an additional week, and has then properly immersed herself in a *mikvah* is she allowed to be intimate with her husband. This process sanctifies sexual relations.

When sexual relations cannot be sanctified, couples are supposed to refrain from physical contact. At these times, women can concentrate more on developing their inner emotional and spiritual potentials and use their *binah* in their relationships with their husbands. In part, this involves introspecting and developing nonphysical forms of communication between husband and wife. (This type of communication should always be present, even when physical intimacy is permitted.) Many women feel spiritually rejuvenated by this monthly process.

Women have total trustworthiness in religious matters and are considered equal to men in this respect. Among the proofs of this egalitarianism is the fact that in so central an area of life, women are given ultimate control over ensuring the sanctity of the marital relationship and sexual intimacy. Observing these laws also helps ensure that women not be viewed as sex objects and that sex is elevated to its maximal spiritual heights. (These ideas will be discussed further in the chapter on *mikvah*.)

It has been suggested that the level of spiritual awareness that women derive from the rituals associated with their bodies can be achieved by men through their observance of rituals using external reminders, such as *tallit* and *tefillin*. By sanctifying their bodies and sexual lives, women bring wells of holiness into their relationships with their husbands and infuse their children with this influence.

Spiritual Contribution of Taking Challah

The second *mitzvah* with which women are especially entrusted is that of taking *challah*. When any Jew bakes bread, he or she is supposed to separate part of it, which is then given to the priests *(cohanim)*.[15] The priests may eat it if they are in a state of ritual purity. It is customary for many Jewish women to bake bread for their families in honor of the Sabbath.[16] This is one of the special commandments by which they bring blessing into their homes.[17] A woman who bakes bread does an act in her home that parallels the priests' baking and setting out the showbread in the holy Temple every Friday.

Judaism strongly emphasizes the importance of elevating the physical world by performing God's commandments. We constantly strive to take our mundane behavior and make it holy. We can sanctify the act of eating to such a point that it is comparable to offering a sacrifice on the altar of the holy Temple.

Taking *challah* is also a way of showing the members of our household that all material blessing comes from God. By separating *challah*, women demonstrate that the ultimate purpose of material blessing is to use it to serve God.

(Since the time of the destruction of the Second Temple, all Jews are presumed to be in a state of ritual impurity. Therefore, the priests are no longer allowed to eat the *challah* that is separated from the dough. For this reason, our current custom is to separate a small amount of dough and then bake it until it is burnt. In this inedible state, it is discarded.)

Judaism wants us to recognize that material success is a divine gift and that pursuit of materialism should not become an end in itself. In domestic realms, women demonstrate that God's providing us with food is not simply so that we can fill our stomachs. His sustenance is a blessing we are supposed to use to serve Him. Part of this service includes sharing our food and material blessing with others, especially those who teach Torah and provide the world with spiritual sustenance.

Theories Regarding Lighting of Sabbath Candles

It has been suggested that women's third special *mitzvah,* that of lighting the Sabbath candles, is an act that sanctifies the realm of time. The Sabbath candles are lit at least 18 minutes prior to sunset on Friday, in order to add time from the secular day to the holy Sabbath. (If a man is unmarried and lives alone or in a dormitory, he is supposed to light Sabbath candles in his domicile. If he is married, or unmarried but living at home, the woman of the house customarily lights the candles for herself and for the men of her family.)

Lighting Sabbath candles brings full circle the woman's means of bringing spiritual blessing into the world. By observing the laws of family purity, the woman elevates her body (as well as her husband's) to a spiritual level. When she takes *challah,* she elevates material objects.

When a Jewish woman kindles the Sabbath candles, she consecrates weekday time and adds to the spiritual illumination in the world. When Adam and Eve extinguished the tremendous spiritual light in the Garden of Eden by sinning, it was left to their descendants to rekindle it. This is partially accomplished by women lighting Sabbath candles.

When a woman does this, she culminates a process that began long before the moment of ushering in the Sabbath. The first three days of the week, we draw our spiritual nourishment from the sanctity of the Sabbath of the previous week. The next three days, we start developing a new reservoir of holiness, that of the Sabbath to come. During the days preceding the Sabbath, we put treasures into our spiritual storehouses, which will be opened on the Sabbath. We invite guests, prepare our homes, buy special food, and cook special meals, all in honor of the Sabbath.

As it approaches, we prepare ourselves to draw on the spiritual blessing we have stored during the preceding week. Judaism tries to motivate us not to content ourselves with allowing that which is neutral to remain so. We are zealous in our efforts to elevate whatever has the potential to be elevated.

By lighting Sabbath candles 18 minutes before sunset, women take the precious moments before the holy day and say, "We can't wait any longer. We need to take from the spiritual and draw from it." When women inaugurate the Sabbath by taking from the weekday and investing it with holiness, they testify that every minute of human existence can be infused with infinite meaning. Every minute of existence can be elevated above the mundane.

By lighting candles prior to the Sabbath, which technically does not begin until sunset, women illuminate and spiritually enrich their homes. They demonstrate that every moment of time is significant. Each moment has its own unique potentials, and it is up to every Jew to take advantage of these opportunities and elevate them. There *is* a difference between the holy and the secular, between light and darkness, between the Sabbath and the six days of Creation. Women demonstrate that it is within human capability to take what is neutral or secular and invest it with so much sanctity that one moment of time can be qualitatively different from the next. When women elevate time by connecting themselves to God, their actions open up storehouses of spiritual blessing that overflow into their homes and into the souls of their families.

Through these three *mitzvot,* Jewish women take their internal awareness of time and sensitivity to others, and use them to sanctify the realms of person, object, and time. By these actions, Jewish women help fulfill God's plan in having created the world.

4

Women as Redeemers of the Jewish People

There are three types of holiness in the world. Certain places are holy *(kedushat makom)*, certain times can be holy *(kedushat zeman)*, and people can be holy *(kedushat adam)*. For example, the holiness of a synagogue is different from the more mundane feelings we have while walking on the street. When we eat in order to nourish our bodies so that we can serve God, we contribute to the holiness of our bodies. When we observe the Sabbath *(Shabbat)*, we experience the holiness of time.

Each type of holiness has subdivisions, and their nuances impact on our lives. For example, we experience and relate to the Sabbath in three different ways. We metaphysically experience it in a progressively different fashion as the Sabbath elapses. On Friday night, we experience the Sabbath as a queen. We passively receive her when women light the *Shabbat* candles. We experience the romance of being sequestered with our beloved Sabbath on Friday night after longing for her the entire preceding week.

Saturday morning impacts on our lives as a king affects the world by commanding us to study Torah. We connect to the intellectual side of Torah by studying it during the Sabbath day.

As the Sabbath ebbs away, we experience the holiness of time both actively and passively. We eat a small meal before the Sabbath ends, but are not focused on learning Torah. This final aspect of the Sabbath portends the coming of the Messiah. The messianic era will usher in a time when God's presence in the world will be so obvious and tangible that the world will be in a state of endless Sabbath. At that time, God's purpose in creating the world will have been fulfilled.

FULFILLING THE PURPOSE OF CREATION OF THE WORLD

What was God's purpose in creating the world, and what is needed in order for it to be fulfilled? As we saw, it has been suggested that God created the world in order to give Adam a place to obey His commands, and thereby allow God to bestow treasures of goodness on humanity. When the first woman helped Adam sin, man and woman lost their opportunity to bring the world to its state of spiritual perfection.

It became the task of all of their descendants to metaphysically rectify this first error. Adam and Eve were created in order to recognize and ratify that there was a singular Creator. It became the task of each successive generation to fulfill their original mission. When people put aside their personal needs and animalistic drives in order to follow God's wishes, they prepare the world for the messianic era.

How does this concept apply to men versus women? How does the Torah's view of their different natures fit in with the plan of Creation?

Adam lived in the utopia of the Garden of Eden, surrounded by its splendor and lushness. He was created directly by the Almighty, brought to life by the Master of the Universe, and was charged with a singular mission. That mission was to enjoy all of the creations that God had placed in the world – the sights, scents, sounds, sensations, and tastes. The First Man had only to restrict himself from taking from one tree, and the rest of the Garden of Eden was his to enjoy forever, as a reward for restraining himself in this one area.

Within hours of her creation, Chavah (Eve) ate from the fruit of the tree of knowledge of good and evil, and gave some to Adam. The rest is history. The subsequent years have been spent trying to make up for the imperfection brought into the world by the First Man's sin. In order for us to rectify this sin, we have to understand not only what the sin was, but what Adam's and Eve's roles with respect to each other were intended to be.

EVE'S DUAL ROLES

Adam was to have been the creature who was to reign over the entire earth as God's appointed surrogate. But he was supposed to have remembered that God was the ultimate decision-maker and ruler. By acquiescing to the rule of his Creator, Adam would have sanctified all earthly existence. Adam was charged with one *mitzvah,* and his task was to serve God directly by keeping it.

Chavah, on the other hand, was created in a different manner than was Adam. She was specifically created as an *ezer kenegdo* – literally, a "help against him." God did not directly command her to keep the *mitzvah* that was given to Adam. (Adam transmitted the command to her.) Rather, she was designated to have two specific roles.

Her first role was to be a helper to Adam, an *ezer kenegdo.* She was created to be an equal partner to her husband. In this role, one of her responsibilities was to help Adam recognize his limitations. The designation of Chavah as a "helper against him" is interpreted to mean that Chavah was to be Adam's helper when he deserved her help, but was to oppose him when he didn't deserve her help. This implied that Chavah, in part due to her objectivity, could have more awareness of God's will than did Adam.

Chavah's name also comes from the word *chai,* meaning life. Chavah's second role was, as her name implies, to be the mother of all people. In encouraging Adam to sin in the Garden of Eden, Chavah was more of a *kenegdo* – an opponent to Adam – than an *ezer,* or help to him. Since Chavah embodied within her the souls of all women who would ever be born, it became the primary task of all of Chavah's female descendants to rectify her error by enabling themselves and their husbands to attain their spiritual goals.

The sages usually translate the term *ezer kenegdo* to mean that a woman supports her husband by helping him, and thereby becomes his *ezer.* A wife who opposes her husband is considered to be *kenegdo* – "his opponent."

The expression *ezer kenegdo* can also be appropriately translated in a different way. Even when a woman opposes her husband, she can be his *ezer.* That is, women can help men by opposing them.[1] Throughout Jewish history, women have stood in opposition to their husbands' misguided actions, thereby enabling their husbands, and the entire Jewish people, to reach spiritual heights that they could not have attained otherwise.

Women rectify Chavah's sin by acting as *ezer kenegdo* as well as by being mothers. These dual roles have constituted the two primary ways that Jewish women act as redeemers of the world and exercise their tremendous power.

Apparent Duality in the World

God created a world that seems to consist of two separate forces – the forces of good and the forces of evil. Throughout the centuries, nations have worshiped these separate forces as independent entities. Zoroastrianism, the religion of the Persians, is a prime example of this. They prayed to one god who controlled good and to a second one who controlled evil. They prayed to one god who controlled light and to a different god who controlled darkness.

In contrast with this, Jews believe that the world will be redeemed when people believe that "the Lord is one and His Name is one." The world will be one step closer to redemption when people recognize that there is only one force in the world. People need to realize that things only happen because there is ultimately a Prime Mover who causes all things to occur.

Beyond the need to simply realize that God is behind whatever happens, we are challenged to recognize that whatever God wills is good. Whatever God causes to happen, even those events that seem by mortal standards to be bad, He intends ultimately to be good.

In the Torah, the biblical man struggles with himself. Part of him wants to attain what he wants, and part of him wants to achieve what God wants for him. The biblical woman, on the other hand, quietly and tenaciously influences and supports men to do what God wants. It is the biblical woman who more readily sees the integration in the world of the apparent forces of good and bad. The man has to develop himself, through trials and tribulations with the outside world, to come to this point. In the Torah, Jewish women seem to comprehend this intuitively. Several illustrations follow.

SARAH'S CONTRIBUTION TO REDEMPTION

In the Bible, women act behind the scenes, quietly and subtly, to bring the world to the state that God envisioned it should attain. One of the first biblical accounts of this occurs in the story involving Abraham and Sarah:

> And Sarah saw the son of Hagar the Egyptian, whom she had born to Abraham, making fun (of Isaac, Sarah's son). And (Sarah) said to Abraham, "Chase out this maidservant and her son, because the son of this maidservant will not inherit with my son, with Isaac."
>
> And the thing seemed very bad to Abraham because it concerned his son (Ishmael). And God said to Abraham, "Let this matter not seem bad in your eyes—regarding this young man, and your maidservant. Everything that Sarah tells you, listen to her, because your children will be called through Isaac."[2]

Abraham is described as the first Jew because he came to an intellectual understanding that the world had a singular creator. He deduced that it was proper to worship only God, and not His creations. However, there was something lacking in Abraham's personal characteristics that did not allow him to father the twelve tribes who would be the progenitors of the Jewish people. It was Sarah, his wife, who provided a corrective to Abraham's character flaw.

Abraham's overwhelming lovingkindness prevented him from seeing the corruption in his son Ishmael. Ishmael was his son from his concubine, Hagar. He could not be allowed to grow up with Isaac, Abraham's younger son. This was because Ishmael was likely to influence Isaac to reject a Godly way of life. It was Sarah's task to tell her husband to send Ishmael away, because she had the spiritual sensitivity and objectivity to realize that Isaac alone was suited to be Abraham's spiritual heir. The Jewish tradition stresses that Sarah's level of prophetic revelation was greater than that of her husband, making her aware of things that he was not.[3]

Since Sarah's time, Jewish women have repeatedly demonstrated their spiritual fortitude. Their moral rectitude has allowed the Jewish people to survive and flourish both physically and spiritually. It is the hallmark of the Jewish woman that she is able to sense God's will and act in consonance with it. She thereby ensures the holiness of the Jewish people and the carrying out of God's plan for the world.

REBEKAH'S CONTRIBUTION TO REDEMPTION

There are many biblical accounts of women devoting their lives to ensuring Jewish survival. After Sarah died, her son Isaac married Rebekah. They had twin sons named Jacob and Esau, who subsequently developed along very different life paths. Whereas Esau became immoral, Jacob strove to sanctify life and serve God.

Before Isaac died, he wanted to bless Esau because he believed that Esau had tremendous spiritual potential. Despite having these potentials, Rebekah understood that Esau would never bring them to fruition. For this reason, she tried to make sure that Jacob received his father's blessing instead of allowing Esau to get it. The story is related as follows:

And Isaac grew old, and his eyes were too dim to see. He called Esau his older son and said to him, "My son." And Esau said to him, "Here I am."

And (Isaac) said, "Behold, I have grown old. I don't know when I will die. Take your tools, your bow and your quiver, and go out to the field and hunt me some game. Make me the kind of tasty food that I love, and bring it to me. I will eat it so that my soul can bless you before I die."

And Rebekah said to Jacob her son as follows, "Behold, I heard your father speak to Esau your brother, saying, 'Bring me game, and make me tasty food, and I will eat, and I will bless you before God, prior to my death.' Now, my son, listen to me. . . . Please go to the flocks, and take me two good kids, and I will make them into tasty food for your father, just as he loves. And you will bring it to your father, and he will eat so that he will bless you before he dies."

And Jacob said to Rebekah his mother, "Behold, Esau my brother is a hairy man, and I am smooth-skinned. Perhaps my father will feel me, and I will appear to be a trickster, and I will bring a curse on me, and not a blessing."

And his mother said to him, "Let the curse be upon me, my son. Just listen to me and go, take (the goats) for me."

And Jacob went, and took, and brought the goats to his mother. And she made tasty food as his father loved. And Rebekah took the best clothes of Esau, her older son, that were with her in the house, and she clothed Jacob her younger son with them. And she put the kidskins on his hands, and on the smooth part of his neck. And she put the tasty food and the bread she made into Jacob's hands.

And Jacob came to his father, and said, "My father."

And Isaac said, "Here I am. Who are you, my son?"

And Jacob said to his father, "I am Esau your firstborn. I have done what you said to me. Please arise and sit, and eat of my hunt, in order that your soul might bless me. . . ."

And Isaac said to Jacob, "Please approach, and I will feel you to determine if you are really my son, Esau, or not." . . . And he said, "Are you my son, Esau?"

And Jacob replied, "I am."

And Jacob approached Isaac his father, and Isaac felt him, and said, "The voice is the voice of Jacob, and the hands are the hands of Esau." And he did not recognize him because his hands were hairy like the hands of his brother Esau, and Isaac blessed him.[4]

This entire episode was engineered through the brilliance of Isaac's wife Rebekah. Rebekah came from a house of shrewd and astute business people, and she quickly discerned that Esau made pretenses of being interested in following a holy way of life. She understood that he was not a fitting heir for the spiritual blessing that Isaac wished to bestow on one of his sons.

Isaac was not as capable as Rebekah of recognizing the danger that Esau's evil represented. Not only did she see through her son's facade, but she also knew that the only way for Jacob to take over Esau's intended role was by using guile. Esau used guile for evil purposes, but it could also be used for good. Rebekah used deception to show her husband and son the power that evil can have when it is harnessed in the service of good, thereby enabling the good to reach its tremendous spiritual heights.

Jacob was unable to harness the spiritual energy that was associated with overcoming evil until his mother forced him to use apparent falsehood in order to serve spiritual goals.

LEAH AND RACHEL

Jacob was the progenitor of the Jewish nation. As such, he was destined to father twelve sons. In one of the most romantic love stories in the Torah, Jacob falls in love with Rachel and works for her father for seven years in order to gain his beloved's hand in marriage.[5]

When the wedding day comes, Rachel's father Laban takes his elder daughter Leah and garbs her in Rachel's wedding dress. He then brings her under the wedding canopy in Rachel's stead. All of this occurs without Jacob's knowledge.

The Talmud says that Jacob had anticipated that Laban would try to trick him, and he gave Rachel certain secret signs by which she could let him know that she was indeed the bride. Since brides were heavily veiled in those days, one could not be sure who the bride was until the ceremony was over.

When Rachel saw that her sister was being brought to the wedding canopy, she thought, "My sister will be horribly embarrassed when she is found out." At that point, Rachel put aside her personal feelings and gave Leah the secret signs that Jacob had prearranged with her.[6] Under these circumstances, Jacob married Leah and did not discover her true identity until after consummating their marriage. A week later, he also married Rachel.

Subsequently, both women gave Jacob their handmaids as additional wives in order to gain children by him. They did this because they were both prophetesses and knew that Jacob was destined to have twelve sons.[7] When Leah and Rachel appeared unable to bear additional children of their own, they still wanted to build the Jewish nation further. They recognized Jacob's unique holiness and the enormous spiritual mission to which they could contribute by giving him their handmaids as his third and fourth wives.

Our sages say that the apparent rivalry between the sisters for their husband's attention was not petty jealousy. Their relationship is detailed as follows[8]:

> And Leah became pregnant, and gave birth to a son, and she called his name, Reuven, for she said, "Surely the Eternal has seen my affliction, and now my husband will love me."
>
> She then had two more sons. When she gave birth to her fourth son, Leah announced, "Now, this time, my husband will become attached to me."
>
> And when Rachel saw that she had no children by Jacob, she was envious of her sister, and she said to Jacob, "Give me children. If not, I will be (like a) dead woman."
>
> . . . And she said, "Here is my handmaid, Bilhah. Take her to wife, and she will bear children, and I will rear them, and I will also have children." And she gave him Bilhah her handmaid as a wife . . . and Bilhah conceived and gave birth to a son to Jacob.
>
> And Leah saw that she had stopped bearing children, and she took Zilpah, her handmaid, and gave her as a wife to Jacob. And Zilpah, Leah's handmaid, gave birth to a son to Jacob. . . .
>
> And Reuven went in the days of the wheat harvest, and found mandrakes (thought to be aphrodisiacs) in the field, and he brought them to Leah his mother.
>
> And Rachel said to Leah, "Give me of your son's mandrakes."
>
> And (Leah) replied, "Is it no small thing that you've taken my husband, that you also want my son's mandrakes?"
>
> And Rachel said, "Therefore, (Jacob) shall sleep with you to-night, in return for your son's mandrakes."

The sages say that Leah and Rachel each wanted to be the fore-mother of the majority of the nation who would have a unique spiritual relationship with God.[9] They poured out heartfelt prayers to God asking Him to grant them children who would carry on the mission of the Jewish nation. In this way, they modeled to us how to pray with intensity, sincerity, and with proper motivations.

Rachel's Uniqueness

Rachel had an incredible desire to bear children who would carry on the mission of serving God. There is tremendous poignancy to the fact that Rachel yearned so deeply to have children, yet was only able to bear two sons. She died in childbirth as her second son was being born, and maintains a unique role among our foremothers.

Of all the people in the Bible, it is Rachel who cries most over the tribes of Israel in their exile. It is by virtue of her tears that God promises to redeem the Jewish people in the future.

The Talmud says that the First Temple was destroyed because the Jews worshiped idols and committed sexual immorality and murder.[10] Instead of destroying the Jewish people, God destroyed their House of Worship and sent the Jews into exile. They passed by Rachel's grave in Bethlehem as they went into the Diaspora.

The *Midrash* reports that at that time, the souls of each of the forefathers and foremothers pleaded to God to bring the Jews back to their homeland and to redeem them from their exile.[11] Abraham first tried to prevail over God in the merit of having personally discovered Him as the Creator of the world. Abraham's act was so meritorious that God made an eternal covenant with him and his descendants. Nevertheless, God did not let Himself be entreated by our first forefather.

Isaac then pleaded with God to redeem the Jews in the merit of his having been willing to be sacrificed as an offering to God on Mount Moriah.[12] His supplication was similarly rejected.

Jacob then pleaded for the Jews' redemption in the merit of his having worked for his uncle for twenty years, and having risked his life to face his murderous brother Esau, all for the sake of his children. Jacob asked God to have at least as much mercy on his descendants as Jacob himself showed. Once again, his words had no effect.

Finally, Moses pleaded in the merit of having been Israel's shepherd for forty years. Once again, his pleas were to no avail.

Rachel's soul then presented itself before God, and pleaded her case. "Master of the Universe," she began, "my beloved husband worked for me for seven years. When the end of those seven years came, it was finally time for the two of us to get married. When I saw my father bringing my disguised sister to my wedding, I could not bear for her to be humiliated. I am only flesh and blood, dust and ashes, whose nature it is to be jealous, yet I was not jealous of my sister when I gave Leah the secret signs that allowed her to marry my husband. I overcame my own feelings and had pity on her for the shame that she would suffer if she had not married Jacob.

"Don't you think, God, who are so merciful, that You can overcome Your 'jealousy' that the Jews are unfaithful to You by worshiping other gods? Can't You allow Your mercy and pity to overcome Your 'jealousy' and allow Your children to come out of exile and return to their homeland?"

Our foremother's plaintive request moved God to pity, so to speak, and He said, "Rachel, for your sake, I will return the Jews to their homeland."

God allowed Himself to be entreated only by Rachel. Her act of self-sacrifice for another Jew, in which she overcame the most basic of human feelings, had a tremendous power that aids the Jews in the Diaspora.

Jacob deliberately buried her on the road leading away from the land of Israel so that she could plead on her children's behalf when they would be exiled. It will also be in her merit that we will be redeemed from the Diaspora in the future.

Leah's Uniqueness

Leah was destined to bear seven of the twelve tribes of Israel. Had this occurred, Rachel would have given birth to only one. Feeling compassion for her sister at a time when Rachel had but one child and Leah had six, Leah prayed that Rachel be destined to bear a second son.[13] This meant that Leah would then be the mother of only six tribes. Through her prayers, Leah spared her sister the humiliation of giving birth to fewer tribes than the handmaids, who each gave birth to two sons. By so doing, Leah reciprocated the compassion that Rachel had showed her in sparing her from humiliation on her wedding night.

Leah's greatness allowed her to be the mother of Levi, who was the progenitor of the priests and Levites who served God in the Temple. Her fourth son, Judah, was the progenitor of Jewish kings, including King David and the Messiah.

DINAH

After giving birth to six sons, Leah gave birth to a daughter, Dinah. Some years later, Dinah was abducted by a non-Jewish prince named Shechem, who raped her.[14]

One explanation as to why this terrible incident occurred is that Jacob had hidden Dinah when he went to meet his brother Esau after the two were separated for many years. Jacob hid her because he was afraid that if Esau were to see her, he would marry her and thereafter corrupt her with his evil ways.

A midrashic explanation says that Jacob should have let Dinah marry Esau. Rather than Esau corrupting her, she might have influenced him to become righteous.[15]

Again, women's virtuousness was deemed sufficient to influence men to actualize their potentials. Were these biblical men to be left to their own devices, they alone could not, or would not, have developed their spiritual endowments to their utmost.

TAMAR

Some years later, Judah, Jacob's fourth son, was involved in a rather unusual incident.[16] Judah was regarded as the leader of all of the tribes. (Several generations later, King David descended from him. Once David was anointed king, all future leaders of Israel were supposed to come only from the tribe of Judah. Throughout Jewish history, Judah and his descendants had a preeminent role as leaders of the Jewish people. Moreover, most Jews today are descended from the tribe of Judah, which is why we are called "Jews".)

Judah had three sons. The eldest, Er, married a woman named Tamar. God killed him for not wanting to mar his wife's beauty by getting her pregnant. According to biblical law, when a man died child-less, his brother was required to marry his widow. The children of that union were then "credited" to the deceased. In Tamar's case, the responsibility of carrying on her deceased husband's name fell to Onan, Er's next younger brother.

Onan married Tamar, but the child who would have been born from their union would have been "accredited" to Er, so he refused to father a child who would not bear his own name. God then killed him as well. The responsibility of marrying Tamar and fathering children with her then fell on the third brother, Shelah.

Initially, Shelah was too young to marry her. However, Judah did not let him marry Tamar even when Shelah grew up because he was afraid that Shelah would die, as did the other brothers when they married her. When Tamar saw that Judah evaded his responsibility to have Shelah marry her, she disguised herself and seduced Judah into getting her pregnant. The male ancestor of King David was born from this union of Tamar and Judah.

Tamar's righteousness in acting out of lovingkindness for the dead, without ulterior motives, transformed what could have been an act of prostitution into a holy sexual union. The souls of her resulting children were endowed with the spiritual potentials to become kings of Israel, who would likewise act for the honor of God without having selfish or ulterior motives.

JEWISH WOMEN IN EGYPT

The Book of Exodus gives an expanded picture of what Jewish biblical women were like. Jacob's extended family went into Egypt, beginning an exile that was to last for 210 years. Even though the Egyptians were renowned for their culture and scientific sophistication, their sexual licentiousness and idolatry were of equal repute.

The overt reason for Jacob and his family moving from Canaan to Egypt was because there was a worldwide famine that did not affect the Egyptians. At that time, Jacob's son Joseph was the viceroy of Egypt. He had engineered a plan whereby previously stored grain was distributed to all the Egyptians so that they could endure the years of famine. Due to his position, he could also ensure that all of Jacob's relatives could get food until the famine ended. Therefore, he invited his entire family to join him in Egypt, and he settled them there.

The men settled a little too comfortably in an Egyptian district called Goshen, where they had a prosperous material existence. The women did not want to trade the spirituality of the land of Israel, even in a time of famine, for the lack of holiness in a land of plenty.

Many years after Jacob died, the Israelite men in Egypt became slaves to Pharaoh. The slavery became more and more oppressive, until the men were so beaten that they had no time or energy to even come home. Their wives were determined not to let the Egyptians destroy the Jewish nation. They prepared food for their husbands and took it out to them in the fields. They also brought copper mirrors with them, which they used to encourage their husbands to gaze at the wives' reflections. When the husbands did this, they realized how beautiful their wives were, and they had relations with them. The women conceived from these unions.

The entire reason for the women's actions was to ensure that the Israelites would continue to reproduce, even under conditions of slavery and oppression. Through these women's efforts, not only did their husbands survive, but they ensured the nation's survival. The Israelites increased from seventy individuals to at least three million people in the space of 210 years.[17]

These righteous women's efforts were formally recognized after the Exodus from Egypt, when the Israelites built the Sanctuary in the desert. Moses made a general announcement for the entire populace to bring gifts, from which God's Sanctuary and its appurtenances would be constructed. The women brought their jewelry (which they had previously refused to donate to the construction of the Golden Calf), as well as the copper mirrors that they had used to seduce their husbands for procreative purposes in Egypt.

When Moses saw the mirrors, he did not want to accept them. He felt that such objects were used for vanity (women's putting on make-up) and that they had no place in God's House of Worship.

God told Moses, "Accept the mirrors. They are more precious to Me than any other contributions (to the Tabernacle). It was due to the women's use of these mirrors that they had many children in Egypt and caused so many people to be brought out of Egypt during the Exodus. What the women did with these mirrors was very holy. They seduced their husbands so that they could fulfill the commandment to have children and bring many Jews into the world."[18]

These mirrors were made into the copper laver and washstand from which the priests washed themselves prior to performing their divine service.

Our sages tell us that the Israelites were worthy of being redeemed from Egypt only in the merit of the women, who were more righteous than the men during the years of enslavement.[19] The Jewish men had become almost as unholy as their Egyptian neighbors. The women had not assimilated themselves into the Egyptian culture to the extent that the men had.

Shifra and Puah

When the population explosion of the Jews in Egypt occurred, Pharaoh decreed that any Jewish males who were born must be killed immediately after birth. There were two Jewish midwives—Shifra and Puah—who were particularly charged with carrying out this royal decree.[20] These women not only refused to implement his plan of murder, but they risked their lives by lying to Pharaoh and saving Jewish babies under his nose.

Miriam

When Amram, a renowned leader of the tribe of Levi, heard Pharaoh's murderous decree, he divorced his wife. Amram did not want to have children if they would be killed at birth. The rest of the Jewish men promptly followed his example and divorced their wives. Amram's daughter Miriam chided her father for this, telling him that his decree was even worse than Pharaoh's. She explained to her father that Pharaoh only decreed that Jewish males be killed. Her father's actions precluded the possibility that either males or females would be born.

After hearing his daughter's argument, Amram remarried his wife, and the other men did likewise with their wives. Through the subsequent union of Amram with his wife Yocheved, the leader of the Jewish people—Moses—was born.

When Moses was three months old, his mother could no longer hide him at home. She put him in a basket and placed him near the Nile, in compliance with Pharaoh's orders. Miriam watched over him from a distance to see what his fate would be.

Shortly thereafter, none other than Pharaoh's daughter discovered the child. At that point, Miriam appeared. She generously offered to find a wet-nurse for the baby. Pharaoh's daughter agreed, and Miriam took Moses back to his own mother. Yocheved nursed him until he was old enough to be raised by Pharaoh's daughter in the royal palace. In this manner, Moses was tended to by his own mother until the time came for him to be raised in Pharaoh's palace.[21]

THE GOLDEN CALF

God gave the Jews the Torah seven weeks after their Exodus from Egypt. Prior to giving it, He made sure that the women would all be present and would witness the event with the same immediacy as did the men. This was to make sure that the mistake that Eve made in the Garden of Eden would not be repeated.

Adam, rather than God, apprised Eve of the prohibition against eating from the tree of knowledge. Had Eve heard the commandment directly from God, she would not have sinned.[22] Therefore, it was necessary for the Jewish women to hear the Torah directly from God. This would enable them to observe the laws better, as well as endow them with the necessary tools to properly influence their children to carry on the Jewish heritage.

God's revelation through the giving of the Torah at Mount Sinai replicated the relationship between God and Adam in the Garden of Eden. Giving the Torah after the Jews were redeemed from Egypt paralleled giving Adam his commandment not to eat from the tree of knowledge of good and evil.

At the giving of the Torah, the Jews agreed to uphold the laws of the Written and Oral Torah. Their accepting God's absolute sovereignty over the world allowed Him to reinstate the relationship with the Jews that He had had with Adam during the sixth day of Creation. Through the revelation at Mount Sinai, God married the Jewish people, so to speak, with the Torah serving as the marriage contract. When the Jews accepted the Torah, it was as if they agreed to be God's wife, and they pledged themselves to an exclusive relationship with Him.

Unfortunately, this proved to be a short-lived marriage in some respects. Forty days after God gave the Torah and revealed Himself, some of the men insisted on making a golden calf. The women did not participate in this.

The Israelite women decided to do what God commanded rather than following the men's impulses. Through their behavior, the Jewish women attained a spiritual level that was worthy of bringing the Messiah.

They commemorated the spiritual elevation that accompanied their lack of participation with the Golden Calf by agreeing to accept the spiritual observance of the holiday of *Rosh Chodesh* – the monthly celebration of the New Moon.[23] It has been a custom since the time of Moses for women to refrain from doing everyday chores on *Rosh Chodesh,* in recognition of the holiday's special significance for them. Thus, they do not launder clothes, iron, sew, or weave on *Rosh Chodesh.* (If they are employed, they do work at their jobs.) It is also considered desirable for Jews of both sexes to eat larger meals than usual on *Rosh Chodesh,* preferably with bread, in honor of the day.[24] Some women also wear special clothes on *Rosh Chodesh* in order to honor its significance.

THE SPIES

The men who participated in the construction of the Golden Calf repeated the same type of mistake that Adam made. They substituted their judgment for God's. The men sinned again in a later incident where they insisted on sending out spies to see if the land of Israel was all that God had told them it would be. Ten of the twelve spies brought back an evil report about the land, and they convinced the Jewish men that they would be unable to take possession of it. Due to this incident, all of the men of that generation were condemned to die in the desert, except for the two righteous spies. These two righteous men were Joshua the son of Nun, who became Moses' successor, and Caleb the son of Yephuneh. They tried to encourage the populace not to be swayed by the reports of the other spies, but their pleas fell on deaf ears. Ultimately, they were the only adult males from the generation who left Egypt to enter the land of Israel.

The ten spies who brought back an evil report about Israel were referred to as an *eidah*. The Torah says that God should be "sanctified in the midst of the Israelites."[25] The concept that a *minyan,* a quorum for public prayer, consists of ten men is derived from the fact that the *eidah* in the Spies narrative consisted of ten men. Similarly, certain public affairs require the presence of ten men, because God is to be sanctified in the midst of an *eidah*—a group consisting of at least ten men.

A possible reason as to why ten men form a *minyan* and women do not is because the entire need to have a quorum in order to bring down God's Presence only applies to males. Women are considered to each be sufficiently holy to not require a group of them in order to say special prayers. This is why the entire idea of public prayer and certain types of sanctification of God's Name are primarily associated with males.

The Jewish women in the desert did not listen to the spies' report. They wanted to go into the promised land. Due to their righteousness, they did not die in the desert, as did their male contemporaries. Due to their love of the land, the women all entered the land of Israel under the leadership of Joshua.

Through the women's demonstrations of their love of God in these matters, they showed themselves to be in tune with His will. Their behavior was so exemplary that had the men acted as the women did, the Messiah would have come during the time of the desert generation.

DEBORAH AND YAEL

Deborah and Yael were two famous women who are described in the Book of Judges.[26] Deborah was the sole female judge in Jewish history and was also a prophetess. She was the greatest Jew of her generation (the *gadol ha-dor*), and she lived during the time when judges ruled the Jewish people. Since no men of her era were qualified to be judges, the entire Jewish nation came to her to be judged.

It is interesting to note that Deborah's husband was an ignorant, simple man. She encouraged him to apply his spiritual potentials in the greatest way he could, so that he would have a share in the Hereafter. To this end, she made very thick wicks for the candelabrum *(menorah)* of the Holy Temple and asked her husband to take them there.[27] The wicks were specially made in order to enhance the light of the flames that were for God's glory. In reward for this, God caused her spiritual light to shine over the entire Jewish people by her being a judge.[28]

During her rule, the Jews were plagued by twenty years of oppression by the Canaanites, whose army captain was named Sisera. God ordered Deborah's husband, Barak, to select an army of 10,000 men to fight the enemy. Even though God promised Barak that his army would be victorious, he was afraid to do as God asked. Deborah was the only one who was able to encourage the Jews to fight the Canaanites. She did this, in part, by promising Barak that she would accompany him in battle. However, since Barak declined to do God's initial bidding, he lost the opportunity to be the primary agent for the promised military victory. Two women, Deborah and Yael, were awarded this honor instead.

When the Jews fought the enemy, they killed all the men except for Sisera himself. The army chief sought refuge in the tent of a woman, Yael, whose family was friendly with the family of the Canaanite king. Yael had sexual relations with Sisera seven times in order to exhaust him, and then she plied him with milk to get him to sleep.[29] Even though such relations were normally forbidden, Yael did so in order to save the Jewish people.[30]

As fatigue overtook him, Sisera asked Yael to be a sentry for him and to tell anyone who approached looking for him that he was not there. He then fell fast asleep. While he was in a deep slumber, Yael took a tent pin and hammered it into his temple, killing him. She was subsequently lauded for her role in her people's salvation.[31] This began a forty-year period of peace for the Jews. Yael's selfless actions, aimed at saving the Jews, resulted in her meriting having the scholar Rabbi Akiva descend from her.

It is noteworthy that when Deborah sang her song of praise to God for their victory, she referred to herself as a "mother in Israel."[32] Even though she was brilliant—a prophetess and a judge—the greatest role she saw for herself was as a mother of the Jewish people. As such, she prayed for her people,[33] had pity on them,[34] and reproved them for their misdeeds so that they would correct their ways.[35]

RUTH

Several hundred years after the Jews settled in the land of Israel, the events in the Book of Ruth occurred. The book begins with a man named Elimelech leaving the land of Israel with his wife Naomi and their two sons. They settled in the land of Moab. Elimelech was a leader of his generation, both economically and spiritually. Many commentators say that he left Israel so that he could preserve his personal wealth. Had he stayed, he would have been asked to support the ubiquitous poor who might knock on his door asking for charity. He avoided this by leaving.

Elimelech's two sons married two daughters of the Moabite king. Elimelech died, either as punishment for leaving the land of Israel, or for his evading his responsibilities toward his fellow Jews. His two sons also died, either as punishment for intermarrying, or for not returning to the land of Israel once their father died, or both.

The Book of Ruth concerns itself with how Elimelech's wife Naomi and their daughter-in-law Ruth rectified the failings of their respective husbands. These failings were the same failings that occurred previously among the generation of men who left Egypt.

One of the first things that these two women did after their husbands died was to return to the land of Israel. This parallels the situation in the desert: the men who left Egypt criticized the land of Israel, and the women insisted on entering it and settling there. Elimelech and his sons were punished with death for spurning the land of Israel, whereas two of their wives subsequently returned to Israel.

Elimelech's second shortcoming was his refusal to support the poor. In contrast with this, Ruth willingly took it upon herself to support her mother-in-law by gleaning in the fields for food. She also forsook her homeland of Moab, where she was a princess (the daughter of King Balak), even though it meant living a life of poverty among Jews.

Had Ruth only taken these two things upon herself, it is doubtful that she would have been considered great. It is likely that her tremendous desire to act as a Jewish woman, *par excellence*, is why she is regarded so positively. She took on the role of being a mother of the Jewish people, and she dedicated herself to doing kind deeds for others. In this way, she demonstrated her special spiritual fortitude to the Jewish people.

Ruth returned to the land of Israel after her husband died. She then gleaned in the field of Naomi's relative, Boaz, in order to eke out sustenance for herself and her mother-in-law. By the time the harvest season ended, Boaz had been kind to Ruth, but nothing more.

In the style of Tamar before her, Ruth sets out to insure that Boaz, her deceased husband's relative, will marry her and father children with her in the memory of her first husband. Like Tamar before her, she is motivated not by her personal desire to have a child, but by wanting to memorialize the name of the deceased.

Ruth repeatedly refers to Boaz as a "redeemer." Her motives in stalking him in a rather unorthodox manner were totally in order to serve God. Not only did she want her husband's name to continue in Israel, but she herself wanted to be a mother to the Jewish people.

Through her maneuverings, Ruth operated as an *ezer kenegdo*—a helper—to Boaz. He did not need much convincing once he realized Ruth's true motives in wanting to marry him. However, had she not initially encouraged him to marry her, he might never have done so.

Boaz and Ruth married, and their union produced King David's grandfather. For this reason, Ruth is known as the "mother of royalty."[36] She merited living until the reign of her great-great-grandson, King Solomon. At the beginning of his rule, she sat on a special seat to the right of his throne.

Ruth was yet another virtuous woman who enabled a man to live up to his potential by her being a mother in Israel and an *ezer kenegdo*. These roles were acted out with no thought of personal reward. Rather, Ruth wanted to help Boaz act in the highest way possible in order to further God's desire for the world to achieve perfection.

CONTEMPORARY WOMEN

How can modern Jewish women redeem the Jewish people without seducing men into levirate marriages and without getting their husbands not to play favorites with the children? They can encourage their husbands spend extra time learning Torah. Some women take on full- or part-time jobs in order to enable their husbands to give up some of their time earning money so that they can devote themselves instead to learning on a more intensive basis. Some women choose prospective spouses according to how much commitment the men will make to learning more about Judaism on an ongoing basis. Other women take on certain domestic or practical responsibilities in order to free their husbands to learn more than they might otherwise be able.

Some women use their domestic talents to draw people closer to learning Torah and growing spiritually. Most organizational leaders know that people who find it difficult to attend Judaism classes may be induced to do so when the classes are followed by home-made delicacies. Similarly, people who might be averse to formally studying about Judaism may be more willing to experience the atmosphere around a Sabbath meal that has been lovingly prepared, and they may be impressed by the harmony and holiness that pervades a Jewish home.

Apart from encouraging men to learn Torah, women can organize their own sessions with study partners. They can also arrange and attend Torah classes for women on a regular basis, or study Torah on their own. For women who find attending classes difficult, cassette tapes on Jewish topics are readily available.

A second area in which women enable men to fulfill their potentials is by raising Jewish families. The love and education that children receive from their mothers at home are cornerstones of their moral and emotional development. The home is the most fundamental school that Jews have, and mothers' interactions with their children affect their personal, social, and spiritual development.

A third area where women can excel is in doing charitable work and encouraging others to do deeds of lovingkindness. For example, a handful of contemporary women have initiated and run organizations in Jerusalem that support thousands of needy families on annual budgets of six figures. They are such adept managers that there are no overhead expenses, and all of the money collected goes to the indigent. These women have amassed over 1,000 volunteers—men, women, and children, religious and nonreligious—to help prepare and distribute food, blankets, money, comfort, and other necessities to destitute families.

Women's lovingkind actions will be a fundamental contribution that brings the Messiah. Their inviting guests into their homes for the Sabbath, doing outreach with unaffiliated Jews, acting selflessly to encourage their husbands to learn more Torah, raising Jewish children, visiting the sick, and giving comfort to mourners . . . all of these are ways in which the modern woman can bring redemption to the world and hasten the coming of the Messiah.

It says in *The Ethics of the Fathers* that the world stands on three things: on Torah, on prayer, and on deeds of lovingkindness.[37] Every day should have a time when Jewish women, and their families if they have them, learn Torah. Every day should have a time for prayer. However, each of these two rests on a third pillar, which is *chesed*—doing kind deeds out of selflessness.

The Book of Ruth is read on the holiday of Shavuot, the day on which God gave us the Torah. The pairing of these two suggests to us that Torah can only exist in a world in which people act with the lovingkindness of Ruth, Naomi, and Boaz.

God wants people to emulate that divine aspect that provides for the world out of selflessness. Once we act with love in helping others reach their spiritual potentials, God will not have to act in a supernatural way to redeem us. Women, with men, will be able to build an everlasting world of lovingkindness.

If we build a world of lovingkindness *(olam chesed yibaneh),* the Messiah and the Divine Presence will hopefully join us as we bring redemption to the world.

II

Relating to Prayer

5

Separate Seating in the Synagogue

Many Jews find separate seating in the synagogue objectionable because it violates their sentiments about togetherness, family, and love. People like to feel that "the family that prays together, stays together." Although Judaism strongly encourages everyone to worship God, the centrality of prayer as a family function is a Christian notion, not a Jewish one. Whereas Judaism is primarily a religion of deed rather than creed, the opposite is true for Christianity. Christianity stresses belief and its expression through church prayer. Therefore, the seat of Christian power and theology is the Church, associating the religion with the edifice in which it is practiced. The church is also the central place where Christian faith is professed.

One might gauge how "religious" a Christian is by how often he or she goes to church. A comparable assessment of Jews would more likely be according to how carefully they observe Jewish rituals. Do they only eat kosher food? Do they observe the Sabbath? The equation of attendance in the synagogue with one's religious stature is not a Jewish concept.

FUNCTION OF A SYNAGOGUE

The synagogue is supposed to be a central place for communal prayer, but it is certainly not the primary focus of Jewish life. Synagogues were not intended to be "Houses of Love and Prayer," where fraternal kinship, neighborly love, and family togetherness are emphasized. In fact, the rabbis condemned those who referred to the synagogue as "the people's house." This appellation suggested that people viewed the synagogue as a place to fulfill their needs, rather than being a place that was dedicated to worship of God.

The framework through which the Jewish family is supposed to "stay together" is via the values and rituals of the home. When families sanctify their food together and thank God for it, it creates family bonds. When Jews celebrate the holidays and Sabbath at home and invite God's Presence to dwell there, they build family ties. When homes are transformed into centers for dispensing charity, and where family members offer kindness to those in need, family unity is reinforced. Unfortunately, when families observe few or no Jewish traditions, and the home is not viewed as a mainstay of Jewish life, what should be accomplished in the home is inappropriately transferred to the synagogue.

Synagogue prayer services originally paralleled the animal sacrifices and prayers offered in the Temple. They were intended to develop a facet of our relationship with the Almighty, not to supplant other facets. The laws that determine the appropriateness of synagogue behavior are designed to foster our sense of reverence for God and to inspire us to do His will. To this end, any thoughts, feelings, or behaviors that distract us from achieving these ends are discouraged.

APPROPRIATE CONDUCT IN A SYNAGOGUE

We are not supposed to kiss a child, friend, parent, or anyone else in the synagogue, because such an act demonstrates love for a person at a time when all of our love is supposed to be directed toward God. When we are in the synagogue, we should concentrate totally on our Creator and direct all of our feelings toward Him.

Synagogues are not supposed to provide us a quiet or solemn place where we can feel content and happy. They are places where we withdraw from the world in order to introspect, work on our relationship with the Master of the Universe, and experience awe and love for Him. One suggested reason as to why God gave us the ability to love is because He wanted us to experience some part of how He "feels" about us and how we should feel toward Him. When we feel grateful for our families and loving toward them in the synagogue, we should relate these feelings to the One Above.

We should experience and develop our human relationships outside the synagogue. We should experience our relationship with God everywhere, but we do this to the exclusion of everything else in the synagogue. Just as a married couple can relate most intimately to each other when they remove any distractions, we do the same when we want to focus our attention exclusively on our Maker.

The synagogue is God's home and we are welcome to sit in His Presence as invited guests. There are rules about how guests should conduct themselves in any host's home, and the same is true about our conduct in the synagogue. God has set ground rules about how He wants us to pray and gave us detailed specifications as to how we should build houses of prayer. Our Scriptures and/or prophets gave our ancestors precise instructions as to how to build the Tabernacle in the desert and how to construct both Temples. In modern times, we are not at liberty to design and engineer our sanctuaries according to our personal preferences. Our contemporary houses of worship are still God's "home," and we therefore build them according to His tastes, not ours.

Thus, there are divine rules about how a synagogue and its worshipers can facilitate God's Presence dwelling on earth. A synagogue must have a certain layout in order for prayers there to be acceptable and for us to be in a frame of mind that is conducive to meaningful communication with God.

Humility is a prerequisite for prayer, and we must incorporate it into our reverence for the synagogue. We are forbidden to do anything in a synagogue that detracts from our sense of awe at being in the Almighty's presence. For instance, it is normally forbidden to converse in a synagogue, with the occasional exception of asking for something we need in order to pray properly (as when asking where the prayerbooks are). We are likewise forbidden to eat or drink in a synagogue, or to use it as a social hall. Nothing that transpires in a synagogue should distract us from feeling that we are humbly standing in the palace of the King of Kings. All of our thoughts, emotions, and speech there should be directed toward building a closeness with, and reverence for, the Master of the Universe.

The Torah commands all Jews "to love the Lord your God and to serve Him with all your hearts and with all your souls."[1] The sages interpret this to mean that all of our powers and feelings should be used to serve God in prayer.[2] These feelings include our desire to do His will, as well as the desire we have *not* to do His will. These latter feelings include wanting to serve our own egos instead of using those feelings to serve God.

For example, if we feel egocentric, and don't want to share what we have with others, or want to get honor so that people will worship us, or want to pursue making money in ways that are immoral or unethical—all of these desires go against God's will. We can acknowledge these drives while changing our motivations as to why we want to satisfy them. In so doing, we can use these feelings to serve God instead of ourselves. For instance, we might desire material comfort not only because we want it, but so that we can host guests for the Sabbath and holidays in a manner where they will be comfortable. Instead of seeking honor so that we will be worshiped, we can live in a way that our personal example to others attains their respect and motivates them to respect the God that we worship.

We should harness those feelings that want to serve God, as well as harnessing those that want to serve our egos, so that we can worship our Creator fully.

One of the Torah's primary functions is to teach us how to be holy. Just as God is holy and the synagogue is holy, so are we supposed to be holy. The requirement to be holy is specifically interpreted to mean that we must keep away from inappropriate sexual relationships. "Whoever fences himself away from immorality is called 'holy.' "[3] Wherever the Torah mentions restraint against immorality, it is preceded or followed by a reference to holiness. This teaches us that any time we want to be in a holy place, or think holy thoughts, we must first "fence" ourselves away from immoral thoughts and behavior.

We are supposed to guard ourselves against mingling with people of the opposite sex when it can lead to immodest behavior or to inappropriate sexual thoughts. Even though many contemporary synagogues also serve as social or community centers, their true function should be as places where we can draw down the Divine Presence and allow it to infuse ourselves with greater sanctity.

The Torah says, "My sanctuary you shall revere,"[4] and the Talmud says that synagogues are to be regarded as miniature Temples.[5] Many of the laws that govern the synagogue's sanctity and the sense of propriety required there are derived from the laws that applied to the Temples.

STRUCTURES OF THE TEMPLES

The two Temples were both constructed as rectangular buildings containing several sections. The western section included an area known as the Holy of Holies. This housed the Holy Ark, with the tablets of the Ten

Commandments. Only the High Priest was allowed to enter there, and solely when he performed a special ceremony on Yom Kippur. It was a capital crime for anyone else to go there. If the High Priest entered the Holy of Holies at any time other than on Yom Kippur, or in other than the prescribed manner, even he would die.

Outside the curtain partition that enclosed the Holy of Holies were the *menorah* (seven-armed candelabra), the incense altars, and a table used for showbread. One exited the inner chamber by descending several steps that led into the rest of the inner court. The eastern end of the inner court had an altar for animal sacrifices and a laver used to ritually wash the priests' hands and feet. Further east was the hall of priests, and at the easternmost end of the inner court was a small "court of the Israelites."

To the east of the inner court was an enormous courtyard enclosed by a wall. This area was known as the "women's court," and it was separated from the Israelite court by a wall. The women's court had a gate in the center, with fifteen steps leading up to the inner court. Thus, the sexes were separated in the Temple by having men congregate in the inner court and women assemble in an outer court. The gates allowed men and women to reach their respective courtyards with a minimum of mingling.

INTERMINGLING

When the Temples stood, ten miracles occurred there daily.[6] The Temple's enormous sanctity and God's manifest Presence through these miracles were obvious to every Jew who lived at that time. Even so, worshipers still entertained inappropriate thoughts and engaged in immodest behavior with the opposite sex when large crowds congregated at the Temple. For this reason, special separations between men and women were added during mass celebrations there. Women normally stood outside the courtyard and men stood inside.[7]

A tremendous celebration was held during the holiday of Succot (Tabernacles). This was known as the "Joyful Ceremony of Water Drawing" (*Simchat Bet Ha-sho'evah*). When this ceremony was originally held, the women stood inside the Temple and the men stayed outside. This arrangement led to excessive levity (*kalut rosh*), which included prohibited physical contact and immodest conduct.[8]

The women were originally in the Women's Court proper, whereas the men were on the Temple Mount and in the area that was enclosed by a rampart. These two areas were also separated by a huge *mechitzah*—a physical separation between the two groups. However, because people had to stand near one of the open gates in order to see the events of the evening, there was "excessive frivolity." This means that men and women interacted immodestly because the *mechitzah* did not fully separate or screen them from each other's view.

The frivolity did not occur simply because the men could look across the women's court while watching the festivities. When the sages permitted the women to be inside and the men outside, they knew that the men would be able to see the women. What they did not anticipate is that the looking would lead to social conversation and a type of mingling that was inappropriate.

Subsequently, the sages arranged for the women to sit outside, behind the men, and for the men to sit inside. They still mingled inappropriately. Finally, the sages enacted "an innovation" for the holiday. They constructed a balcony; the women sat upstairs and the men downstairs. A *mechitzah* had originally separated the sexes, but it was inadequate to prevent immodest levity between them. Therefore, the sages required women to stand in a balcony in the Temple.

It was forbidden to make engineering or architectural innovations in the structure of the Tabernacle or Temples, since they were built to exact specifications based on divine instructions.

When they were built, the Tabernacle and both Temples had separate areas for the sexes, but no balcony. When the Talmud says that the sages enacted an "innovation" in the Second Temple, it means one of two things: the Women's Court of the Second Temple originally had no walls, so they were added in order to construct balconies, or fixtures were added to existing walls of the Women's Court, to which balconies were then attached. Since it was forbidden to add anything to the Temple that was not divinely mandated, the sages had to ensure that there was a scriptural basis for making additions to the Women's Court.

SCRIPTURAL BASIS FOR *MECHITZAH*

The requirement to physically separate the sexes during prayer is based on a scriptural verse: "The land shall mourn, every family apart – the family of David by itself, and their wives by themselves, the family of the house of Nathan by itself, and their wives by themselves. . . ."[9] One interpretation says that this mourning refers to the eulogy for the Messiah, the son of Joseph.[10] He is destined to be killed in the War of Gog and Magog that will immediately precede the advent of the second Messiah, who will descend from King David. One might think that people would be too sad to be frivolous at a time of such great mourning. Nevertheless, it was prophesied that the men and women should mourn separately at that time.

Another talmudic interpretation says that this mourning will occur when people's inclinations to do what is wrong will no longer exist. If both sexes must mourn separately when they have no desire to do what is wrong, how much more is separation required when we have the desire to act inappropriately!

King David spoke to his son Solomon, who was to build the First Temple. " 'Take heed now, for the Lord has chosen you to build a house for the sanctuary. Be strong and do it.' Then David gave Solomon his son the pattern of the porch, and its houses, and its treasuries, and the upper chambers, and the inner rooms, and the place of (the ark with its) covering. . . . [David said,] 'All this is written by the hand of the Lord who made me wise, even all of the works of this pattern.' "[11]

The sages understood from these verses that they were not allowed to alter the Temple plans revealed to David, since they were God-given. They deduced from the verse in Zechariah that the requirement to physically separate men and women in the Temple was a pre-existing biblical law. They thereby realized that the Temple should have a separation between the sexes to prevent levity.

According to some opinions, the only reason for the *mechitzah* and balcony in the Temple was to prevent the sexes from inappropriate conversation and touching. Maimonides gives two reasons for having a women's balcony in the Temple: The first reason was to preclude the sexes from mingling.[12] The second reason was to prevent the men from looking at the women.[13] To achieve this aim, the women's balcony was built above the men's section.

RECENT RULINGS ABOUT SYNAGOGUE *MECHITZAHS*

Rabbi Moshe Feinstein wrote that synagogues must have a physical structure that separates men from women.[14] This is preferably achieved by having a balcony, such as was done in the Temple, with the women being above the men. If this is not feasible, and men and women must be seated on the same plane, there must be a physical separation that precludes the possibility of any type of interpersonal contact or conversation. Even if men are on one side of a synagogue and women are on the other, biblical law still requires them to be separated by a barrier. It must extend at least five feet from the floor, to approximately shoulder height. Anything lower than this will not prevent levity, since men can still converse easily with women, and this constitutes a type of mingling.

Rabbi Feinstein noted Maimonides' comment that one reason for separating the sexes was to prevent the men from seeing the women. However, Rabbi Feinstein concluded that the sages were not concerned about the men viewing the women. The barrier's only function was to prevent men from mingling with women.

Throughout Jewish history, any synagogue that was attended by women had either a balcony for them or a *mechitzah*. According to Rabbi Feinstein, it is not necessary for women in a balcony to be screened from view as long as their being seen will not lead to frivolity. However, if men can see women's exposed upper arms (or upper legs), a curtain must be put up to hide those limbs from view. This is because men are forbidden to say the *Amidah* (most central of the prayers) and the *Shema* (declaration of the unity of God) in a place where women's bodies are inappropriately exposed.

Rabbi J. B. Soloveitchik ruled that a synagogue with separate seating but no *mechitzah* forfeits its sanctity and status as a miniature Temple. Since its holiness derives from the laws that governed the Temples, a synagogue can only be holy if it has discrete sections for women and men, separated by a physical barrier.

It is better to pray alone than in a synagogue without a *mechitzah*. We are even prohibited from attending services on Rosh Hashanah and Yom Kippur (New Year's and the Day of Atonement), two of the holiest days of the year, if they are held in a synagogue that lacks a *mechitzah*. This is true even if our only opportunity to hear the blowing of the *shofar* on Rosh Hashanah (which the Torah requires) would be at such a service.

Since the Reform movement began mixed seating in the nineteenth century, every rabbinic authority who has ruled on the matter has forbidden us to pray in a synagogue that does not physically separate the sexes. Such synagogues are not holy, nor are any prayers that are said there.

The abrogation of separate seating in synagogues has its roots in Christianity.[15] When the early Christians started gaining adherents, they maintained many Jewish traditions. However, they began introducing their reforms by having men and women sit together during prayer services.

Certain archaeologists have claimed that they discovered ancient synagogues that did not have balconies or women's sections. There is no reason to assume that all ancient synagogues were regularly attended by women, just as certain synagogues today are attended primarily or exclusively by men. On those occasions when women did pray there, they presumably erected temporary *mechitzahs* or made makeshift women's sections, just as we do today. (It is not necessary for synagogues that are not attended by women to have a separate women's section.) Not even the original Reform Jews in Europe seated men and women together during services. Isaac Mayer Wise initiated the change when he used a Baptist Church to house his Reform services in Albany, New York. He liked the fact that Baptist men and women prayed together, and he initiated their seating pattern in his own temple.[16]

ARGUMENTS RAISED AGAINST *MECHITZAH*

People who object to a *mechitzah* often maintain that no one gets distracted or has sexual thoughts merely by sitting next to someone of the opposite sex. Whether the biblical law requiring separation of the sexes in the synagogue makes sense to us or not, it stands on its own merit. Nevertheless, many people want an intellectual understanding of why God commanded such a law.

One explanation could be that the presence of someone of the opposite sex can distract us or even stimulate our sexual fantasies. People who don't believe this should sit in a therapist's chair (or locker room) and hear what uncensored men and women fantasize about the opposite sex in "nonsexual" situations. Healthy human beings are sexually responsive to their environment. It is difficult enough to banish ourselves from having sexual fantasies when no object of these fantasies is in view. It is much more difficult to do so when they are within reach.

All normal people have sexual fantasies and feelings. The Jewish laws that seem so restrictive about sexual expression and mingling preserve the excitement, sensuality, and meaning of physical intimacy for married couples. They also help channel these wonderful feelings within the framework of marriage.

Unfortunately, people in secular societies often become desensitized to the excitement inherent in something as "insignificant" as a touch. Bombarding people about sex through advertising, music, movies, books, and the like has inadvertently led people to lose their appreciation for various types of intimacy.

For a sensitive person, the brush of a hand against the skin, the feeling of a knee against a leg, the touch of a woman's hair accidentally skimming a man's body can and should be exciting. It is a sad comment on current times that contact that should be suggestive and arousing is often reduced to utter meaninglessness. Even though many people have become desensitized to what should be intimate behavior, this does not justify creating situations that degrade it even further. That is, just because certain men have lost their appreciation for the sexual excitement of sitting next to a woman, or vice versa, this is not a reason to institution-alize this loss by sanctioning mixed seating in the synagogue. When men or women who retain this sensitivity pray in a synagogue without a *mechitzah,* it detracts from their true worship of God.

SEPARATE BUT BETTER

The idea of *mechitzah* was never intended to be discriminatory to women. Certain problems that result from *mechitzahs* that are not esthetically or practically appealing are unfortunate pragmatic developments that are not mandated by Jewish law.

Some women interpret the separation of men from women during prayer as denigrating to women. There is no mention in any of the scriptural, talmudic, or rabbinic writings that a *mechitzah* is required because of anything lacking in women. If anything, it is men who are regarded as needing greater protection than women in order to pray properly, because they are more likely to be distracted. Women are generally considered to be less distracted by the physical attractiveness of men, whereas men are viewed as being very sensitive to external stimuli. (In the author's experience as a therapist, women tend to be more affected by men's emotional attractiveness than by their physical appearances.)

People sometimes express concern about the structure of certain *mechitzahs.* Although the law requires either a women's balcony or a *mechitzah* of shoulder height, some women's sections make it impossible for women to see or hear the services. This unfortunate situation can sometimes be resolved. There is nothing wrong with women (or men) suggesting architectural or design innovations that eliminate these prac-tical problems, as long as the solutions fulfill the spirit and letter of Jewish law.

One reason why certain *mechitzahs* effectively relegate women to small and perhaps unattractive places of worship is because men generally attend the synagogue more frequently, and in greater numbers, than do women. Women are not required to pray in the presence of ten men, and if they have small children or consuming domestic involvements, they are often unable to come to the synagogue.

If a woman has no concurrent obligations, such as taking care of her children or tending to domestic responsibilities, it is preferable for her to pray with a *minyan* if she is able to do so. However, many women do have concurrent obligations that take precedence over the preference to pray with a *minyan*. Whatever the reason, women typically constitute a minority of the congregants at most synagogues. The majority of the space must then be allocated to the regular worshipers, who tend to be men.

In places like Stern College for Women, the women's section occupies the majority of the synagogue. There are synagogues and college *minyans* that have altered the size and design of their women's sections and *mechitzahs* when significant numbers of women regularly attend services, provided that space and money are available to do so.

Synagogues usually have limited space and money. When they build or remodel a facility that is used 365 days a year, the planners usually do so by allocating the most resources to those who will use it the most. When women attend synagogue regularly, rather than only a handful of days a year, synagogues will often accommodate them by expanding the women's sections in a way that invites greater attendance and comfort.

In certain synagogues, it is difficult for the women to see what happens on the other side of the *mechitzah*. One of the very purposes of the *mechitzah* is so that men will not be distracted by women, but this does not mean that women should not be able to see. Insofar as women cannot see what those conducting the services are doing, accommodations can be made. In some cases, the upper part of the *mechitzah* can be made of lattice-work or special fabric. This allows women to see the goings-on in the men's section, while preventing the men from seeing the women. At least three well-known synagogues have *mechitzahs* of one-way glass. From the men's side, the glass reflects like a mirror, but it is completely transparent from the women's side. Thus, the women can observe the services with an unobstructed view.

OUR AVERSION TO RESTRICTIONS

There is one final reason why people tend to oppose the concept of *mechitzah*. This is rarely articulated, but it is probably a strong rationale for some people who stage bitter opposition to physically separating men and women in the synagogue.

We like to feel that we have ultimate control over our lives. We learn from the story of Adam and Eve that as soon as a person is limited as to what he or she can have or do, that which is forbidden becomes irresistibly desirable. We know that "forbidden fruit is sweetest."

The *Midrash* (a homiletical commentary on the Torah) says that when God gave the Jewish people the laws of sexual morality, they wept. The Talmud says that the Jewish people engaged in idolatry during biblical times only so that they would have an excuse to engage in illicit sexual relations, which were an integral part of idolatrous rites. In contemporary times, it would not be surprising to have vehement opposition to the notion of installing a *mechitzah* in synagogues that do not yet have one. It is as if God once again commands us to physically separate the sexes, and people weep.

A rabbi of a non-Orthodox synagogue might suggest to his congregants that only kosher food be served at synagogue affairs. Chances are good that even if people oppose the idea, it will not be met with venom and rancor. Similarly, he might require any boy or girl who wishes to have a *bar* or *bat mitzvah* ceremony at the synagogue to attend a certain number of Judaism classes. This, too, may be opposed by certain individuals, but probably more out of inconvenience than conviction. Let him suggest installing a *mechitzah*, and he may need to fear that he will lose his position. Why does this recommendation meet with such a different emotional response than other recommendations for a return to tradition?

Perhaps the reason for this is because the *mechitzah* is an irrefutable reminder that we can't be the ultimate determiners of how we should behave. When people oppose having a *mechitzah*, it is because they don't want to accept God's terms for how He wishes to rule the world. Such people want to maintain ultimate control over every facet of their lives, while allowing their Creator limited access into their personal domains. It is part of human nature to want to control God rather than letting Him control us.

Many Jews adhere to traditions because the rituals make rational sense, or because they feel emotionally fulfilling. The idea of doing a commandment solely because it was commanded, without being able to make sense of it, is anathema to many Jews. We want to understand and control what we do.

The concept of *mechitzah* implies that some things are absolutely prohibited, whether we find them intellectually reasonable or emotionally acceptable. Those things that we like most—heterosexual interactions—can often be a barrier to holiness. Many Jews find regulating these relationships emotionally unacceptable. They want to retain ultimate control over their emotional and interpersonal lives and are not willing to turn these areas over to God's dominion.

The *mechitzah* stands as a reminder that Judaism gives us little say about how flexibly we can interact with people of the opposite sex. God has set down the rules about which relationships are permitted and which are forbidden, and such rules are absolute. Whether we like it or not, Judaism does not permit us to determine the absolute parameters of our sexual behavior.

The *mechitzah* represents a major confrontation between our desires to chart our own courses and our need to be humble enough to let God direct our behavior. We must recognize His greatness by letting Him tell us what pleases Him. If we really want God to "be One, and His Name One," we have to be ready to accept His authority to rule us, and trust His judgment as to what is best for us. Worshiping the Almighty in the presence of a *mechitzah* ratifies His rule, rather than telling the Master when we will allow Him to reenter His palace.

6

Making Traditional Prayer Relevant

It is difficult for many contemporary Jews to relate to traditional Jewish prayer. This is partly due to what motivates people to pray and to what they expect of prayer. Many people pray only when they feel they lack something. Since "there are no atheists in a foxhole," some people pray only when they face life-threatening crises.

For college students, an impending final exam in a difficult course might suddenly transform them into fervent members of God's fan club. If they don't get an A in the course, they may decide that it is not worth their time and effort to pray in the future.

Single men and women of marriageable age might pray that God send them their future spouses, preferably by that weekend. They might even tell God what is on their "wish list," in case His idea of what they need is different from what they think they should have.

Similarly, when a lottery jackpot reaches $10 million, God certainly gets many prayers. Some people surely negotiate with Him about getting a runner-up prize if He doesn't see fit to help them win outright.

It is appropriate to pray in order to get what we want or need. However, we often do this as if we are submitting a shopping list of our desires to God and are testing Him to see whether He will really be there for us. We often expect Him to give us exactly what we want simply because we want it and have asked for it. It is likely that someone with these expectations will feel rejected or ignored if their wishes are not fulfilled.

When God does not give us what we want, we might feel that He does not really exist, or if He does, He has better things to do than to be concerned with us. Otherwise, why didn't He grant us what we asked for? It is hard to feel close to the Master of the World when He does not conduct it the way we think it should run.

Modern Jews who recite the traditional Jewish prayers have even more struggles. One needs to be fluent in ancient Hebrew in order to pray this way. Even when this is not an issue, the prayers still seem primarily relevant to an earlier place and time. Our liturgy is filled with references to forefathers who lived over 3,000 years ago, our Exodus from Egypt, and our hopes for a restoration of the sacrifices that were offered in the Temple. The Temple was destroyed and the sacrifices ceased almost two millennia ago. How are we supposed to feel that these prayers are relevant to us in modern times?

Because praying under these circumstances can feel so frustrating and ungratifying, many people find it impractical or impossible to pray the traditional prayers in a meaningful way. If they pray at all, they do so using abridged versions, or make up their own spontaneous prayers as they see fit. Sometimes these prayers are consistent with authentic forms of Jewish prayer; at other times, the words and the ways they are said verge on blasphemy.

Because trying to form a personal relationship with God through traditional prayer seems so difficult, people sometimes confer that role onto religious figures, especially rabbis and cantors. The rabbi and cantor are often viewed as proxies for making an authentic connection with God, whereas lay people become responsive spectators at prayer services. At best, the congregants may feel emotionally inspired by the cantor's (and choir's) singing, but not necessarily spiritually closer to God than if they had attended a concert. These were never the roles that religious figures or lay people were intended to have. Cantors, choirs, and houses of worship are important only insofar as they are vehicles for inspiring the worshipers to make their own personal connections to God through prayer.

Traditional Jewish prayer can be meaningful. It should impact us personally and nationally, and metaphysically affect the entire world. However, in order for this to happen, we must learn what our Hebrew prayers mean and change our attitudes about how to use them to connect to God.

WHAT IS PRAYER?

Lehitpallel means "to pray" in Hebrew, but it also means "to judge oneself."[1] This suggests that prayer should not be our way of trying to convince God to change how He runs the world. Rather, it should be a process by which we introspect and then change who we are, thereby allowing God to respond to us differently than He otherwise would.

We begin this process by first assessing how we have used what God has already given us. We take stock of our talents and resources and ask ourselves, "What am I doing with my life? What are my material, intellectual, and emotional assets, and how am I using them to further my spiritual growth?"

It is legitimate for us to ask God to provide us with what we need; however, if we pray so that we can get the Master of the Universe to do what we want, without being interested in what He wants, this is not prayer. Prayer is supposed to forge a relationship with our Creator. We should yearn to connect with Him because He "yearns," so to speak, to have a relationship with us.

Our traditional prayer services begin with our recognizing and expressing many of the good things that God does for us. He gives us our lives, with many gifts, not merely for our pleasure, but so that we can thank Him for all of the wonderful kindnesses that He does for us. We reciprocate this behaviorally by observing the commandments of the Torah.

Just as a mother hopes that her children will develop positively and benefit the world, so does God put us here with the same intentions. If a child does not appreciate what a parent does for him, and destructively uses what he is given, the parent should stop giving to him. If the child pleads with the parent to continue, the parent would be most responsible by saying "no" to the child's requests.

We each have a unique contribution to make to the world. To this end, no two of us have the exact same challenges or paths for expressing our spirituality. God wants each of us to see His Presence in every facet of our lives, yet we must be interested in looking for it. He created the world such that it would obscure how He acts behind the scenes in directing our lives. Yet, we can still discern His presence, should we only want to find it.

God's greatest desire in creating the world was to give to us, since we are the crowning achievement of His six days of Creation. When we take what God gives us physically, materially, intellectually, and emotionally, and use these gifts to serve Him, we bring His goals for the universe to fruition. On the other hand, when we pray to God to give us what we want, with the intention of using it to do what is contrary to what He wants, we are asking Him to help us dismantle His world.

This is one of several reasons why our prayers are not always answered in the way that we would like. We often ask for things that will not ultimately be to our benefit. If God were to grant us what we ask for, we might direct our energies into pursuing what makes us emotionally happy but could destroy us spiritually.

For example, if we pray to win a lottery, who will we be after becoming rich? Would we use our new-found wealth to form a closer relationship with God? Would the money stir us to become more meticulous in our observance of religious commandments and be more conscious of God's presence in our lives? Perhaps He knows that a year after winning the money we would feel like self-made men and women and forget about the Being that made it all possible.

GOD'S PERSONAL INVOLVEMENT IN OUR LIVES

God's response to our prayers reflects His running the world according to principles of general and specific supervision. Jews believe that God not only created the world, but continues to supervise it in a general way. This is necessary because He has an overall plan for it, in which every person will recognize God's Presence in all aspects of daily existence by a certain time.

God is also intimately involved in guiding the details of what happens to every Jew. He confronts us with situations every day, many of which are inherently neutral. If we are spiritually aware, we can use these opportunities to grow spiritually. If we choose otherwise, these opportunities will remain unutilized, or we may even use them destructively.

To illustrate this idea, suppose that someone gets a good job. Some people would attribute this to their abilities, good references, impressive interviewing skills, and so on. Observant Jews, however, believe that our abilities are factors, and we must make appropriate efforts in order to secure a job, but it is ultimately God who determines the outcome.

Once we have such a job, we can become very immersed in it, and view it as an end in itself. We shouldn't forget to ask, "Why did God help me get this? How can I use my work situation to further my spiritual growth? How would God like me to show that I appreciate the meaning of this gift?"

Ideally, we should view a good job as a God-given opportunity that will allow us to have more money to give to charity, more time or peace of mind to study Torah or teach it to others, or more opportunity to serve other spiritual ends. Perhaps we got the job so that we can set an example to our Jewish and Gentile co-workers about what a Jew can be, thereby sanctifying God's Name. Among other things, our co-workers can see that it is possible to eat only kosher food, to refrain from working on the Jewish holidays and Sabbath, to be honest in business and sensitive in interpersonal relationships.

God might also help us get a good job in order to challenge us spiritually. Will we keep our religious resolve when we are pressured to eat nonkosher food at parties or work functions? Will we take a job that offers a wonderful salary if it requires us to work after sunset on Fridays and holidays? Will we decline to participate in unethical practices in the work place?

We sometimes think that getting what we want is always beneficial. Sometimes it is and sometimes it isn't. Its ultimate goodness depends on how we use the opportunities to overcome the challenges that it presents. If we use a gift to destroy ourselves spiritually, it is no blessing. To quote a famous author, "There are two tragedies in life – getting what you want, and not getting what you want."

People often view vocational or financial success as an opportunity to have a materially better or more emotionally gratifying life. It should be much more than that. When God gives us money, and we don't give a tenth of it to poor people, or our jobs allow us a lot of leisure time, which we then use to further our own self-interests, this is not a good investment strategy for God. The more blessing He gives us, the greater is our responsibility to make sure that we use it properly.

When we view our jobs as means to an end, as gifts that can allow us to more easily pursue a religious way of life, we should show God that we are making full use of whatever He gives us. Since His nature is to want to bestow goodness, if He sees that we dedicate what He gives us to higher spiritual purposes, then He may give us more. Ideally, we should serve God not only so that He will give to us. But when God provides us with what we desire, and we put it to good use, He may continue to provide for us in ways that make our lives easier or more comfortable rather than our having to develop ourselves and serve Him through hardships or unpleasant challenges.

If God grants people financial prosperity, for example, and they devote their money to pursuing hedonistic goals, He may not want to throw good money after bad. He may decide not to continue bestowing material blessing on such people until they develop their spiritual sensitivities so that they will again be worthy of receiving His blessing.

With this in mind, we can now understand prayer in a deeper way. Prayer is first and foremost an opportunity to verbalize to God that we recognize the many good things that He does for us. Secondly, we create a relationship with Him through prayer. Our relationship allows us to ask for things that will enable us to grow spiritually. Since God wants to give of His goodness to us, this allows us to deepen our relationship when He responds to our requests.

There are times when God knows that it is not in our best interests to give us what we want. How often do parents have to turn down the tearful and heartfelt pleas of their children because they know that acceding to them will not be good? Children's intense emotions and lack of experience and wisdom make them certain that what they want is essential, and they feel disappointed, angry, and/or devastated when their desires are rejected.

In the same way, our desires can be so intense that we don't consider the possibility that what we so poignantly request of God might not be beneficial. King Solomon, the wisest man who ever lived, verbalized this idea when he dedicated the Temple.[2] He asked God to always listen to the prayers of individuals according to His knowledge of what they truly needed, not according to what they prayed for, since people might ask Him for things that were not in their best interest. This was elucidated to mean that Solomon asked God to never give Jews what they ask for when it is not good for them. On the other hand, Solomon asked God to always grant Gentiles their requests. Gentiles were permitted to have sacrifices offered on their behalf. Since they sometimes made an enormous effort to come to the holy Temple, and traveled great distances in order to do so, they would not believe in the true God if He did not grant what they asked for.[3]

When God declines our requests, we can further our spiritual growth by accepting that He has heard our prayers but has chosen not to do what we ask. When He says no to us, we develop ourselves by accepting that He has good reasons for His decision.

THE RELEVANCE OF ANCIENT LITURGY

There are several reasons why our liturgy refers to Jewish historical events and why our prayers were codified in Hebrew. In general, the daily morning prayer service tries to make us aware of how much God does for us every day. The preliminary prayers underscore how this happens to us personally, and the later prayers highlight how He manifests His goodness and power through nature. The latter section of the prayers reminds us of how God has intervened on behalf of the Jews throughout history. Since He has a 3,000-year track record with our people, we should trust that He is also capable of and interested in responding to us in the present.

With rare exceptions, almost all of our standard prayers are in Hebrew. (The others are in Aramaic.) This is because Hebrew is a holy language, whose ideas cannot be expressed precisely in any other tongue. Even if we don't fully understand what we are saying in Hebrew, our prayers can have metaphysical effects and reach God in a manner that no other language can.

It is beyond the scope of this book to explain the meanings of the prayers or the specific reasons why they make mention of certain historical events. However, we can learn a critical lesson from the fact that our prayers refer to our ancestors' lives.

Since the time of the first Jew, our belief in God has been challenged. Our forefathers, foremothers, and the Israelites who left Egypt all had to overcome barriers to their relationships with God. Our ancestors were challenged by the same problems that we have relating to Him. For example, most of our foremothers were initially barren, and our forebears had to uproot themselves from their homelands. They were faced with wars, were pursued and enslaved, and had to live through years of famine. Nevertheless, they achieved spiritual and personal growth by developing more mature views of God via these challenges. This teaches us that we do not have such unique problems that we cannot communicate to God about them or relate to Him through them. It also teaches us that we can grow spiritually through the challenges that God puts in our lives.

Our forefathers, foremothers, Moses, and the sages who composed our prayers all struggled with their own personal tragedies, and in many cases, with national ones as well. They all had to discover God's presence in their lives and find ways of accepting and responding to Him when His behavior did not meet their hopes or expectations. Through these struggles they came to understand that God does not run the world the way that mortals think is most appropriate. His wisdom, love, and justice require Him to gratify our every desire and demand, and to create difficulties through which we can grow.

God loves the Jews so much that He wanted our ancestors to experience Him as He truly is, not only as people want Him to be. The more you love someone, the more you want to really share your essence with the other person and let the other person know you. Similarly, God sometimes revealed Himself to our ancestors through His lovingkindness and sometimes through exercising power and justice.

When God holds Himself back from giving, we often experience Him as being punitive or absent. When we were children, we had to learn that when our parents did not give us what we wanted, it did not mean that they didn't love us. We must develop the same feeling about God. As long as we are interested in trying to find Him, He is interested in our seeking Him. He is only absent from our lives to the extent that we shut the door on Him, or misinterpret His not giving us what we want as meaning that He doesn't care about us.

Our standard prayers teach us how our ancestors searched for and related to God. We can use these same approaches whenever we are unable to establish a relationship with God using our personal resources alone.

Our sages were aware of the difficulties inherent in saying the same standard format of prayer three times a day. For this reason, they told us that we must constantly strive to imbue new meaning in our prayers.[4] Our standard prayers then become a springboard from which we embark on a personal journey through individual, original prayers, said in whatever language we feel most comfortable.

Many of us struggle to form a relationship with God through prayer. This is one reason why another Hebrew term for prayer is *avodah shebalev*—"work of the heart." We must truly work on ourselves in order to make prayer relevant; we must find a way of using it as a vehicle to connect to God. This process involves our appreciating what God has done for us, contemplating what He might want of us, and committing ourselves to doing it. We must also develop an inner sense that as we undergo trials and tribulations, God is with us in our distress.

Patients in psychotherapy often want the therapist to tell them what to do, or explain to them why certain things have occurred. When the therapist supplies them with answers, the patients' curiosity might be satisfied. On the other hand, when patients are willing to struggle with finding their own answers, they end up feeling much better about themselves than they could have otherwise. They feel more self-confident at having discovered their own solutions, which, by the time they find them, are personalized.

Sometimes God acts as the ultimate psychologist. He puts us in many life situations that raise theological and emotional questions. However, He also gives us the necessary tools to find meaningful and correct answers. We simply have to be patient enough and willing enough to keep working at finding them.

When therapists don't give certain patients answers, they get intolerably frustrated and abandon therapy. Some people similarly lose their patience with God and assume that He's not listening to them whenever He doesn't do what they think He should.

Unfortunately, some people give up praying as soon as God doesn't answer them in the way that they think He should. Such people do not realize that His conduct with them is a sign that He is aware of their spiritual needs and is giving them exactly what they require at that moment–an opportunity to grow yet further with the challenge of disappointment.

Some people negate everything that God does for them by virtue of the few things that they perceive He does not provide for them. This is analogous to a first grader who is asked what his mother does. Unless his mother is employed, he will probably say that his mother does nothing. If his mother were asked what she does, she would probably respond that she does everything. She is aware of how dedicated she is to making the child all of his meals, helping him dress every day, going over his homework, taking him to the doctor, nursing him when he is ill, arranging play dates with his friends, reading to him, and so on. Her day revolves around providing for all of his needs. Because the child expects her to do all of these things, he gives her no credit for her actions.

A fundamental part of being a Jew is learning to appreciate what others do for us and expressing our gratitude for it. This applies to our relationships with both God and people. We should periodically contemplate how much God does for us, and not focus on what He does not do. He put us here, and He tends to us as a loving parent does to a young child. He gives most of us functioning bodies and food to nourish them. He provides clothes for most people to wear and furnished homes in which to live. If we are alive, it is because He has nursed us through sickness and watched over us every night, giving us back our souls after keeping them safely each evening. He puts all kinds of pleasures in this world for our benefit. The least we can do is to think about this every day and thank Him for it.

There is a beautiful anecdote about a famous rabbi. When he was a little boy, he played hide-and-seek with his friends. He found a wonderful hiding spot and concealed himself in it. A long time elapsed and no one discovered where he was. He finally emerged from his hiding place to find out why no one had found him. Much to his dismay, all of his friends had given up searching for him and had left long ago.

He went home to his father, where he burst into tears. His father asked him what was wrong, and the young boy replied, "I was playing hide-and-seek with my friends, and I hid in a great spot. A long time passed, and I realized that all of my friends had gone away without finding me. It was bad enough that they all left without me, but the worst part was that they didn't even care enough about me to try to find me. . . . Now I know how God must feel."

ELEMENTS OF JEWISH PRAYER

The *Shemoneh Esrai* (the main prayer in each of the three daily prayer services) contains at least three important elements of prayer. We begin the *Shemoneh Esrai* by saying that God is "blessed." This means that God is the Source of all blessing that comes into the world. The Hebrew word for *blessing* comes from the word *braichah,* which means "that which flows or gushes." "Blessed are You, God" means that we acknowledge God as the source of all blessing, whose nature is to let this blessing flow into the world.[5] We ask God to allow His blessing to flow so that we can be conduits for Him to do what He most wants to do, which is to give to us. In this sense, reciting a blessing is not merely a way of praising God. It is also our way of beseeching Him to give so that we can use His blessing to actualize our spiritual goals, such as doing more of His commandments, learning more Torah, and improving our character traits.

We begin every prayer service by praising God. This is not because He needs our praise, but because we need to acknowledge that He is the source of everything that happens to us. In the next part of prayer, we petition Him to give us what we need. If God is the only one who has the power to grant us what we need, we must then ask Him to provide it for us, including giving us material things. When we do this, we have to make sure that we are worthy recipients of the Almighty's blessing.

When we ask for knowledge, health, wealth, and the like, we should only do so if we have developed ourselves into recipients who will make good use of these gifts. Our asking God for things implies that we have taken stock of ourselves and can assure Him that whatever He gives us will be used to its fullest potential.

The third element of prayer is thanks. We thank God at the conclusion of our prayers, even before we know if He will grant our requests. Our doing this shows that we recognize that whatever God does is ultimately for our benefit. Some of this we see quite readily, whereas other aspects don't make sense to us. Nevertheless, we transform prayer from our trying to control God to demonstrating that we accept how He runs the world.

Whether we understand His ways or not, we appreciate the importance of whatever He grants us. This makes it easier to accept that whatever He does is for our good. This attitude also helps us develop the trust that is a prerequisite for our being able to love God, even when He deprives us of what we think we need or puts challenges in our lives. The more we trust Him, the more we simultaneously allow Him to manifest His love for us in ways that encourage us to grow further.

ALTERING OUR PERCEPTIONS OF GOD

There is a well-known story about a man who dies and goes to heaven to meet his Maker. Once there, God shows him an instant replay of his life on a movie. While the man sees his life reenacted in front of him, he also sees two sets of footprints in the sand. Each time he goes through a difficult period of his life, he sees imprints of both his and God's footprints on a beach. This tells the man that God was standing by his side as he underwent each hardship.

Finally, they come to the most difficult period in his life, and there is only one set of footprints in the sand. When the man sees that the second set has disappeared, he begins to cry. "Master of the Universe," he asks, "how could You have abandoned me in my time of greatest need and travail?"

God responds by saying, "My beloved son, I didn't abandon you. Where you see only one set of footprints in the sand, that is where I picked you up and carried you."

If we approach prayer properly, we can transform our perspectives about God, the world, and ourselves.

7

Women and Prayer

The manner in which Jews traditionally pray presents a tremendous conflict for many modern women. They often feel that only men have been given the opportunity to really connect with God, and only men are allowed to pray to Him in ways that truly foster an intimate relationship. If women are excluded from leading public prayer, being counted in a *minyan* (quorum), and being called up to the Torah, how are they supposed to approach God meaningfully?

The Torah's position about women's role in prayer can only be understood within the overall purpose of being Jewish. Since one possible reason why God created a world was to allow Him an opportunity to give to His creatures, all of its creations testify to His love for us. When we observe and appreciate the diversity of people, plants, and animals, the awesomeness of nature, the sweet smell of flowers in the spring, the majesty of a sunset over the ocean, the feel of a cool, summer breeze, God "hopes" that we will understand that He put it all here and that we will thank Him for these kindnesses.

If this is where the story ended, we would pray to God out of love, thank Him, and go on our merry little ways. However, unrestricted taking on our parts with periodic thank you's was not God's ultimate intention for us. He also gave us commandments to observe so that we could feel that we earn the good things He grants us.

One of the major purposes of the Jewish nation is to sanctify God's Name by doing His will. To this end, we are each supposed to serve God with our personal strengths, by which we fulfill both individual and national missions.

Originally, each of the twelve tribes used a slightly different version, or *nusach,* of prayer. Each *nusach* was designated as the particular vehicle by which each tribe was supposed to communicate to God through prayer. The reader may be familiar with Ashkenazic, Sephardic, and Lubavitch *(Nusach Ari)* variations in prayers. These and other versions of standardized prayers derive from the original twelve versions that were said by the Jews, according to their tribal heritages. We are not normally allowed to change from a *nusach* our personal ancestors used to a version that belongs to another group. This illustrates the uniqueness of each tribe's path for gaining access to God.

DIFFERENT CONTRIBUTIONS BY DIFFERENT GROUPS

In addition to using different styles of prayer, each tribe had unique strengths with which they served God. For example, two tribes, Yissachar and Zevulun, had a partnership. Yissachar studied Torah all day, and Zevulun engaged in commerce in order to support Yissachar's learning. (It should be noted that the tribe who worked, and thereby enabled his brother to study Torah full-time, earned the same spiritual reward as his brother.)[1]

Another tribe was renowned for its military strength. It made its unique contribution by conquering the Israelites' enemies in order to allow the Jews to settle peacefully in the land of Israel. Since the time of King David, Jewish kings can only be descendants of the tribe of Judah. Part of the tribe of Levi became priests and offered sacrifices in the Temple. The remainder of the Levites sang praises to God there and ministered to the priests.

By combining all of their differential strengths and observing the commandments that pertain to them, Jews can serve God personally and nationally. A priest cannot decide that the rules barring him from contact with corpses are too restrictive and thereby decide to renounce his priesthood. (Many contemporary Jews of priestly lineage avoid becoming doctors due to the prohibition against contact with corpses.) Every priest has a unique contribution to make to the world through his priestly duties and restrictions. Similarly, he cannot decide to abdicate his priesthood because he falls in love with a divorcée and wants to marry her. (Priests may marry widows but are forbidden to marry divorcées.) By the same token, Jews who are not from priestly families are forbidden to serve as priests in the Temple, on penalty of death, and are disqualified from conferring the priestly blessing on the Jewish people.

It is important to stress that whenever Jews have roles that confer power, status, and visibility, these are always accompanied by corresponding restrictions. The restrictions insure that the roles will be used as vehicles for serving God, not as means for gaining greater personal power, prestige, or honor.

For example, Jewish kings had one of the most prestigious and powerful positions in Jewish society. Unlike many secular kings, a Jewish king was not supposed to use his position as a vehicle for personal aggrandizement. The king was held to a standard of moral behavior that was generally more stringent than what God applied to the people at large, and he was divinely punished accordingly for any infractions. Moreover, there were special laws that applied only to kings, such as their needing to have two Torah scrolls in their possession, carrying one with them at all times. The effects of such laws reminded kings that their power should enable them to model exemplary moral behavior to others and help the people maintain that high level themselves.

USURPATION OF OTHERS' ROLES

Judaism stresses the importance of each of us making our unique contributions to the world, not somebody else's. We may not fully understand why God chose us to have a given role or be faced with certain challenges in life. Yet, we accept that whatever role, challenges, and strengths He assigned us we should use to do His bidding.

There are historical examples of Jews usurping roles that were rightly intended for others. An example of this occurred over 2,000 years ago after the Maccabees achieved a military and spiritual victory over the Greeks, resulting in the institution of the holiday of Chanukah. The Maccabees were priests, descendants of Levi, whose role was to minister to God in the Temple. After their victory, they rededicated the Temple and reinstated the services and sacrifices there. However, they also usurped the monarchy and set themselves up as kings over the Jewish people.

According to Nachmanides, a medieval Jewish commentator, once kings from the tribe of Judah reigned over the Jews in Israel, members of other tribes were not allowed to rule.[2] This meant that once King David ruled, long before the Maccabean era, the monarchy belonged to the descendants of Judah, and was not to be usurped by any other group. The Maccabees risked their lives, and in some cases died, zealously fighting the Greeks, and they rededicated the Holy Temple, which had been desecrated by the pagan enemy. Nevertheless, those who survived usurped the kingship and were severely punished for this. Their entire dynasty perished within several generations because they misappropriated a role that was forbidden to them.

Similarly, a previously righteous king by the name of Uziah decided one day to usurp a priestly role by burning incense in the Temple. Eighty-one priests confronted him and told him to leave because he was appropriating a role that was permitted only to priests. "It will not be an honor for you from the Lord God," they admonished. When he refused to desist from his attempt to offer the incense, God afflicted him with leprosy. He lost his preeminence as a king and remained a leper until he died.[3]

When Jewish women try to feel better by abandoning their given roles and insisting on gaining recognition by usurping men's commandments and roles, they miss the point of what being a Jew is all about. From the Torah's perspective, our actions are only valuable insofar as they reflect God's will. Our actions can only serve Him insofar as we do what He asks of us, rather than doing what is independent of His will, regardless of how emotionally satisfying it may feel.

GAINING IMPORTANCE

The fact that men are obligated to perform more commandments than women is not a statement that men are more important than women. In Judaism, status is determined by how well we fulfill the mission that we were given, not how well we do someone else's task.

This highlights one of many conflicts between the secular world and Judaism. Some people believe that Judaism does not accord women status. This is not true. It does accord women status, but not always in the manner that the secular world values it. In part, this reflects the fact that Judaism doesn't value what the secular world values.

For example, one of the ways in which the secular world determines one's status is by how visible he or she is (fame). Judaism doesn't equate visibility with status. To the contrary, privacy is considered to be an ultimate condition for which both men and women should strive, with rare exceptions. The spiritual heroism of the Jew primarily takes place in private, as we learn to control our drives and direct them to serve God. Women are supposed to cultivate a private relationship with the Almighty as a primary value. Men do this as a secondary value.

For Jews, strength is admirable only insofar as it represents moral fortitude in overcoming the inclination to sin. Men's performing priestly functions, leading public prayer, and saying *Kaddish* (the sanctification of God's Name) are not important because they allow men to be granted public prestige. They are important only because God commanded or invited men to worship Him in these specific ways. Women may seek status by increasing their visibility in public prayer, by joining men in going up to the Torah, or by becoming cantors or "rabbis." Doing this may grant them status in the eyes of the secular world and may make them feel good, but these actions don't serve God because He did not ask them to worship Him in these ways.

As Jews, our success in praying results from how well we forge a relationship with God according to how He wants us to connect to Him. When He invites us to pray, we are not free to express our personal feelings in any way we please. Just as there is a protocol for how one has an audience with a mortal king, there are rules that govern how we may stand in the presence of the King of Kings. We should not think that just because He is God, we can approach Him in any way we like and that He will be pleased by our efforts.

Our standard daily prayers offer us a regularly scheduled audience with our Creator. There are certain rules that pertain to these meetings, including how we must dress, when we should say various prayers, where we may not pray, and so forth. If we want to say prayers with a group such that it constitutes public prayer, additional rules apply. One of these says that public prayers may only be offered in the presence of at least ten men, known as a *minyan*.

THE ORIGINS AND IMPLICATIONS OF *MINYAN*

A *minyan* is a quorum of ten men who are equally obligated to pray publicly. Women cannot be counted as part of this quorum because they are not obligated to participate in public prayer. Various rabbinic authorities state that men are required to pray with a *minyan*,[4] whereas others do not concur.[5] Even though it is generally considered to be a rabbinic edict that ten men, and no number of women, constitute a *minyan,* the concept of a *minyan* was based on the biblical episode involving the ten male spies. (See Chapter 4.) These ten men brought back an evil report about the land of Israel to the Jews, thereby causing the other men to despair about conquering and settling the land of Israel. As a result, all of the adult men of that generation died, thereby delaying the Jews' entry into the land of Israel by an additional thirty-nine years.

This incident led Moses (or a later leader) and his court of law to realize that male Jews were apparently deficient in their ability to worship God, based on their having acted evilly when they convened as a group. To rectify this, the Jewish leaders wanted men to train themselves to convene as a group only for holy purposes. This would require the same minimal number of men who had previously gathered in order to do evil. In order to guarantee that men would congregate, they were prohibited from saying certain prayers without a group. This might also have been initiated to emphasize men's degradation and lack of perfection. They were no longer individually capable of communicating properly with God. Only by gathering together with the force of a group would they be worthy of having God join them.

With respect to women, however, the Jewish leader and his court said, "You never sinned. You never gathered together in a group to do evil. Therefore, we have no reason to decree upon you that you must gather together to do good. No individual woman has anything inherently lacking in her ability to communicate with God without anyone else's assistance."

These women did not sin because each one independently decided not to be persuaded by public opinion. They did not have to assemble publicly in order to form a group consensus not to follow the men. They saved themselves by individually deciding to leave the mob and return to their houses. Therefore, the decree that requires men to join a *minyan* in order to pray never applied to them.

Over the course of centuries, the original rationale for this decree was forgotten, and people made up all kinds of reasons as to why women were not obligated to pray publicly. One such rationale is that a woman's obligation is primarily to her home. In actuality, women were never obligated to pray in a *minyan.* They retained the original status of being allowed to pray alone, as our Patriarchs and Matriarchs did, when individuals of great stature were able to pray individually to God.

The Talmud expresses this concept by saying that all people were originally created from one individual in order to emphasize the importance of each person being a complete world unto himself or herself.[6] A woman possesses such holiness and purity that she does not need a *minyan*. It is therefore ludicrous for a woman to want to be counted in one. The entire decree was enacted on men because they require ten males in order to ameliorate their original deficiency.[7]

We can readily understand how the value of a *minyan* is not because it makes men visible, ergo important. Its value is that men have an opportunity to create an environment where God promises to hear any member's prayers, regardless of his personal, individual merit.

When any Jew prays with a *minyan,* part of God's covenant with our people obligates Him to "hear" those prayers. This does not mean that God will automatically do whatever the group asks of Him. However, if an individual is not personally worthy of having God hear his or her prayers, or does not pray with appropriate concentration, God will still give him or her an "ear." This is because a quorum represents the Jewish nation at large, which collectively has merits that exceed those of any individual. These collective merits might allow God to consider requests that would not otherwise be heard if they were not said with proper sincerity.

Throughout Jewish history, there have been individual men and women who have gained an audience with God through their personal prayers, independent of whether or not they prayed in a *minyan*. However, since most people find it hard to pray with sincerity and concentration, it is to our benefit to pray in a forum where we are guaranteed that our unworthy prayers will be at least be noted.

That it is not men's greater importance that allows them and not women to form a *minyan* is highlighted by the following situation: If a Jew is ever called upon to choose between violating a Jewish law in private or being killed, he or she must violate the law rather than be killed, unless the required act involves idolatry, committing adultery or incest, or murdering another person. On the other hand, if the Jew is given the choice between violating the law publicly or forfeiting his or her life, the Jew must allow him- or herself to be killed. Under these circumstances, many authorities consider that either ten women or ten men constitute a public group,[8] in whose presence a Jew must forfeit his or her life, rather than transgress any Jewish law. Thus, there are times when ten women constitute a public group, as a representation of the Jewish nation at large. However, they never do this with respect to prayer. If they were not deemed of equal importance with men, they could not represent the Jewish nation at large when the sanctification of God's Name was at stake.

PUBLIC VERSUS PRIVATE

Women were not obligated to perform commandments that require public involvement. This is possibly because such involvement could conflict with their first priority to develop their internal and family roles. Nevertheless, if a woman wishes to pray with a *minyan,* it is laudable for her to do so, provided she has the time and the inclination. At the same time, our rabbis felt that women can pray more authentically when they are alone than can the typical man. The Talmud even tells us that God counts a woman's tears, suggesting that He is sensitive to what women feel even when we do not bring ourselves to formally verbalize it. Therefore, when women insist on being counted in a *minyan,* they denigrate their abilities to communicate with God. If the Almighty tells us that we have enough merits to be heard when we pray sincerely in private, why clamor to insist that He only hears us when we participate in public prayer?

Since women are obligated to pray, but not in public, the secular world interprets this as a denigration of women's capabilities. This attitude reflects a lack of understanding of the Jewish concept of obligation and prayer. In the secular world, that which is private has little status. In the Jewish world, that which has importance is whatever fulfills God's will. Sometimes our divine mandate is to serve God in private, and at other times it is to do so in public.

From a Jewish perspective, serving God in private is sometimes more important than serving Him in public. For example, although the Written Law was given in front of the entire Jewish nation at Mount Sinai, the Oral Law was given to Moses in private. God taught it to him in a "face-to-face" encounter where Moses was hidden from the people. Although the Written Law is important, it is the Oral Law that explains how the Written Law is actually observed.

A second example of the importance of private prayer was reflected in the Yom Kippur services that took place in the Tabernacle in the desert, and subsequently in the two Temples. This was the holiest ceremony of the year, in which the High Priest atoned for the entire Jewish nation. The central ceremony of the day occurred in private in the Holy of Holies, where no observers were allowed.

A third area in which privacy was stressed was in prophetic communication. In most biblical instances of prophecy, God communicated to the person while he or she was alone. For example, the forefathers and foremothers all received prophetic communication from God (and the level of prophetic knowledge of the foremothers was sometimes higher than that of their husbands). Such prophetic communication was almost always transmitted when the recipient was alone.

Moses' first encounter with God at the burning bush, as well as most of God's subsequent communications with him, occurred privately. Even the prophetic visions the Jews perceived at the Red Sea and the Giving of the Torah can be viewed as private, direct communications by God to masses of individuals, who received prophecy simultaneously.

Just as prophecy occurred with many individuals, each of whom received a private communication from God, public prayer allows many individuals to pray simultaneously, while each person relates to the Almighty on his or her level. Although the forum for public prayer requires at least ten men, the laws about how both men and women should pray the central daily prayers *(Shemoneh Esrai)* were derived from the private prayer of a woman. We emulate the style of a woman named Chanah, who prayed in solitude and in silence. (It is unclear if Chanah invented her particular mode of prayer or simply modeled a preexisting one. Nevertheless, the Talmud uses her as the exemplar of how to pray the *Shemoneh Esrai*.) This was because she demonstrated tremendous sensitivity to the essence of prayer and used it to supplicate the Master of the Universe.

CHANAH

Chanah was married to a man named Elkanah, who also had a second wife, Peninah. Peninah had ten children, whereas Chanah remained childless for almost twenty years. Every year, Elkanah and his wives would go to Jerusalem for the pilgrimage holidays, where Chanah always felt anguished because she had no children. Even though her husband was a prophet, his prayers supplicating God to give her a child were not answered and she remained barren.

One pilgrimage holiday, Chanah realized that she could not depend on her husband or any other intermediary to beseech God on her behalf. She went to the holy Temple and prayed to have a son. She moved her lips in silent supplication and challenged Him: "Did you create me to be an angel or a woman? If I am childless because I am an angel, then I must be destined to live forever. However, since You created me with the body of a woman, why don't You fulfill my purpose in having this type of body and give me a child?"

Chanah prayed with tremendous fervor, and ended her prayer with the promise that if God would grant her a child, she would dedicate him to serve Him in the Temple.[9]

Not only were her prayers answered by giving birth to the prophet Samuel, but she subsequently had four more children as well. Something about her prayer so impressed the rabbis that when they compiled the most central daily prayer, they taught that we should pray it as Chanah did. To this day, we pray the *Shemoneh Esrai* with our hearts dedicated to God, our lips moving, and with our prayers audible only to ourselves, in imitation of Chanah.

The significance of Chanah's prayer can be better appreciated after reading an incident that involved two priests named Nadav and Avihu: Shortly after the Torah was given, the Jews sinned grievously by making a golden calf. The following Yom Kippur, God forgave them. When they later consecrated the Tabernacle in the desert, built according to God's command, it signaled that He was willing to dwell among the Jewish people once again, despite their having sinned. At the consecration ceremony, God sent down a form of divine fire, thereby showing His pleasure with how the consecration had been performed.

Meanwhile, two of the High Priest's (Aaron's) sons, Nadav and Avihu, decided to offer God a sacrifice that He had not commanded. Our sages tell us that these two men made their offering with the purest of motives, in an attempt to serve God with the loftiest of spiritual motivations. The Almighty's response to their well-intentioned endeavor was to kill them instantly.[10]

It seems shocking that God punished these two men so severely for expressing their religious fervor in this personal way. We normally think that God wants us to pray to Him from our hearts, with spontaneity and initiative. If this is true, why did they get such a response? We will return to the incident of Nadav and Avihu after a discussion of the meaning of prayer.

THE MEANING OF COMMANDMENTS

When we pray to God, even out of love, we are still not at liberty to forget that we are praying to the Creator of the Universe, its Master and

Director. We are obligated to recognize His power in various ways, which include our following His commandments.

Jews frequently observe parts of the Torah because they make sense or are emotionally satisfying. For example, people might not murder because it makes sense not to take an innocent person's life or to destroy the social order by killing. They might observe a Passover *seder* because it creates a warm family atmosphere. Similarly, people observe other Jewish traditions because they lead to a more cohesive family unit. As satisfying as it might feel to observe the Torah in this way, this is not truly serving God. Such conduct depends on the laws making sense or feeling gratifying, rather than for the sake of obeying God's will.

We are supposed to perform *mitzvot* to demonstrate our belief that God has the authority to command us. It is easier to do this when we find *mitzvot* emotionally appealing or sensible, but we are still required to observe *mitzvot* that don't feel good or aren't overtly rational. This demonstrates our willingness to accept God's authority to command us, and it ratifies our trust in Him. If He commands us to do 100 things that make sense to us and that benefit us in appreciable ways, we can likewise assume that the laws that we can't fathom must also be beneficial. When we only observe those laws that we like, and pick and choose among the others, we reduce God to the level of an enlightened human being who gave us some interesting suggestions about how to lead a fulfilling life.

Picking and choosing the *mitzvot* we like and observing them while ignoring those we don't like is serving ourselves, not God. We are supposed to observe all of the *mitzvot* that apply to us, whether or not we find them emotionally or intellectually appealing.

We should similarly worship God in the way He wishes, not in the way we decide is most appealing. If our first thought before praying is, "How can I feel good praying?" a major function of prayer is missing. Our first question should be, "How must I pray so that my words will be pleasing to my Creator?" Following that we can ask, "How can I pray within that context so that my words will be personally meaningful and will establish a close connection with the Almighty?"

PREREQUISITES FOR PRAYER

We must have certain intentions and concentration (*kavanah*) in order to fulfill our obligation to pray.

Maimonides says that there are two types of *kavanah* in prayer. One type of concentration requires that we minimally understand the meanings of the words in the first of the nineteen paragraphs of the *Shemoneh Esrai*.[11]

However, there is a second type of *kavanah*. If we lack this when we pray, we have not fulfilled our obligation, no matter how well we might understand what the words mean. This second type of *kavanah* is the realization that we are praying before God. If we say the words of the prayers, and do not feel that we are standing in God's presence, our words are not prayer, no matter where we are or what we are saying.

When we pray to God, we recognize two ideas: First and foremost, He is the most powerful Being in the world. Since He created us, we owe Him our very existence. Second, we recognize His goodness and that everything that happens to us is ultimately for our good. When we stand in awe of Him, we feel humble and motivated to praise Him. When we appreciate His omnipotence, we realize that we can turn to no one but Him in order to get what we want or need.

When we contemplate that God wants to give us what we need, we are overcome with love and we thank Him. The more we rely on God for our sustenance, the more we learn to trust Him and the more we love Him. Our first feeling of awe encourages us to praise God. Our second feeling encourages us to make requests of Him and to thank Him. Both feelings together enable us to pray.

WOMEN'S OBLIGATION TO PRAY

Women are equally obligated with men to pray the morning and afternoon *Shemoneh Esrai* every day.[12] The *Magen Avraham* suggests an innovative idea to defend the fact that most women don't pray every day.[13] He attributes women's obligation to pray at least once a day to a Torah law that requires every Jew to pray on a daily basis. According to that opinion, any words a woman says that praise God, make a request of Him, and thank Him fulfill her daily obligation to pray.[14] According to the currently accepted opinions, however, women are obligated to say the *Shemoneh Esrai* twice a day.[15] They are also encouraged to say the *Shema* (Unification of God's Name) twice a day.[16]

The previous chapter discussed our need to introspect when we pray. When we examine our motives for praying, is it to serve God or ourselves? Do we pray in a synagogue because we want to be visible to our friends and community, because it provides a convenient place to socialize, or because we want honor and prestige? The latter have nothing to do with serving God. Prayer begins with the humility of recognizing who we are and what we are, and using that knowledge to relate to our Creator.

As was mentioned earlier, the word *avodah* (work) means prayer. When Jews had a central court in Jerusalem (known as the Sanhedrin), the rabbis spent nine hours a day praying. They spent an hour preparing for prayer, an hour saying the *Shemoneh Esrai,* and an hour drawing themselves away from prayer at each of the three daily services. Even when they prayed in a *minyan,* each individual underwent a personal and private process whereby he developed his unique connection with God and appreciated what God had done for him. Then he had to recognize and rectify his personal shortcomings in his service to his Creator. Finally, each had to petition God for whatever he and the community required for their survival and spiritual growth. It required tremendous work on the part of each individual to create and sustain this intense bond with God every day. These people exemplified the "work" of prayer.

MAKING PRAYER MEANINGFUL

How can the contemporary woman develop her ability to connect herself to God through prayer? Four methods will be discussed here.

The first method requires studying what prayer in general is all about and what specific prayers mean. This can be done by attending classes. Reading books and listening to the numerous audiotapes about prayer are good substitutes when classes are not available. Regardless of where a woman prays, if she doesn't appreciate what the prayers mean and how they are relevant today, it is impossible to use them to connect to God.

Second, we must take the time to engage in the "work" of prayer. Ongoing, meaningful prayer doesn't just happen, and it doesn't come easily to anyone. We must work on ourselves in order to relate to the standardized prayers. The more time we spend trying to pray with devotion and understanding and the more we strive to relate to the prayers, the more meaningful they will be for us.

Third, learning the melodies to various prayers and letting oneself be moved by them can flesh out the nuances of prayers. Listening to Jewish music and sung prayers can bring people to very powerful emotional states that are conducive to connecting to God. The more prayers are connected to music, the greater is their meaning for many people and the stronger is their emotional bond with God. Even melodies that we learned as children can still move us to deep feelings of connection with God when we are adults.

Fourth, we need to observe and appreciate how God set up the world around us. If we want to appreciate our Sponsor, all we have to do is to look at how He created nature. We can see His "hand" in every part of Creation. The diversity of plants and animals, the marvel of a seed becoming a tree, the beauty of spring flowers, and the majesty of mountains all exemplify God's love for us. We can partially reciprocate this by showing our gratitude to Him for giving us such wonderful gifts.

When we study the sciences, it moves us to praise God for the genius of His handiwork in making each creature, organism, and cell. It is especially marvelous to appreciate the concert of all of the parts of a body working together to make a functioning human being.

Mothers can use their unique experiences to shape how they pray. They can feel wonder at the creation and molding of a little person as he or she grows up. They can see the beauty of the world through a child's eyes. They can experience the unique pleasures of raising children.

From this, they can appreciate how God must feel when He watches His world develop and unfold. Mothers can imagine how God must overflow with joy, so to speak, when His children develop positively, and how "pained" He must feel when they rebel and reject Him. Women can praise God for the happiness they feel watching their children, holding them and caring for them. They can thank God for the stamina that He grants them and for protecting their children through daily miracles that save them from injury or death. Women can make requests of God based on their individual needs, which change and mature as they and their families do.

It is not our physical proximity to the Holy Ark or to the Temple that opens up the gates of prayer in Heaven. It is our appreciating God's grandeur and goodness in our everyday lives and our wanting to connect to Him that open up channels of communication with God.

We see from Nadav and Avihu that zealousness alone is not what God wants. We have the right to pray to Him only because He invites us to do so. Yet, even when He invites us to pray, we are only allowed to do so in the way that the Almighty permits.

Women sometimes feel that the way the Master of the Universe has asked them to serve Him is not good enough. They can insist, like Nadav and Avihu, that they have to add to God's command. When people approach God in this way, their behavior is not prayer. When women feel that they have to legitimize their role by taking over the role of men in the synagogue, replete with *tallitot* (prayer shawls), *tefillin,* and the like, they are emulating Nadav and Avihu. This approach negates the humility with which we are supposed to come before our Creator. It also negates the inherent sanctity in the way that God commanded women to pray. Such actions broadcast a belief that the way that God has asked us to pray is insignificant.

Not everything about Nadav's and Avihu's prayer was negative. We can enlist their fervor in trying to achieve closeness to God and self-perfection through prayer. Nevertheless, we must be careful not to overstep the bounds of our egos; we must allow God's knowledge of what is in our best interests to determine how we pray.

SAYING *KADDISH*

Women frequently ask if they can say *Kaddish* for a deceased relative, and if so, can they be counted as part of a *minyan?* For the reasons stated earlier, women are never counted as part of a *minyan.* They are, however, allowed to say *Kaddish* under certain circumstances, but this requires further elaboration.

The recitation of the *Kaddish* prayer is of relatively late origin. Our literature indicates that Rabbi Akiva was once approached by an orphan shortly after his father's death. The child wanted to bring merit to his father's soul, so the rabbi told him to recite the *Kaddish.*[17]

At some point, the rabbis subsequently determined that whenever a parent would die, the son should recite *Kaddish,* an Aramaic prayer that publicly sanctifies God's Name. Prior to this time, the cantor was the only one who recited the *Kaddish,* and he did so on behalf of the entire congregation. In order to benefit the soul of the departed, it was eventually decided that orphans should also do this. The *Kaddish* prayer should be recited at least once a day, and can only be said in the presence of a *minyan.*

The purpose of reciting this prayer is to bring the merit of sanctifying God's Name to the deceased's soul. If a parent dies and leaves behind a child who is concerned about sanctifying God to the world, it reflects well on the parent. Since the parent's death motivates the child to sanctify God's Name, the parent's soul is rewarded for this. The rabbis specifically enacted that only sons and not daughters were obligated to say *Kaddish.* They recognized the hardships that it would place on women to have to abandon their families or other pursuits to search for a *minyan.* Therefore, they did not require women ever to say *Kaddish.*

If a daughter wishes to say *Kaddish* for a deceased parent who left no sons, she may do so, provided that she recites *Kaddish* in a *minyan* where a man is also saying it.

If a woman wants to say *Kaddish* for a parent or other relative who left no close kin, she may also achieve the same benefits for the deceased's soul by attending a *minyan* every day and answering "Amen" to the *Kaddish* of another mourner. Under these circumstances, a woman who answers "Amen" is as if she personally sanctified God's Name.

If a man or woman whose parents are still alive wish to say *Kaddish* for someone other than a parent, their parents must give their consent for the children to say *Kaddish* for someone else.

Since it is no simple matter for most women to say *Kaddish* with a *minyan* every day, it is generally recommended that they elect one of several other options, in order to confer the same benefits on the soul of the deceased. The preferred option is for them to arrange for a man (usually one who has lost one or both parents himself) to say *Kaddish* in their stead. Most *yeshivot* (men's schools for higher Jewish education) can arrange for one of their students to do this. (It is customary to make a contribution to the *yeshivah* or to the person who does this.) Some Jewish charities will make similar arrangements.

Another meritorious option when anyone dies is for a relative to observe an extra religious precept that was formerly neglected, or to do it more scrupulously than one did it previously. One can also give extra money to charity or sponsor Torah learning or lectures in memory of the deceased.

WOMEN'S PRAYER GROUPS

Since the seventies, there has been a great deal of interest in establishing women's *minyans* and egalitarian *minyans*. Most of these violate Jewish law by having women and men sit together during the services, women leading services in which both men and women participate, women being counted for a *minyan* when ten men are not present, and women being given *aliyot* to the Torah along with men.

No matter how many women gather together, they can never constitute all or part of a *minyan*. Thus, there is no such thing as a women's *minyan*. It is prohibited for Jews to recite certain prayers when not in the presence of a *minyan*. These prayers include the *Kaddish* (whether said by mourners or by the representative of the congregation, known as the *shaliach tzibur*), the *Kedushah,* the repetition of the *Shemoneh Esrai,* and the invitation to prayer known as *Barchu.* The Torah is likewise not read publicly if no *minyan* is present.

A small number of Orthodox women have set up women's prayer groups that do not involve most of the above violations. They tend to stress that their groups do not constitute a *minyan,* and they provide opportunities for women to pray more intensely than they might otherwise. Most of these groups have women publicly reading the Torah for other women. Some of these groups also prohibit men from attending, obviating certain technical problems that would arise from women singing in the presence of men.

During the mid-1970s, certain religious authorities condoned women's prayer groups, provided that they followed the same rules that apply to women praying individually. In addition, these groups were typically led by a woman, and women read from a Torah scroll. When the women were called up for *aliyot,* they recited the blessing over studying Torah prior to the Torah portion being read.

It is technically permissible for a group of women to organize a prayer group with a woman leading them. Since women are required to learn Torah, they should recite the blessing over so doing, and say a short selection from the Torah and *Mishnah* every morning upon arising. In the women's prayer groups, women said these blessings when they got their *aliyot* instead of early in the morning. Those women who wished to wrap themselves in a *tallit* were also permitted to do so, provided the *tallit* was specifically made for a woman and not for a man.

With the passage of time, the rabbis saw that these innovations in prayer groups were more often than not so that women could act like men and thereby prove their equality with them. The source of the desire to pray in women's groups was often a response to secular feminism, not an authentic desire to pray more purely as a Jew. As this became generally apparent, the technical compliances with Jewish law became subject to an overriding objection to women's praying with their own cantors, reading from the Torah scroll, and wearing *tallitot* in public.

There is a principle that prohibits Jews from emulating gentile customs. Once women's prayer groups were viewed as a means for achieving equality by doing what men do, they became forbidden because they imitated non-Jewish ways. Imitating the non-Jews includes incorporating the secular philosophy of feminism into Judaism. This was an application of alien ideas to Judaism, aimed at forcing changes that were not necessary. There were no inequities or inadequacies in the preexisting Jewish ways of praying that logic would have required changing. Therefore, it is currently prohibited for women to pray in groups where they read the Torah from a scroll. Women are generally discouraged from wearing female *tallitot,* since their motivation to do this is usually to elevate themselves by making a statement to the world that they are on par with men. When a woman is fully observant of all of the other commandments that apply to her, certain rabbinic authorities allow women to don a *tallit* in private when her intention is to take on yet one more avenue by which she can serve God. Since it is only worn in total privacy, her motivation is not to impress anyone else by her equality, which is something that Judaism already grants her.

Should a woman desire to stand in front of God and offer heartfelt prayers, she should certainly do so. We don't need to be visible to others in order to connect ourselves to our Creator. Should we wish to study Torah, we should likewise pursue that desire. However, the best framework in which to do this is privately, in concert with a study partner, and/or in a class.

STANDING IN GOD'S PRESENCE

A story is told about a famous rabbi who used to keep a slip of paper in each of his pockets. One slip read, "For my sake was the world created." The other slip read, "I am but dust and ashes." When we approach God with the humility that comes from believing that we are but dust and ashes, we can stand in front of our Maker and be pleasing in His sight. Once we have gained an audience with the King of Kings, we can then have the audacity to ask Him to grant our petitions and change the world for our sake.

We can now understand why Chanah's prayer was viewed as the model for all subsequent prayer. Her initial belief was that God was the Creator and Director of the world, and she felt humble recognizing this.

When some people feel overwhelmed by humility and think no further, they perceive themselves as being too unimportant and unworthy for God to hear their personal prayers. When this happens, it is impossible to pray. Such people will feel that they have no right to ask God to listen to them.

What was special about Chanah was that in her humility, she realized that if God is all-powerful, she *must* supplicate Him for her personal needs. If God would not help her, how else could she get what she wanted? Realizing that God wanted her to ask Him to provide for her, and understanding that He wanted her to believe that He would listen to her prayers, Chanah knew that she merited having the world be created and altered for her sake. With this insight, she was able to pour out her heartfelt prayers.

Chanah's mode of praying was chosen as the ultimate. This teaches us that it is what we bring to individual prayer that makes it legitimate. It is not intermediaries, standing in a visible place in front of a congregation, fancy apparel, the Temple, or pyrotechnics that compel God to answer our prayers. Our prerequisite to being heard is simply having the humility of Chanah in coming before God – first as dust and ashes, and then with the audacity of, "For my sake was the world created" – that invites Him to listen to us.

8

"Blessed Are You . . . Who Did Not Make Me a Woman"

Perhaps one of the most challenging issues that confronts modern Jewish women is a blessing men say every morning. The preliminary morning service has a series of blessings that praise God for various acts of kindness He does for us every day. Jews of both sexes are supposed to recite them every morning.

The fourth blessing in the series has two different versions to be said by men and women, respectively. Men say, "Blessed are you, God, King of the Universe, who did not make me a woman *(ishah).*" Women say, "Blessed are You, God, King of the Universe, who made me (with the qualities that exemplify) His will *(kirtzono).*"

People who are unfamiliar with Jewish history, liturgy, and biblical Hebrew frequently misinterpret the content as well as the intent of the above two blessings. They mistakenly assume that men thank God every morning for not having made them so unfortunate as to be female. Such critics further maintain that the blessing said by women demonstrates their passivity in resigning themselves to a second-class role.

RECEIVING WITH DIGNITY

It has been previously mentioned that God created the world, and people, in order to bestow goodness on humanity. If God simply gave to us

113

unreservedly, without our doing anything to deserve it, we would feel like freeloaders. The Talmud tells us that a person would rather have a smaller quantity of something that he or she personally produces than a greater amount of the same thing that comes with no personal investment or toil.[1]

In order for us to receive God's goodness with dignity, He created us with the ability to make choices. When we choose what accords with His will, we can earn the goodness that He gives us. When we make the wrong choices and act at odds with His will, we become unworthy of receiving many of His gifts. We also forfeit the emotional pleasures of earning God's beneficence through our efforts.

If it were our nature to only want to do what God wants of us, and we were totally clear about what that entailed, we would follow His will in every aspect of our lives. However, this would not be due to our free choice because we would not be tempted by any other alternatives. In order to ensure that we would truly have free choice, God created each of us with two inclinations. We each have an inclination to do what God wants and a competing inclination that does its best to convince us to act contrary to what He wants. These two inclinations are respectively known as the *yetzer hatov* and the *yetzer hara*.

THE TWO INCLINATIONS

The *yetzer hatov* is the inclination that motivates us to achieve greater understanding of and closeness to God. It pushes us to do what He wants and elevates us to greater spiritual heights. The *yetzer hara* includes, but is not limited to, that part of our psyches that psychologists call the "id." The id consists of our physical desires and the impulses that demand immediate gratification. People's desires to eat whatever and whenever they please, to have sex when and how they wish, and to express their anger and aggression without restraint are examples of id impulses.

The *yetzer hara* motivates us to gratify our physical desires in an unbridled manner. It makes us want to be the ultimate masters of our lives, the ultimate determiners of what we can and should do; it encourages us to satisfy our drives for power, status, materialism, and the like.

The *yetzer hara* has many ways of operating. When Adam was created, the desire to oppose God's will was not an integral part of him. The *yetzer hara* existed as a theoretical idea, a potential force, but it was not a facet of the human being. The *yetzer hara* was internalized into people only after Adam and Eve sinned in the Garden of Eden.

The biblical narrative about the serpent enticing Eve to eat the forbidden fruit was intended to be understood literally as well as allegorically. In that story, the serpent is termed a *nachash*. The Hebrew word *nachash* not only means "serpent," but also "to guess," or "to create doubt." The serpent was a representation of the *yetzer hara*, who attempted to create doubt in Eve's mind as to whether or not she should follow God's will.

The machinations of the serpent and Eve were also prototypical of how the *yetzer hara* operates and how it tempts the human being to respond to it.

The sole reason for the *yetzer hara*'s existence is to make us doubt whether we should follow God's will. The *yetzer hara* is supposed to tempt us to go against His will simply so that we can recognize the evil inclination for what it is and refuse to succumb to it. The *yetzer hara*'s *modus operandi* are beautifully illustrated in the serpent's encounter with Eve.

HOW THE EVIL INCLINATION WORKS

The serpent used four arguments in its attempts to persuade Eve to sin. These four methods are paradigms for how the *yetzer hara* generally entices people to disobey God. The evil inclination first tries to convince us that God forbids so much that it is impossible to follow His commandments. Thus the snake asked Eve, "Didn't God forbid you to eat of every tree in the Garden?"[2]

In actuality, God had only told Adam not to eat from one tree. The snake wanted Eve to believe that what God prohibited was simply too onerous and that she would never be capable of adhering to it all. Through this ploy, he wanted Eve to feel that if she couldn't obey everything that was expected of her, she should not bother with any part of it. The *yetzer hara* undermines what we accomplish by focusing on, and then exaggerating, what we cannot do.

The snake then told Eve that if she would eat of the forbidden fruit, "You shall not surely die."[3] The *yetzer hara*'s second ploy was to convince her that violating God's commandments would have no negative consequences.

The snake's third argument was that eating the forbidden fruit would result in Eve's "eyes being opened."[4] This means that the snake wanted Eve to believe that the sensual pleasure from tasting the forbidden fruit would justify eating it. The *yetzer hara* convinced her that the fact that sensual pleasures felt so good proved that she should enjoy the forbidden acts.

When we focus only on the short-term effects of our actions, we are sure they will be positive and enjoyable. By doing this, we lose sight of how bad their long-term consequences will be.

The snake's final argument to Eve was that by sinning, she "will be like God."[5] One of the commentators explains this to mean that she would be able to create worlds.[6] This was especially appealing because God made human beings with the need to be creative and productive.

People often complain that a moral way of life is too limiting and that it interferes with their ability to be creative and productive. Sin promises to open up new vistas for us, if we only avail ourselves of its opportunities.

In general, the *yetzer hara* convinces us to fall prey to the illusions of what sin can offer – knowledge, power, and sensual pleasure, all to be enjoyed without negative repercussions.

FIGHTING THE BATTLE

Since God created us with the ability and desire to serve Him, but with a tremendously strong, competing drive that motivates us to sin, our lives have been likened to battlefields. We engage in a battle between wanting to do God's will and wanting to indulge our own desires until the day we die. This is the challenge our Creator wants us to overcome in order to be worthy recipients of the tremendous blessing that He wishes to give us.

Had God created us with these two competing desires, with no knowledge of how to win the battle, our lives would be chaotic and purposeless. However, He made His will known to us and gave us guidelines for how to win the war when He gave us the Torah.

The Torah commands us to observe 613 commandments, which express God's will. There are 365 commandments that tell us what not to do and 248 commandments that tell us what we must do. Since the time when the Second Temple was destroyed (over 1,900 years ago), we can only observe a fraction of these laws because many only apply when the Temple is standing or when the majority of Jews live in the land of Israel.

No single individual can personally observe all 613 commandments because many of the laws apply only to certain people. For example, certain laws apply only to kings, whereas others apply only to high priests. Some laws are relevant only for Levites, while others apply to nonpriests. Certain laws apply only to women, whereas others apply only to men.

Therefore, apart from the battles that we as individuals fight between our two inclinations, we fight a national battle as well. Every Jew is supposed to play a role in this national battle of doing God's will. In this national war, men are considered to be the front-line soldiers. In any war, the front-line soldiers have rigidly prescribed schedules of when to report for duty. In Judaism, men act as front-line soldiers by having rigidly prescribed times when they must report to God. They must pray three times a day and say the *Shema* (Unification of God's Name) within specific time frames every morning and evening, reporting for duty to the King of Kings.

In this analogy, men attending synagogue can be viewed as their mustering for inspection and briefing several times a day. This constantly reminds them of their duties and charges.

In a war, soldiers cannot exercise much personal choice as to whether or not to accept their responsibilities. Soldiers cannot make excuses, even when they prefer not to accept their missions. In this sense, commandments are neither suggestions nor personal preferences. They are requirements that, once delegated to people, need to be adhered to in order for the soldiers to be victorious. This is why we were given the Ten Commandments, not the Ten Suggestions.

Jewish women are like generals who are removed from the front lines in order to oversee the war away from the trenches. They cannot objectively evaluate how the soldiers are faring unless they are far enough away from the battlefields that they can view the war *in toto*. Women must be able to see the forest for the trees, whereas the men attend to more of the details.

This is one suggested reason as to why women are relieved from certain time-bound positive *mitzvot* and from public positions. Both of these situations might otherwise detract from their ability to oversee the total progression of the battles. Women are in charge of maintaining the troops' morale and for replenishing their supplies.

THE TWO TORAH SCROLLS

The Torah requires a king to possess two Torah scrolls. Whenever he goes out to war, he must take one of them with him. He keeps the second scroll in his treasury and is supposed to refer to it whenever he is not away. One reason why this is necessary is because whenever the king goes out to battle, the scroll he takes with him is likely to become worn and tattered. After a certain amount of time, the war-torn scroll may become illegible. Therefore, when the king returns from battle, he has a pristine Torah scroll in his chambers from which he can read. It is an unadulterated version of what the Torah originally said, without the distortions that accrued on the battlefield.

Men and women have different individual and national roles through which they serve God. Men can be viewed as analogous to the Torah scroll that goes out to battle. After interacting with the outside world for a certain amount of time, they can lose sight of what their true objectives should be. Jewish women can be viewed as analogous to the Torah scroll stored in the king's treasury. They are supposed to serve as the guardians of the uncompromised, original Torah.

When men come home from their days on the battlefield, their wives can offer opinions as to whether or not the men have become distorted by the pulls of the outside world. Women are models of what God's true will is supposed to be, and they are endowed with the capability of continually drawing their husbands and children back to proper standards. Through this process, women have always been the backbone of Jewish survival.

THE MEANING OF THE BLESSING "WHO DID NOT MAKE ME A WOMAN"

Since a woman must depend on her intuition and internalized values to maintain a proper perspective about what God really wants, she has a much more difficult role than does a man. The regimentation of men's lives by religious schedules makes it much easier for them to successfully battle their negative inclinations.

This is one reason that has been offered as to why men praise God for not making them women. They are grateful that He gave them the easier task of being foot soldiers rather than generals. Men have additional, specific commandments to help them conquer their negative drives. Women must act as generals, and they have fewer specific instructions as to how to plan their battles. They must use their intuition and intelligence in spiritual endeavors to a greater degree than do men, and their job is therefore fraught with much greater dangers.

As has been noted, Hebrew is a very precise language. A man recites a blessing every morning that says that God did not make him an *ishah*. There is no precisely comparable word in English for this term. Had the blessing used the word *female (nikeivah),* it would be a praise of God for not making men of the female gender. As we saw in the Creation story, *ishah* refers to a woman at the pinnacle of her spiritual greatness, just as *ish* refers to man at his spiritual finest.

One reason that has been advanced as to why the blessing is worded negatively (that God "has not made me"), rather than praising God for creating man as an *ish,* is because the Talmud says that it would have been easier for man had he never been born, because then he never would have sinned. However, insofar as man has been created, the Talmud concludes that he should examine his deeds and serve his Creator.

The struggle that a man undergoes in being born, only to fight a lifelong battle, is one about which he has very mixed feelings. On the one hand, he is glad to have an opportunity to live a meaningful life. On the other hand, life is filled with unending challenges, only some of which he may overcome successfully.

This situation can be likened to that of a chaplain who is drafted into a war. He can't thank the president of his country for drafting him because, although he doesn't have to fight, he would rather have stayed out of the war altogether.

Similarly, a man cannot praise God for making him a man because he does not know until the day he dies if he will succeed in accomplishing what he was put here to do. In other words, he can't be grateful for something he may never achieve – becoming a man of great spiritual accomplishment *(ish).* Therefore, a man does not praise God for making him a man.

No one can say that he was created as someone of great spiritual achievement, because no one is born great. We may have tremendous potentials, but until we actualize them, they have no intrinsic value. In Judaism, our achievements are much more important than our potentials. Therefore, we should develop our positive qualities in order to bring our potentials to fruition.

CARRYING OUT GOD'S WILL

One suggested reason as to why women praise God for making us with characteristics that are consonant with His will is because we were created spiritually similar to God. His will in creating the world was to give life to His creations, upon whom He could then bestow goodness. Women resemble this ideal more than men, insofar as women can give birth, and they tend to be more nurturing to others than are men.

When understood in this context, it becomes quite obvious that the different blessings of the sexes do not disparage women (or men) in any way. If anything, they highlight the fact that when we arise in the morning, we have significant accomplishments to achieve in the course of the day ahead.

In fact, our reciting these blessings simply continues a theme that begins when we open our eyes upon awakening every morning. The first words we say are, "I thank you, living and everlasting God, that You returned my soul to me. Great is Your faith (in me)."

Our first words every morning are that God has faith in us. He believes that we are worthy of living another day and are indispensable agents for carrying out His plan for the universe. For this reason, He restores our souls to us on a daily basis, as a way of telling us that we have a mission. This short declaration affirms that we can individually and collectively make a unique and indispensable contribution to the world every day.

Thus, when a man praises God every morning for not making him an *ishah,* he demonstrates his acceptance of his mission. He simultaneously expresses his gratitude to God for being given many guidelines to help him achieve spiritual greatness. When a woman praises God for making her according to His will, she expresses her belief that she has a more difficult task than the man. Yet she accepts her extra responsibility with enthusiasm because she knows that God gave her the gifts to be successful in her endeavors.

III

Marriage and
Procreation

9

Modesty and Self-esteem

Psychologists and sociologists have long been aware that people project their personalities through their body language and appearance. People make personal statements that reveal their inner character, feelings, or attitudes through the clothes they wear and by their nonverbal communication. Many therapists can partially diagnose patients before they even say a word, based on what they project about themselves through their clothing and demeanor. One woman might dress quite flamboyantly, whereas another may be blatantly seductive. A third woman may not seem to care at all about her appearance, whereas a fourth may be meticulously groomed and dressed according to the dictates of corporate culture. A man may present himself as the ultimate executive, but may wear shoes that indicate his nonconformity to the expectations of his workplace. Another may dress casually in an attempt to appear relaxed, but his nervous cough still belies the inner chaos and anxiety he feels.

Whether we admit it or not, we all make statements to the world about who we are via our clothes and body language. Our clothes define and describe us to some degree. Numerous books have been written about "dressing for success," and there are even specialists who coach and advise others about how to dress to maximize a certain impression to the world.

Movies present stereotypes of various individuals based on the images that certain groups of people typically project. The reader has certainly seen portrayals of the librarian whose hair is tied up in a bun, who wears manly glasses, and dresses asexually; the "mathematical nerd," who wears thick glasses and whose clothes are rumpled and out of style; the "corporate" executive; and the preppie, to name a few.

Books and movies capitalize on these stereotypes. Certain psychologists are even trained to advise lawyers as to how trial defendants should dress in order to achieve a particular effect with juries. Advertising agencies predict the image that the public would like to see promoted by a given product. Business deals are likewise clinched or abrogated according to whether or not the negotiators conveyed the right image to one another.

Whether we like it or not, society is very image-conscious. When we don't convey the images that we desire, we often pay the price in how others react to the discrepancy.

Therapists frequently treat people who project a certain image and then can't understand why the world reacts to them accordingly, instead of to how they would like to be perceived. Two illustrative stories immediately come to mind.

The first involved a very creative, middle-aged man who came to therapy complaining that others had thwarted his longed-for success in his profession. As soon as he walked in the door, it was immediately apparent that he flouted authority in the very clothes that he wore. He came from a very proper white Anglo-Saxon Protestant background, and his way of rebelling against it was by refusing to wear suits and by refusing to dress in the "executive" mold. Despite being brilliant, he never stood a chance of being taken seriously. Clothes may not make the man, but they certainly influence his ability to climb up the corporate or professional ladder.

The second story involved a woman who lamented to her therapist that men never took her seriously. She was a beautiful woman with a stunning figure, and she invariably wore low-cut blouses, high-heeled shoes, tight skirts, and heavy makeup. She couldn't understand why men tended to proposition her rather than listening to her suggestions about how management could improve the work environment!

The way we dress conveys a very strong message about how we feel and what we value about ourselves. How we dress also shows how we have internalized or rejected societal values. We may wish to project a certain message about ourselves, but if society consistently interprets it otherwise, our intentions are irrelevant. We will be misunderstood and unappreciated. Some women may wish to dress in a sexy manner and have men focus on their minds or their personalities. This feat rarely occurs. There is a presumption in Jewish law, as well as a societal reality, that men find it difficult to remain unaffected by a woman displaying her body. Even when men try not to attend to women's features, it is difficult to ignore them when they are flaunted.

THEORIES ABOUT MEN'S AND WOMEN'S BODIES

God created men in a way that they are attracted to women. He wanted these feelings of attraction and arousal to be put to productive use within a marital relationship. Therefore, a woman who wants men not to be overly distracted by her sexual qualities should downplay those aspects of herself rather than try to change human nature.

Jews believe that the differences in the anatomy of men and women are not biological flukes but were intentionally designed by God. It has been suggested that they were meant to reflect differences in the way they can express their respective souls' potentials. One theory suggests that men's anatomy reflects their being more outer-directed than women. If men are especially attentive to the details of the world around them, this implies that they will be attracted to women's external appearances. That attraction can strongly influence their decision to further a relationship. Women's anatomy, on the other hand, reflects their tendency to develop relationships based on inner qualities and then to generalize those feelings to externals. This suggests that women often find men emotionally appealing and then become physically attracted to them.

Numerous groups capitalize on the presumption that men are more susceptible to sexual influences and physical appearances than are women. For instance, American advertisements frequently include sexual messages, even when the advertised product or event has little or nothing to do with sex. Soft drinks, liquor, cars, boats, and even cigarettes are sold with suggestions of sex, or at least with beautiful women alongside them. Women's products are advertised with the message that if women will only use them, they will become beautiful and/or loved by men. The subtle difference between these two approaches results in partially clad women appearing in advertising for men's products, whereas scantily clad men rarely accompany marketing for women's products. Advertisers have discovered that the promise of sex sells products used by men, whereas the promise of beauty or of being loved sells women's products.

Another phenomenon that reflects differences between women's and men's attraction to sexual stimuli is prostitution. The most ancient of societies had female prostitutes, and prostitution is still present today. Few societies have had gigolos (for women) in more than scant numbers. This is one of the phenomena that suggest that many men are willing to have purely sexual relationships with women and are even willing to pay for them. Women are much less apt to desire strictly sexual relationships, and they are even less wont to pay for them than are men.

The numbers of homosexual men who have casual sex with other men, sometimes with numerous men in a day, are not paralleled by lesbians who are similarly promiscuous. Psychotherapists and sociologists have observed that it is much more frequent for heterosexual and homosexual men to seek relationships based only on sex than is the case for women. This is even reflected in an old adage that says, "Men give love to have sex; women have sex to get love."

Jewish law presumes that men will be sexually attracted to women's physical appearances. Jewish law is also structured such that women (and men) should downplay their sexuality in public. One outgrowth of this is that men can more easily take women seriously and more fully appreciate their nonsexual attributes. Whereas many women wish men would look beyond their physical endowments and not be affected by them, these wishes don't change human nature.

PROJECTING A GODLY SELF-IMAGE

The world in which we live is known in Hebrew as *olam*. This word comes from the word *he'elem,* meaning "hidden." This world is known as an *olam* because God's presence is always hidden behind it to some degree. It has been suggested that God obscured His presence so that people would attain reward for searching for and finding Him.

The Hebrew word for modesty is *tzeniut*. This can be translated as "hidden in its proper place." It has been suggested that the laws of modesty and Judaism's emphasis on them were enacted so that people would allow their internal essences to emerge, rather than being focused on physical coverings. Covering the body reminds us that our external, physical appearance is not our essence. Our essence is within. Just as Jews are encouraged to look for God's image behind the screen of the physical and material world, so can we look for the divine image behind the facade of our bodies and those of others.

Our bodies are vehicles by which we express our souls, and they should not be viewed as ends in themselves. We must look within our own "hiddenness" in order to find God's essence inside us. We can similarly look behind others' physical facades to discover the divinity that fuels their existences. We should not obscure our inner Godliness by focusing on our appearance as if it is our essence. Our facade should project our truest essence – that of our souls.

This concept is equally applicable to both sexes. Judaism obligates both men and women to project ourselves in a way that we take responsibility for how others view us. This includes creating a self-statement through which others notice our inner Godliness rather than focusing on our external distractions.

Besides attending to the divine essence within us, we should strive to discover the same in others. A partially clad body can be misinterpreted as representing someone's essence, instead of simply being the external garment that covers one's truest self.

THEORIES ABOUT WHY WE COVER THE BODY

The first time the Torah speaks about the need to cover the body is after Adam sins in the Garden of Eden.[1] After he ate the forbidden fruit, thereby demonstrating that his physical drives controlled his spiritual ones, he hid himself. When God asked Adam where he was, he replied that he had hidden himself "because I knew that I was naked."

Prior to eating the forbidden fruit, Adam and Eve were both naked, and the Torah tells us that "they were not ashamed." This is because, prior to sinning, their bodies had only one function, which was to serve God. Once they indulged their physical drives in a way that was at odds with their spiritual missions, they internalized inclinations that were independent of serving their Creator. At that point, they could misuse their bodies to serve their animalistic drives. Once they created a division between their physical and spiritual drives, they had to cover their bodies. They needed a constant reminder that they should use their bodies as vehicles for accomplishing their divine missions, rather than indulging in physical pleasures as ends in themselves.

God would not have allowed Adam and Eve to remain naked from the time of their creation until they sinned if bodies were inherently sinful or distasteful. Clothing only became necessary once people demonstrated that their physical desires needed restraints lest they be misused. When God expelled Adam and Eve from the Garden of Eden, He made them clothes. This suggested that once people could potentially use the body as an end in itself, they would need to be reminded to use it properly.

There is a very interesting *Midrash* that addresses the changes that came about due to Adam's sin in the Garden of Eden. Adam had tremendous physical and spiritual stature before he sinned. After he sinned, God diminished his physical stature to reflect his simultaneous diminution in spiritual greatness. The only part of Adam's body that did not stop reflecting his spirituality was his face. To this day, people's faces, and especially their eyes, are viewed as reflections of their souls. Perhaps this is one of the reasons why the Jewish laws of modesty never required a woman to cover her face, even though doing so with a veil was a common practice in the Middle East. Perhaps when a soul can be glimpsed behind the body's facade, we have no need to cover it. We need not fear that our body will obscure our soul when the soul's presence is so apparent in our faces.

Thus, one outgrowth of the Jewish laws of modesty is that they assist us in creating a proper image to project to the world—that is, one that reflects our divine potentials. The more our self-image is consistent with imitating God, the more we will act in accordance with it.

COVERING WHAT IS PRECIOUS

A second suggestion as to why the body must be covered has to do with accentuating its preciousness. When we own something very precious, we shouldn't flaunt it. The more we flaunt something, the less valuable it appears to us. When we own beautiful silver, jewelry, or rare paintings, we normally exhibit them only on special occasions. Were we to display and relate to them on a daily basis, they would cease being so special. For example, if we go to a black-tie affair once a year, it can be exhilarating. People who go every week typically feel that such events are social chores.

Just as familiarity can breed contempt, or at least dampen our excitement about material objects or events, the same thing can happen in religious domains. Many Jewish laws effectively reinforce our awareness of the holiness of various objects. For example, when a prayerbook is not being used, we keep it closed. When *tefillin* (phylacteries) are not being worn, they are put away and covered in a cloth bag. When a Torah scroll is not being read, it must be covered. All of these actions help preserve a feeling of reverence for the covered object. The holier something is, the less familiarity and casualness we are allowed to have with it.

An example of this type of reverence was exemplified by the Holy of

Holies, the *sanctum sanctorum* of the Tabernacle and two Temples. This was the most holy place in the entire world because God's presence was most manifest there. The Torah set down rigorous restrictions regarding who could enter it and when. It was only entered on Yom Kippur by the High Priest after he had ritually immersed himself and undergone stringent preparations. Perhaps because the body houses the Divine Presence, exposing it is similarly limited. By covering the body, its holiness is less susceptible to degradation or diminution.

Not only did the Temple have its own tremendous sanctity, but those who entered it had to maintain the highest standards of modesty. The Torah commanded the Temple altar to be built with a ramp approaching it, rather than using steps. This was so that the ministering priest's leg would not be exposed as he ascended to offer a sacrifice. When the priest approached the altar via a ramp, his garments were not displaced.

The Torah also required the priests' garments to cover their entire bodies, with the exception of their faces, hands, and feet. These laws suggest that the closer one is to God's manifest Presence, the less one is permitted to expose him- or herself. The greater the potential for holiness, the more care must be taken to insure that the body acts only as a vehicle for the soul.

Another example of this occurs when a man wears a prayer shawl. It ordinarily covers at least the upper half of his body, starting at his shoulders and extending down to his hips or legs. When a man prays the holiest of the prayers (the *Shemoneh Esrai*) or is given an *aliyah* (ascension) to the reading of the Torah, he typically covers his head as well with his *tallit*. Whenever men or women approach greater holiness, we protect ourselves with extra reminders of humility and modesty.

This idea is not limited to our conduct in a sanctuary. The Code of Jewish Law says:

> It is written, "You should walk modestly with your God."[2] Therefore, it is every person's duty to be modest in all of his ways . . . (even when getting dressed or undressed) one should be careful not to expose the body unduly. . . . One should never say to oneself, "I'm all alone behind closed doors—who can see me?" For the glory of the Holy One, blessed be He, fills the universe, and darkness and light are alike to Him.[3]

This means that we should constantly perceive ourselves to be in God's Presence[4] since He is aware of our comportment at all times and in all places.

There are thirty-two commandments we may fulfill every day by merely thinking about them. One of these is to make ourselves a throne and a sanctuary for the divine presence.[5] This is based on the verse, "You should make Me a sanctuary, and I will dwell within you."[6] Among other things, this requires that we act modestly.

THE CENTRALITY OF MODESTY

The Jewish concept of modesty is unrelated to the secular one. Colloquially speaking, modesty is often equated with repressing one's feelings, having poor self-esteem, or being incompetent. Judaism considers modesty to be a prerequisite for true religious observance for Jews of both sexes. This idea is communicated quite vividly in the verse from the Prophets, "What does God ask of you? To love doing lovingkindness, to do justice, and to walk modestly with God."[7] In order for a person to observe the commandments of the Torah in a way that pleases God, he or she must have a sense of modesty. That sense includes having a consciousness of the One Above.

A second reference to the importance of modesty says, "When a person does a premeditated sin, the result is shame, but with modesty comes wisdom."[8] We must have the humility and dignity that come with a sense of constantly standing in God's presence in order to relate to the essence of life. Such modesty helps us develop the ability to regularly contemplate how to make our lives most meaningful.

Relating to life superficially is easy. Relating to life in terms of its transcendent value requires a great deal of work and is much more challenging. Many people are attuned to gaining others' approval rather than to doing what is right in God's eyes. The more we try to derive our self-esteem from gaining the approval of those around us, the less meaning and self-control our lives will have. Developing our sense of modesty is one way that we can examine and refine our inner values, as opposed to looking outside ourselves to find approval from external sources. Modesty teaches us how to transcend our physical selves to search for the deep, internal values that are the lifeblood of our Jewish soul.

UNIQUE CONTRIBUTION OF WOMEN

Judaism believes that women were created to bring a number of qualities into this world. One of these qualities is modesty. Eve was purposely created from Adam's rib—a part of him that was concealed and internal.[9] Perhaps this was done so that we would have the capacity to bring "innerness" (modesty) into the world in a greater way than could Adam and his male descendants. It has been suggested that not only did Eve's physical construction reflect her greater potential for modesty, but so did her emotional and intellectual construction.

Eve and her female descendants were especially endowed with *binah*.[10] We can only use this faculty if we can see beyond others' external presentations into their true selves. We can do this best when we have learned how to see beyond our own external trappings.

Psychotherapists use *binah* all the time, and it is the quality they rely on most in working with patients. This is because therapists must be able to empathize with others in distress and understand where they are "coming from." It is only when they can truly appreciate another's background, thoughts, and feelings, that they can put the person's life into context. They can deduce from someone's inner workings how he or she deals with situations and people. Once someone's thoughts and emotions are understood, they can be modified so that the patient can lead a more meaningful and productive life.

Therapists cannot be truly effective unless they are already aware of what goes on in their own psyches. The almost universal requirement for therapists to be analyzed is a secular version of using *binah* to enhance one's self-awareness. Just as a therapist must introspect to understand what his or her deepest desires, feelings, and conflicts are, and how these affect their interactions with patients, so must we understand how our inner workings enhance or impede our spirituality and affect our interpersonal relationships.

A Jew who embodies true modesty has already developed an inner sense of security, self-esteem, and meaning in life. These traits are based on realizing and internalizing the feeling of having been created in the image of God, and trying to live up to that calling.

LAWS OF MODESTY

The Jewish laws and attitudes about modesty pertain to several areas of life. Both men and women are required to act and dress modestly; however, the details differ as to what each should and should not do. Both sexes are required to dress and comport themselves modestly and to speak in a refined and dignified way.

Men are prohibited from being in situations where they will view women who are dressed immodestly or are behaving immodestly.[11] Women are similarly enjoined from watching men who are sexually provocative or stimulating. Men are even prohibited from praying in the presence of anyone whose "nakedness" is exposed[12], be it another man, a woman, or even the man himself. A woman's "nakedness" (*ervah* in Hebrew) includes any exposed body parts that she is normally required to cover (e.g., upper arms, thighs, and torso). Men are also prohibited from reading or thinking about things that will stimulate them sexually. The sole exception is that a man may think about his wife and allow himself to be aroused in her presence, provided that she is sexually available.

The laws of modesty require women to wear clothing that covers their arms down to the elbows, with necklines not much lower than the collarbone, and with hems that reach to the middle of the knee joint or below.[13] These areas must remain covered even when a woman is bending, reaching, sitting, and so on. This means that if a dress will not constantly cover the requisite areas during the course of daily activities, it should not be worn. For instance, a woman should not wear a skirt that covers her knees while she is standing, but hikes up several inches when she sits down. Similarly, a woman who is a teacher or professor will probably need to write on a blackboard. Certain types of half-sleeves will not cover her elbows when she's writing on a board, even though they may while her arms are at her sides. Thus, when choosing clothes, a woman must consider not only what they look like when she's standing still in a dressing room, but what they will look like when she actually wears them elsewhere.

The Torah requires married women to wear something that covers their hair.[14] This is usually accomplished by wearing a hat, a scarf, or a wig. (Technically, this law is a requirement that is independent of the laws of modesty; however, it is a generally accepted extension of modest dress.) It is a widely observed custom in many communities that women wear knee socks or stockings.[15] In some communities, women's pants are not worn because they are not considered to be modest.[16] Nevertheless, there are many communities where observant women do not make a point of wearing stockings and do wear modestly tailored women's pants.

Women are also forbidden to sing individually in the presence of men other than their husbands.[17] Some authorities interpret this prohibition to extend as well to two or more women singing together in the presence of men.[18] As a general rule, women are required to comport themselves in a manner that is not sexually suggestive or arousing in the presence of men besides their husbands, and men are expected to do likewise with women. The demeanor and speech of both sexes is supposed to reflect the dignity that comes with being created in God's image.

A Jewish man is required to cover his head as a sign of modesty. One interpretation of this requirement is that a man needs to know that he is finite, with limited abilities and knowledge. He needs to constantly be aware that there is a God who is above him. A wig (or hair covering) serves the same purpose for a married woman.

Some people wonder what a married woman accomplishes by covering her hair if she is more attractive wearing a wig than when exposing her real hair. There is no reason that women should not look *attractive;* they are prohibited from looking *attracting.* As long as the wig increases her attractiveness without being seductive, it can still make her more aware of God's presence. This, in turn, encourages her to comport herself modestly and to accentuate her spiritual beauty at the same time that her physical beauty is apparent.

Many laws of modesty govern how women should dress and comport themselves in the presence of men. However, the concept of modesty also applies to a woman's relationship with other women, as well as to her relationship to God. The laws of modesty are basic guidelines that help women present themselves with dignity to the world. Just because women are not in a man's presence, it does not mean they shouldn't be dignified.

The laws of modesty technically permit women to expose body parts that are normally covered, as long as men (other than their husbands) cannot see them. Nevertheless, certain women develop such a sensitivity to the idea that their bodies are temples that house God's image that they don't display them even to other women. For this reason, some women are careful to cover their hair, as well as other body parts normally covered, even when they are in the total privacy of their homes. Such women (and men who act similarly) imitate the Temple priests who were careful never to expose their bodies in God's presence.

The Jewish laws of modesty help us internalize and project a dignified image to others. This image helps us to be taken seriously by the world at large.

RATIONALE FOR DETAILS IN MODESTY

A common criticism of the laws of modesty is that they seem obsessively concerned with details and are too bogged down in minutiae. For example, many people ask, "What difference does it make if a woman wears sleeveless blouses as opposed to sleeves that cover her elbows? Did the rabbis really think that men would get sexually aroused by seeing a woman's biceps?"

One response to this question is that every commandment is designed to create specific spiritual effects, and sometimes emotional, intellectual, and physical ones as well. We rarely know what all of these effects are. We can measure cause and effect in the physical world, but not in the spiritual one.

We can imagine going to an opera, ballet, or show and noticing that all of the performers' costumes are several inches too short. Does it really matter that those extra inches of leg are exposed? Would the singers, dancers, and actresses perform differently while wearing inappropriately short costumes? Would the audience react differently to them?

We know that in any business or profession where appearances are important, it matters a great deal how everyone is dressed. A store does not advertise a dress unless the sleeves are long enough to complete a certain look. A movie director does not shoot a scene until every detail of hair, clothing, and makeup are in place. Actors and actresses try to prepare themselves for their roles by walking, dressing, and comporting themselves in ways that are consistent with their characters. This allows them to identify as fully as possible with the people that they are trying to portray.

Similarly, the laws of modesty help us achieve certain effects. In order to do this, the laws needed to be very specific, and they have provided us with necessary guidelines for 3,300 years. They have insured that the body's degradation by the secular world has not been accompanied by the same for the Jew.

Any legal system, Judaism included, has rules as guidelines, but its adherents must also extrapolate from the letter of the law to the spirit of the law. The legalities exist as important entities in their own right; they also protect the spirit of the law and the effects it is designed to foster.

It has been suggested that women, due to their endowment with extra *binah,* have intuitive sensitivity about what types of nonlegislated behavior and clothing are or are not modest. It is certainly possible for women to wear clothes that cover the requisite parts of their body, yet attract attention in a way that is anything but modest. Provocative clothes can cover the major parts of one's limbs, but that doesn't necessarily make the clothing modest. At the same time, the laws of modesty do not require that women make themselves ugly or unattractive. Jewish women should be attractive, but not attracting. To that end, there may be specific items of dress, such as a beautiful wig or makeup, that enhance their physical appearance. As long as these enhancements don't make women look provocative, they are permitted.

The laws of modesty have at least two effects—one for the woman herself and one for men who might see her. Certain men may find women more attractive when they see less of a woman's body than when nothing is left to the imagination. Other men may find certain women more attractive when they wear wigs rather than showing their own hair. In any event, women project less dignity and self-respect and develop less awareness of their inner essence when they wear fewer clothes.

MODESTY IN ROLE

Jewish law mandates what body parts must be covered, and this instills a sense of modesty about our physical selves. Similarly, there are laws that help create a sense of modesty about a woman's role. Judaism obligates men and women to be holy and to bring holiness into the world. Men have roles that bring holiness to people, places, and objects in the public, external world. Women have roles that emphasize bringing holiness into realms that are hidden from public view. This implies that we should develop roles for ourselves in which our inner self is active.

We each have a finite amount of energy and time. The more we develop our outer self, the less time and attention we have to develop our inner self. The more we are preoccupied with how we appear to the outside world, with others' opinions of us, and with their approval, the less time and emotional energy we have left to focus on our inner selves. The more attention we devote to our internal selves, the less we will concern ourselves with getting attention from others.

When society relegated women primarily to the home, they did not have positions of public power and were not active politicians. It should be noted that Judaism discourages both men and women from partici- pating in positions where public honor or prestige is a perquisite of the job. Perhaps this is because modesty and humility are viewed as virtues for both men and women. The more people's roles encourage them to view themselves as important because of how others react to them, the more these roles can detract from people's awe of and obedience to God.

Traditionally, public religious positions were almost invariably held by men, although there were occasional exceptions to this (such as the judge Deborah). Women were not excepted from public office because they were deemed too unstable, stupid, or incompetent to make decisions that affected society. It might be because Judaism believes that women should develop their capacity to influence people using their personal, internal qualities, and not value themselves according to how much external power they wield. Women were dissuaded or prohibited from powerful external roles so that they would focus themselves on developing their essential internal influences and use them to further the spiritual development of the Jewish people.

As society changed, and women became much more active in its social, economic, and political fabric, many of the traditional roles women occupied expanded beyond their domestic realms. Nowadays, there is no religious reason why women cannot occupy any role in secular society as long as it allows them to preserve their adherence to Jewish standards of morality and ethics. (The same applies to men.) Thus, women can be secular lawyers and judges, businesswomen, physicians, politicians, and the like as long as their chosen professions do not compromise their adherence to Jewish law. In the religious world, it is accepted that women can be teachers, even of male students, and can render decisions about Jewish law, if they are sufficiently knowledgeable in such areas. As an example, the biblical scholar Nechama Leibowitz has lectured in many *yeshivot* throughout Israel for decades.

When women or men gain positions of power or prestige, they need to ask themselves how they can serve God through these roles and be exemplary models to others of how Jews should live. Their positions should not be viewed as opportunities to gain personal respectability because others give these roles credence.

One theory about why women are excluded from certain roles of visible power and prestige in synagogues and religious organizations is because these roles disproportionately affect men. For example, the policy-making of most synagogues primarily affects the male worshipers, since they tend to use the synagogue in greater numbers and more regularly than do women. It would be inappropriate for women to have an equal say with the men about such policies. However, insofar as synagogues or organizations spend money on programs that equally affect men and women, there is no reason why women cannot be their treasurers or other policy makers in areas that do not determine ritual observance.

THE POTENCY OF INTERNAL POWER

The process of psychotherapy recognizes and rewards the potency of internal power. Patients who seek therapy are frequently viewed as having emotional disturbances that resulted from their early home environments. Using the power of personal influence, parents can mold children in ways that will affect them positively or negatively for the rest of their lives. The seeds for adult patterns of thinking, feeling, and acting are set down in early childhood, and it is often the mother who profoundly influences them. Numerous studies have also shown that it is a therapist's personal relationship with patients that effects change more than any other variable in therapy.

The ability to mold and change someone's life is a very potent type of power, and it is distinct from that which occurs at corporate or political levels. People can wield tremendous power if they help others recognize their potentials and assist them in actualizing themselves based on this knowledge.

Women have been granted the preeminent positions of molding people's lives on an individual basis in the home; men have been granted the position of doing so on a societal level. Both exercise their abilities to influence others through teaching and role modeling.

WOMEN IN NONMATERNAL ROLES

Although many books about Jewish women focus on their contributions and self-fulfillment through mothering, this emphasis needs to be redefined for many modern women. There are many contemporary women who do not marry until later in life, if they marry at all, or who never have children, or whose children have left home. How are they supposed to modestly exercise their God-given talents and capabilities?

It is important for all women, whether they are married, have children, or neither to find a way to express themselves modestly. Some women do this by bringing surrogate family members into their homes and offering them hospitality. Others do it by introducing singles to each other in a discriminating and sensitive way. Still others do it through careers that allow them to be sensitive to the needs of others and be models for how Jews can express an inner focus.

Neither Jewish women nor men should be satisfied with living only for themselves and feeling content with their secular career achievements.

Our greatest achievements are in sharing our Godly essence with others and helping others realize the same in themselves. It requires a great deal of effort to engineer our lives to do this, but it also keeps us from stagnating personally and helps us reach our spiritual potentials. We cannot simply wait for these opportunities to fall into our laps – we must make them happen.

FINDING THE GODLINESS WITHIN

The more spiritually developed we are, the more we are aware of our worthiness due to the fact that God put a part of Himself within each of us. The Torah says that God breathed into Adam's nostrils *nishmat chaim* – a soul of life.[19] God put some of His spiritual essence into each of us, and this is what keeps us alive. The more we appreciate our intrinsic self-worth due to the "image of God" in us, the more we can appreciate others' essential worthiness because of the divine image in them.

Modesty helps us find the Godly spark in ourselves and in others. The manner in which women dress, speak, and conduct ourselves encourages this process. When we try to emulate God, we can connect to our divine soul and use our inner resources to nurture our spiritual growth. Once we identify our inner goals and our potentials for nourishing them, we can do the same for others.

When we transcend our self-absorption to help others get in touch with their divine image, we expand modesty into a role. One way in which we fulfill this role is by listening and communicating empathically with others. When we attune ourselves to our divine image, we can see it in others and help them find it, also.

10

The Jewish Marriage Document and Jewish Marital Obligations

Marriage is one of the most important milestones for Jewish men and women. Yet, despite its centrality, and the many years that most people spend being married, few Jews know how a Jewish marriage is contracted or what rights and obligations it entails.

Perhaps in part to create a unified and holy society, the Torah prescribed certain laws that determine how a husband and wife can create a family with a minimum of discord. These laws include role divisions, inheritance rights, how financial support of the family should occur, and how they should treat each other emotionally. Some of these marital obligations are so ancient that they date back to the time of Moses.

Jewish husbands and wives rarely know what is written in their marriage documents (*ketuvot*). By understanding the *ketuvah* and Jewish marital obligations, we can appreciate how concerned the Torah and the rabbis were with protecting women financially, emotionally, physically, and socially. Not only are these laws often biased in favor of women, but they were truly revolutionary in the societies in which the Jews lived.

EFFECTING MARRIAGE

There are three imperative components of a contemporary Jewish marriage: the marital contract *(ketuvah)*, the giving of a ring by the groom to the bride, and sexual intercourse. Judaism requires the absolute commitment of a husband and wife to each other in order for marriage to be valid. During the marriage ceremony, the groom gives his bride a ring. When she accepts it, they implicitly agree to have an exclusive relationship with each other from that point forward. Once the couple has pledged themselves to this exclusivity, the obligations of marriage begin. Some of the husband's marital obligations to his wife are spelled out in the *ketuvah.*

WHAT IS THE *KETUVAH*?

Ketuvah means "that which is written." The *ketuvah* is a legal document signed by two valid witnesses. (Among Sephardic Jews, the groom also signs it.) It delineates some of the obligations that a husband assumes when he marries, and it also stipulates that he will pay his wife a lump sum of money in the event of his death or divorce from her. This sum consists of a preestablished amount of money, plus whatever capital and personal possessions she brings to her husband's estate when they marry. It also includes whatever she or her family spent for the wedding.

In ancient times, the amount of the divorce settlement was enough for the woman to invest and derive a steady income from it.[1] Although the actual sum could vary, it was at least enough to support her for a year. This was especially important in societies where women could not support themselves through paid employment, and it also allowed them the freedom to raise their children without needing to work outside the home.

It may have been customary for men to give their wives *ketuvot* prior to the time that the Torah was given.[2] However, it was formally required by legislation enacted by the Sanhedrin (the Jewish Supreme Court) in the time of Shimon ben Shetach (approximately 100 B.C.E.). Prior to this time, a husband had to give his wife's father or agent a certain amount of money at the time of marriage as a lump sum payment in the event of his subsequent death or divorce from her.

Approximately 2,100 years ago, the Sanhedrin altered this arrangement. They determined that, from then on, a man would mortgage his estate to his wife's *ketuvah.* This allowed her to collect her *ketuvah* money when her husband divorced her or died. This same legislation may also have required the *ketuvah* to be a written document,[3] even though a binding oral agreement was originally sufficient.[4]

The *ketuvah* was considered so important that the Sanhedrin forbade a husband and wife to live together without the wife (or her agent) having it in her possession.[5] It was designed to make it expensive for a man to divorce his wife,[6] thereby protecting women from many of the negative financial, emotional, and social consequences of divorce.

WHAT A *KETUVAH* SAYS

Ketuvot are written almost entirely in Aramaic because that was the vernacular at the time of the Sanhedrin's legislation. A standard *ketuvah* for a first marriage says approximately the following:

On the _____ day of the week, the _____ day of the month of _____, the year _____ from the creation of the world, according to the way that we count here in _____, the groom Mr. _____, son of _____, said to this virgin, Miss _____, daughter of _____ , "Be my wife according to the law of Moses and Israel. I will work, honor, feed, and support you in the manner of Jewish men, who work, honor, feed, and support their wives faithfully. I will give you the marriage settlement *(mohar)* of virgins, 200 silver *zuzim,* which is your due according to Torah law, as well as your food, clothing, necessities of life, and conjugal needs, according to the custom of the world."

Miss _____ , this virgin, agreed, and became his wife. The dowry *(nedunya),* which she brought from her father's house, whether in silver, gold, jewelry, clothes, furnishings of the dwelling, or bedding, Mr. _____, our groom, accepts upon himself as (being worth) 100 silver *zekukim* altogether.

Our groom, Mr. _____ , agreed, and added to hers, from his (money) an additional 100 silver *zekukim,* to match them (her 100)–in all, 200 silver *zekukim* together.

And thus said Mr. _____ , our groom, "The obligation of this *ketuvah,* this dowry, and this additional amount I accept upon myself, and upon my heirs. It can be paid from the best part of the property and possessions that I own under the heavens, that I (already) own or will own in the future. (It includes) possessions that can be mortgaged and that cannot be mortgaged. All (of it) will be mortgaged and secured to pay this *ketuvah* document, this dowry, and this additional amount from me, even (taking) the shirt from my back, during my life and after my life, from this day and forever."

And the obligation of this *ketuvah* document, this dowry, and this additional amount was accepted by Mr. _____, our groom, upon himself, in the strictest (manner) of all marriage documents and additional amounts that daughters in Israel are accustomed to, that are made according to the enactments of our sages, of blessed memory. (This is) neither a speculation nor a sample document.

We have made an acquisition from Mr. _____, son of _____, our groom, to Miss _____, daughter of _____, this virgin, about everything which is written and spelled out above, with something that is appropriate to make this acquisition.

And everything is proper and established.

(Signed) _____ son of _____witness

(Signed) _____ son of _____witness

THE MAN'S MARITAL OBLIGATIONS

In order to ascertain what a Jewish husband's marital obligations are, one could study various sections of the Talmud. However, these laws are not codified in one central place. Maimonides, a Jewish scholar who lived in the twelfth century, compiled Jewish law into an organized book called the *Mishneh Torah,* which organizes many of the marital obligations into several chapters. The laws presented from this book differ somewhat from current practice. Nevertheless, they provide an excellent illustration of how the rabbis regarded Jewish women thousands of years ago. The following is a free translation from Maimonides' *Mishneh Torah, Hilchot Ishut,* chapters 12–14.*

Laws of Marriage[7]

When a man marries a woman, whether she is a virgin, or was previously married; whether she is older than 12 years and a day or is a minor; whether she is a convert or a freed slave – in all cases the man is responsible to provide her with ten things, and he is entitled to four. Of these ten, three are obligations based in Torah law, and they are: To provide her with *sheirah, kesutah,* and *onah.*

Sheirah means that he must provide food for her. *Kesutah* means that he must clothe her, and *onah* means that he must have sexual relations with her.

The seven remaining obligations are rabbinic, and all of them are conditions made by the Jewish court of law. The first of these is the essence of the marriage document *(ekar ketuvah).* (He must pay his

---

*The sentences in parentheses are the author's comments and are not part of Maimonides' text or comments.

wife) 200 *zuz* (if he divorces her or he dies), as long as she was a virgin (when he married her). (He must pay her) 100 *zuz* if she was not a virgin (when he married her).

The remaining six obligations are known as the conditions of the marriage document, and they are: to pay for her medical care if she becomes ill; to redeem her if she is taken captive; to bury her if she dies; to provide for her needs from his estate; and to allow her to remain in his house after he dies for as long as she is a widow. Also, their daughters are to be provided for from his estate after his death, until they are betrothed. Their sons inherit the money promised in her marriage document, above and beyond the inheritance shared with his sons from other wives. That is, whatever their mother brought into marriage from her personal prenuptial possessions, including anything that her father gave her, belongs to her sons, not stepsons, if their parents die. (These prenuptial possessions are known as *mulug* and *nedunya*.)

He is entitled to four things by dint of rabbinic decree, and they are: whatever she makes (or earns) belongs to him; whatever she finds belongs to him; he can enjoy all of the interest on the capital she owns while she is alive; and if she dies while he is still alive, he inherits her estate. He takes precedence over any other person in inheriting her.

(Some of the wife's rights are paralleled by corresponding benefits that the husband receives.) The sages decreed that (the woman gives up) the work of her hands (and earnings) in return for (her husband's providing her with) food. He redeems her (if she is taken captive) in exchange for his being allowed to use the interest on her possessions. He buries her in exchange for inheriting her prenuptial possessions, which are documented in the marriage contract.

Therefore, if the woman says, "I don't want you to provide food for me, and I don't want to work for you," we listen to her, and she is not forced to work.

(A Jewish woman is not required to be employed outside of the home. However, she is then required to do certain domestic work. If she chooses not to work outside of the home, her husband is still required to feed her. If she chooses to work outside of the home and wishes to keep what she earns, her husband is not required to feed her.) But if the husband says, "I don't want to support you, and I will not take from the work of your hands," we do not listen to him, since we are concerned that her earnings or findings will not provide enough food for her. Due to this edict, providing food is considered to be a conditional responsibility of the marriage document.

(Thus, the woman was empowered with the choice to waive several of her husband's obligations, in order to waive her corresponding responsibilities; however, the husband could not waive his obligations toward her without her consent.)

When a woman marries, the man is (automatically) entitled to the above four things, and the woman is automatically entitled to her ten. This is true even if the above were not written in the marriage document. It even (holds true) if no marriage document was ever written and the woman married without stipulations. It is not necessary to detail the marital rights and obligations (in order for them to apply).

(Indeed, one can see by the above translation that most of these rights and responsibilities are not mentioned in a modern *ketuvah*.)

A man can make a prenuptial decision not to be obligated by his (normal) responsibilities if his wife agrees to it. Alternatively, she can make a condition not to be entitled to rights that her husband is (normally) required to provide for her. Such prenuptial agreements are valid, with the exception of three things. The man's obligations to provide these three responsibilities may not be waived, and anyone who does so has made an invalid stipulation.

The three things are: the husband must fulfill his wife's sexual needs, pay her the essence of the marriage document (100 or 200 *zuz* in the event of his death or divorce, as previously mentioned), and retain the right to inherit her property (if she predeceases him).

If a man made a prenuptial stipulation that he need not fulfill his wife's sexual needs, it is invalid and he is required to fulfill them. If he made a prenuptial agreement with her that he would give her less than the usual amount stipulated in a marriage document, or if he wrote that he owed her 200 (*zuz*) or 100 (*zuz*) as the essence of her marriage contract, and she wrote that she had already received some of that amount when in fact she had not, his stipulation is invalid. The sexual union of a man with his virgin wife when he has promised her less than 200 (*zuz*), or with a wife who was previously widowed (or divorced) if he promised her less than 100 (*zuz*) is considered to be prostitution.

Clothing, Shelter, and Household Necessities[8]

What monetary amount of clothing must the man provide for his wife? – clothes worth 3 *zuz* every year. . . . He (is required) to give her new (warm) clothes in the rainy season and lightweight ones in the hot season. . . . And (he is required to) give her a belt for her waist and a head covering, and shoes each holiday. The Jewish court of law says that these requirements apply in those days and in the land of Israel, but at other times and in other places the monetary amounts are not (what is) essential. There are places where clothes are very expensive or very inexpensive.

What is essential is that the husband is required to give her clothes that are appropriate for the rainy (cold) season and for the hot season, at least commensurate with the manner in which a married woman in that country dresses. The *kesut* (covering) that he is required to give her (also) includes household objects and a dwelling for her to live in.

Household objects include a bed, a mattress, and a mat to sit on. Eating and drinking utensils include a cooking pot, a plate, a cup, and a bottle, and the like. And the dwelling place that he rents for her must be a house of (at least) 4 cubits by 4 cubits, and there should be a wide space outside it that she can use. It also must have a toilet outside of the house(!).

Similarly, the man is required to give her adornments, which include colored scarves to wrap around her head, and something for her forehead, and eye shadow, and rouge, and the like, that she not become repulsive to him. The Jewish court of law says that these stipulations are (what must minimally be provided by the) poorest man who lives in Israel. A wealthy man must provide for his wife according to his wealth. Even if this means that it is appropriate for him to buy his wife silk and embroidered clothes, and vessels of gold (and he does not), the court can force him until he gives these to her. Similarly, (he must provide her) with a dwelling place according to his (level of) wealth, and (similarly) jewelry and household items, all according to his wealth.

In a place where women are accustomed to go out to the market wearing not only a covering on their heads, but also with a garment that covers their entire bodies like a prayer shawl, (the husband) must give her a shawl that is at least comparable to those of others. If (the man) is wealthy, he gives her according to his wealth in order that she be able to visit her father's house, or the home of mourners, or a house of feasting.

It is every woman's right to visit her father's house, a house of mourning, or a house of feasting in order to do good deeds to her friends or relatives, in order that they will also visit her. A woman is not in a prison that she should not (be able) to come and go.

Sexual Obligations[9]

The (man's) sexual obligations, which are mentioned in the Torah, (apply) to every man according to his strength and according to (his) type of work. How so? The marital obligation of men who are healthy, refined men of leisure who don't do work that weakens their strength, but rather eat, drink, and sit home is (to have sexual relations with their wives) every night. Workers such as tailors, weavers, builders, and similar men whose work is in the (same) city are obligated to be sexually intimate (with their wives) twice a week. If they work in another city, their sexual obligation is once a week. . . . Torah scholars are obligated once a week because Torah learning diminishes their strength. It is the way of Torah scholars to have sexual relations with their wives on Friday nights.

A woman is allowed to prevent her husband from pursuing a trade that is not nearby in order that he not be prevented from fulfilling his sexual obligations to her. He may not go away except with her permission. Thus, she can prevent him from leaving work that requires him to be with her frequently in order to work where his sexual obligation is less frequent.

There is probably no other society in the world where the wife's sexual needs determine her husband's obligations. All of the above requirements for a husband to fulfill his wife's sexual needs are predicated on her desire to have sex with such frequency. The husband's sexual needs are considered to be of lesser importance, and he is required to regulate his sexual relationship with his wife according to her desires, not according to his own. This is truly a revolutionary idea.

From the above selection, one can appreciate how concerned Judaism was with the physical, emotional, financial, and sexual needs of women even 3,300 years ago!

Now that the *ketuvah* obligations to "provide food, clothing and conjugal needs" have been partially explained, the financial obligations of marriage can be addressed.

JEWISH INHERITANCE LAWS

According to Jewish law, when a man died and his sons survived him, they automatically inherited his estate. Daughters inherited only if there were no sons. Surviving widows retained use of their husbands' houses and lived there for the rest of their lives, supported from the estate in the manner to which they had been accustomed. Unmarried daughters could do the same. Sons only inherited whatever was left of the estate after their sisters and mother were provided for, even if this meant that the sons had to beg for a living. (It was considered beneath a woman's dignity to have to beg.)

When a woman married, her husband was responsible for housing, clothing, and feeding her, and the courts could make him fulfill his obligation if he shirked it. By requiring men to support their wives (unless the wives waived this), and by depriving women of certain property and inheritance rights, Jewish law attempted to assure women's financial well-being. Effectively, this system was designed to prevent women from becoming impoverished if a man died and left only a small estate that would otherwise have to be shared with sons. It also freed women to concentrate their energies on raising families without the necessity, albeit with the option, of working outside of the home.

FINANCIAL PROVISIONS OF THE *KETUVAH*

When a daughter was betrothed, her father customarily gave her some type of gift. This capital, money, and/or other gifts were known as *nedunya*. Shimon Ben Shetach instituted the husband's right to use all of the premarital gifts that his wife's father had given her. Nevertheless, if the husband sold or disposed of these gifts, or if they were damaged or lost, he would have to replace their original monetary value if the marriage were dissolved.[10] He was granted the right to use her possessions as compensation for having to redeem his wife if she were taken captive. If she refused this exchange because she wanted the money for herself, she waived her husband's obligation to redeem her, and any losses she incurred on her possessions were hers.

Thus, if a father gave his daughter an apartment and $10,000 as *nedunya,* and the husband wished to rent out the apartment and invest the money, he was free to do so. The income from the property, and the interest and accrued capital from the investment then belonged to him. Although he became the portfolio manager, rental agent, and safekeeper of his wife's property and money, he was also liable for any losses or damage that were incurred during his proprietorship.

For example, imagine that the husband invested the $10,000 in the stock market, but when they got divorced the stocks were only worth $6,500. He was then responsible for repaying his ex-wife the missing $3,500, in addition to her owning the stocks. If she owned property and it became damaged or destroyed, he was liable for all of the losses and had to replace the worth of what was lost. In the event of a normal divorce or the husband's death, all of the *nedunya* capital reverted back to the woman.

In the event of the wife's death, her husband inherited her estate. When he died, her *nedunya* was then passed on to her sons, even if he had other children by another wife.

The standard *ketuvah* specifies that a virgin brings *nedunya* worth 100 *zekukim kesef* into marriage. For a widow or divorcée, this amount is 50 *zekukim*. According to one estimate, 100 *zekukim* is the equivalent of 500 silver dollars. At $6 an ounce, 100 *zekukim* would be worth approximately $3,000, and 50 *zekukim* would be worth half that amount.[11] Other estimates of these amounts determine each *zekuk* of silver to equal half a troy-pound, or $4,800 for 100 *zekukim* at $6 an ounce.[12]

The Marriage Settlement

In addition to the *nedunya* that the father gave his daughter, the groom also paid the bride's father a marriage settlement known as *mohar*. In biblical times, this was money the groom gave his father-in-law at the time of marriage. This was essentially his wife's money, which he left in safe-keeping with her father. (If the groom were to give it directly to her, it would revert back to him once they married. This is because unless the *ketuvah* were negotiated to stipulate otherwise, a husband owned any-thing that belonged to his wife once they married.)

In the days of Shimon ben Shetach, men became reluctant to marry and to stay married due to the financial obligations of so doing. Prior to this time, a groom gave his father-in-law money to keep for his bride at the outset of marriage. It was difficult for many poor men to acquire this amount of money at their young ages. On the other hand, once men gave this money to their fathers-in-law at the start of marriage, they lost subsequent use of it. Therefore, they had no financial incentive not to divorce their wives at whim. Once they had paid their initial marriage settlement, divorce incurred no monetary penalty since divorced men no longer had to support their wives or pay alimony. Thus, men had no financial obligations to their former wives once they were divorced.

Shimon ben Shetach began the current custom of having the *ketuvah* specify that the marriage settlement would be directly payable to the wife in the event of divorce or his death. This replaced the previous system of having the money paid up front to the father-in-law. The current *ketuvah*, then, is essentially a promissory note that the groom gives his bride that is payable only if their marriage dissolves. This removes some of the previous financial discouragement for men to marry, but applies it if they want a divorce, thereby protecting women from being divorced against their will. It also strengthens the institution of marriage and the stability of families.

The Additional Amount

Apart from the marriage settlement and the *nedunya,* the *ketuvah* specifies that the groom contributes additional money to his wife should she ever collect her *ketuvah* money. This contribution parallels her dowry and is known as the *tosefta.*[13] The groom gives this to show his love for his bride.[14] It equals the amount of the *nedunya* that the bride brings into marriage.

Thus, three elements comprise the *ekar ketuvah*—the financial obligations of the marriage contract. (1) The *mohar* is the marriage settlement the groom pays, and equals 200 *zuz.* Its exact value is the subject of great rabbinical debate. Some authorities maintain that it is however much a woman needs to support herself for one year, whereas others say that it represents a specific monetary amount. (2) The *nedunya* is what the bride brings into marriage and the groom agrees to repay her if the marriage dissolves. (3) Finally, the groom contributes his *tosefta.* According to one estimate, in the event of divorce or the husband's death, the wife receives about $6,200 from him or his heirs if this is her first marriage, and half that amount if she was previously married. (Other estimates assess much higher values to the marriage settlements, ranging from $10,000 to $50,000.) Since the *ketuvah*'s value depends on the value of silver, its worth fluctuates according to the market value of silver at any time.

The actual worth of the *ketuvah* is ambiguous because it is rarely relevant to current Jewish divorce settlements. Almost all divorcing couples elect to dissolve their marriages according to considerations other than the *ketuvah*'s monetary stipulations.

MODERN PRENUPTIAL AGREEMENTS

In order to reduce problems in the event of divorce, certain couples sign prenuptial agreements such as the one below:[15]

> The undersigned, namely _____ and _____ , hereby agree that should a petition of divorce be entered in the civil courts, they will immediately contact an Orthodox Jewish Religious Court and arrange to receive a Jewish divorce. Failure of either party to do so will obligate that party to pay the other party a sum of $100.00 a day (United States currency) until the Jewish divorce is agreed to and granted.
>
> Both undersigned parties voluntarily agree to this clause and agree that it should be enforceable by the secular courts.

Signed on _____ in the town of _____ in the State of New York.

Bride: _____ Witness _____
(Name) _____ Witness _____
Groom: _____ Witness _____
(Name) _____ Witness _____

This document was signed in triplicate. The groom retains one copy, the bride a second, and Rabbi _____ who officiated has the third.

MODERN ANTENUPTIAL AGREEMENTS

Certain modern rabbis give couples English summations of the *ketuvah*'s obligations after it is given to the wife. The following is one such example:[16]

This contract is an accurate summation of the obligations assumed by the husband to his wife pursuant to the signing of the traditional marriage contract—the *ketuvah*.

It is added to the *ketuvah* document to assure full comprehension by the husband of his obligations; to remove any ambiguity of intent in the original Aramaic language text of the *ketuvah;* and *to underscore the valid nature of this contract,* so as to facilitate adjudication in the secular courts of the United States of America.

Article One: This agreement is binding on _____ , hereinafter referred to as the husband, and his estate, until all clauses are fulfilled.

Article Two: Upon dissolution of this marriage by the husband's death, or by a legally executed divorce in accordance with secular and Jewish law (Torah law), a minimum lump sum settlement equivalent to the dollar value of one hundred pounds of silver or the amount specified in the *ketuvah* document, whichever is greater, is guaranteed to _____ , hereinafter known as the wife.

Article Three: Upon the husband's death, or complete dissolution of this marriage by secular and religious divorce, the monies, articles of value, and real estate contributed by the wife to the joint property are to be returned in full value to her. This is understood to include all marriage gifts from her family and friends, in addition to all property owned by her at the time of the marriage or acquired thereafter by independent means. It also includes any wedding expenses paid for by the wife or her family.

Article Four: Any dispute as to the true value of the wife's estate is to be submitted to binding arbitration in a rabbinic court.

Article Five: Until complete dissolution of his marriage, the husband assumes full responsibility for the wife's:

(a) Food and clothing budget in keeping with the social and economic status of the husband and the previous economic standard of the wife.

(b) Domiciliary accommodations commensurate with the social and economic status of the family.

(c) Ransom payments in the event of her being held captive.

(d) Full medical expenses.

(e) Burial expenses.

Article Six: Dissolution of the marriage because of the death of the husband does *not* void Article Five. The wife may remain in the marital home and continue to receive from the estate all benefits under Article Five, until she remarries or agrees to accept the settlement sum specified in Article Two.

Article Seven: In case of separation or abandonment by the husband, all of the above obligations remain in full force until the completion of all divorce proceedings and the removal of all impediments to the remarriage of the wife. *Any residual restrictions to such remarriage, be they secular or religious, maintain the support provisions of this agreement in full force.*

Duly witnessed and signed:

on this _____ day of _____ in the year _____.

Witness _____

Witness _____

Husband _____

The *ketuvah* was designed to accomplish several goals: It encouraged men to stay married and provided for women's financial security during and after marriage. It also allowed women to receive risk-free management of their capital by their husbands.

In general, the *ketuvah* is a husband's pledge to be financially, emotionally, and physically responsible to his wife. Women do not give their husbands corresponding documents stipulating their responsibilities to their husbands, nor do they sign the *ketuvah*. One reason for this may be because Jewish law assumes that women know how to comport themselves as wives even without a written document stipulating their responsibilities and obligations.

11

Sexual Intimacy and Mikvah

Throughout the ages, Jewish women have been the pillars of the Jewish people. Until fairly recently, Jews prided themselves on the unique strength of their families. Not only were Jewish husbands known to be kind and faithful, but alcoholism was virtually unheard of, and violence and delinquency were almost unknown among Jewish ranks.

In modern times, Jews have become highly assimilated. Alcoholism and drug abuse rates are now approaching for nonobservant Jews what they are for the population at large. Intermarriage rates are over 50% for Jews in most other countries, and they are close to that in the United States. Child abuse and juvenile delinquency are no longer problems that are anathema to Jews. Furthermore, the inability of Jewish parents and children to relate to one another is very evident in many families.

It would be naive to say that these problems would be eradicated if all Jewish women went to the *mikvah*. However, the laws that govern family purity and sexual ethics teach husbands and wives how to relate to each other emotionally, spiritually, and sexually. If people take them to heart, they can go a long way toward making the home a place where lasting values can be taught and where positive impressions can be made. Jewish tradition recognizes that it is women, more than men, who have the ability to make the home and family life a mini-sanctuary for God's presence and for the development of family members' self-esteem and respect for others.

Children should not know when their parents have or abstain from sexual relations. Nevertheless, the laws of family purity contain within them a foundation of interpersonal ethics that govern how a couple relates to each other. Therefore, when parents observe the laws of family purity with all of their interpersonal components of respect, their stress on loving communication, and mutual appreciation and self-control, it teaches children that Judaism has something that the rest of the world does not. It teaches that sex should not be enjoyed simply because it feels good and that the physical world is not here merely so that we can indulge our hedonistic drives.

The laws of family purity teach us that we are here to sanctify the world and relate to one another as people rather than as objects. These laws underscore how we take functions in which all other creatures engage instinctively and raise them to the highest levels of holiness.

For Jews, sexual relations are sanctified when a woman is intimate with her husband after properly immersing herself in a *mikvah*. A couple that sanctifies their sexual relationship can imitate God's role as a Creator in one of the highest ways possible. Unlike in Christianity, we believe that sexual intimacy is valuable in its own right, not only when it can result in pregnancy.

This is not just romantic hyperbole. God intended sex to be an ennobling experience where a man and woman can bring His holy presence into the world by joining together in the most gratifying of physical pleasures.

ENLIGHTENED PERSPECTIVES

Imagine women having the opportunity to receive an all-day pass to the most luxurious health spa in the world. Once there, they can leisurely regain their peace of mind, reestablish their psychological equilibrium, luxuriate in private baths with a personal attendant, and be pampered like queens. How many women would turn down such an offer? When they hear that the place to do this is not at a spa in California but rather in a *mikvah,* how many would still accept the invitation?

Women who are unfamiliar with modern *mikvahs* may recall upsetting stories about them from a previous generation. Some uninformed women still think that *mikvahs* are filthy, disgusting places where women who are dirty from having their periods go to get clean. Today, there are few *mikvahs* that are not spotlessly clean, nor are they lacking the most modern conveniences. Those who maintain *mikvahs* are usually exquisitely sensitive to this issue. In fact, a *mikvah* in Australia was retiled at a cost of thousands of dollars because the previous green tiles made the water look dirty, even though it was pristine. Despite most *mikvahs* being cleaner than most health spas, women don't immerse in them so that they will become physically clean. Women must be scrupulously clean prior to immersing. The effect of ritual immersion is to create spiritual purity.

Some people think that since we are so aware of hygiene these days, there is no longer any need to subject women to such demoralizing and degrading customs as the laws of family purity. This is similar to the misconceptions that people have regarding laws such as circumcision and keeping kosher. They erroneously think that the rationale for circumcision was that it promoted greater sexual hygiene, or that eating pork was prohibited because ancient Jews did not know how to properly kill trichinosis. None of these laws is based on hygienic reasons, even though those who observe them sometimes derive medical benefits as a result.

THE CONCEPT OF RITUAL IMPURITY

Even though Jews no longer observe the complex laws of ritual purity and impurity, it is helpful to understand them conceptually. This allows us to better appreciate the meaning and function of the laws of family purity—those laws that govern the physical relationship between husband and wife.

What do the terms *ritual purity* and *ritual impurity* mean?

The words *purity* and *impurity* are actually poor translations of the Hebrew words *taharah* and *tumah*. Spiritual purity and impurity are not states where a person is wholesome or degraded. The word *tumah* cannot be translated well into English; yet we have some idea of what it implies.

Ritual impurity exists on seven different levels, only several of which apply specifically to women. Men produce and contract spiritual impurity as well. In Temple times, both sexes went to the *mikvah* in order to regain states of purity.

For example, a man who had a seminal emission became ritually impure, as did a couple who had sexual relations. A woman who experienced a flow of blood from her uterus, even when not menstruating, became ritually impure. A person who came into contact with a dead animal or corpse also became impure. Becoming ritually impure did not mean being considered taboo, evil, or corrupt.

The most serious source of ritual impurity is a dead person. A corpse is totally unable to express its soul's potentials because death completely disrupts the body's ability to utilize and express the soul's power.

During times when the ritual laws of purity were observed, someone who had been in close contact with a corpse became ritually impure for a week. Such individuals were forbidden to enter the Temple and could transfer spiritual impurity to other people and to objects until they reinstated their spiritual purity.

There is a common secular misconception that corpses, or Jews who touched them, were considered taboo inasmuch as they contracted or transferred ritual impurity. In contemporary times, some people likewise misinterpret the fact that Jews of priestly lineage (*cohanim*) are forbidden to be in the same room with a corpse as meaning that a corpse is taboo.

To illustrate how the impurity of death has nothing to do with taboos, Jewish law requires that the living treat a corpse with the utmost respect. Even though being in the same room with a corpse rendered someone ritually impure, we are prohibited from leaving a corpse unattended for even a moment between the time of death and burial. Also, burial must normally occur within 24 hours of death. This is because it is considered denigrating for a corpse to remain unburied any longer than is absolutely necessary.

Moreover, there are numerous laws that govern our conduct when we are near a corpse. We must comport ourselves with the utmost dignity in its presence and do nothing that would cause grief to its soul, since the soul can no longer express itself through the body. For example, we are forbidden to study Torah in a corpse's presence because it is painful for its soul to be aware of how blocked it is from reaching greater spiritual heights via the body.

THEORIES ABOUT LEVELS OF IMPURITY

Death is viewed as the ultimate source of impurity, perhaps because it renders the soul completely unable to influence the body. When the soul's potential influence is partially disrupted, it creates lesser levels of ritual impurity. For example, there used to be a skin condition known as *tzaraat* (usually mistranslated as leprosy). This condition afflicted the person who spoke slanderously or negatively (*lashon hara*) about another person. It has been suggested that *tzaraat* was the body's way of expressing that its soul's influence on it was blocked.

Spiritual Sensitivity and Rectification

Judaism theorizes[1] that over the millennia, people have become more technologically advanced, whereas their spiritual awareness and stature have diminished. In biblical times, people were actively aware of the connections between their bodies and souls. In modern times, people instead develop psychosomatic illnesses; their emotional states create physical manifestations of their anxiety, depression, and so forth. In biblical times, there were physical manifestations not only of emotional states, but of spiritual ones as well. Over time, people's sensitivity to body–soul connections diminished. Therefore, physical symptoms no longer invariably reflect disruptions of the soul's ability to affect the body.

During our lives, we encounter many situations that we might prefer not to experience. The Torah gives us guidelines that help us react positively when these undesired situations arise. The Jewish laws of *tumah* (literally, blockage) and *taharah* (literally, free flow) allow us to take potential spiritual blockage and use it to grow to greater spiritual heights.

Ritual Impurity Due to Contact with Death

The primary source of ritual impurity, or *tumah,* is a dead person. Priests are forbidden to come into contact with death. The law technically prohibits them from being in the same room with or touching a corpse, although it is likely that such proximity will result in viewing the dead body. Seeing a dead body is disturbing and can, for the moment at least, cause one to question whether there are really an afterlife and a God.

Since priests minister to God, there is no room for them to have even a shadow of a doubt about His existence and Providence over the world. This was especially true of the High Priest, who was never allowed to have any personal feelings or doubts intrude on his service to God on behalf of the entire Jewish nation. Perhaps this is why he was not even allowed to defile himself for a close relative, as other priests were permitted to do.

Thus, it has been theorized that the state of *tumah* has an element of spiritual doubt attached to it. When we confront death, and our own mortality, we can be overcome by despair and a lack of faith. When we have close contact with a corpse, we might feel that life has no purpose, since everyone eventually dies. This sense of futility could result in our blocking our access to our soul.

Alternatively, confronting death can stimulate us to contemplate the true purpose of life and to draw ourselves away from what is only ephemeral. It can awaken us to accomplish more, and allow our souls greater influence over our bodily functions and physical life. The laws of ritual impurity can focus us on appropriately responding when we confront mortality and death.

Tzaraat

When people were punished with the skin condition of *tzaraat* for abusing their power of speech, they were isolated from others for a week or more. This helped them experience the effect that their misuse of speech had on those they had slandered. Just as their slander caused others to be shunned by the community, the slanderers themselves experienced this same feeling of isolation. When the isolated individuals stopped misusing their speech, the *tzaraat* disappeared. They were then able to rejoin the rest of the Jewish community.

It is noteworthy that if someone did not stop abusing his power of speech, the *tzaraat* might spread on the body. As long as it continued to spread, the person was kept out of the community. However, if the *tzaraat* spread until it covered the entire body, the person returned home. It has been suggested that this indicated that he was unwilling to learn the message that the *tzaraat* was supposed to teach, so further isolation would serve no purpose.

THEORIES ABOUT THE POTENTIALS OF SEX

Besides death and *tzaraat,* sex also has the inherent potential of blocking spiritual influences. God created sex as a powerful drive that would be a vehicle for holiness. It was designed to encourage people to build worlds and unite with each other in the way that God desired. When properly directed, sex has such tremendous spiritual potential that it can result in the creation of a child and the drawing down of a soul. Some describe sexual intimacy as the ultimate ratification of God's belief that we can unify the most diametrically opposed forces within ourselves—the most intensely physical act with the greatest spirituality.

All aspects of the physical world, including our physical drives, contain potentials for infinite good and holiness. However, the more potential something has for holiness, the greater is its potential for unholiness. Since the potential for misusing sex is so great, its spiritual accomplishment when it is channeled correctly is correspondingly profound. Sex can facilitate a couple's desire and ability to love, nurture, and give to each other, and it can result in the creation of a child. At its other extreme, it can be reduced to the narcissistic fulfillment of one's animalistic drives.

Sex is an act that must either enhance or detract from a couple's spiritual and emotional potentials. It cannot leave a couple spiritually untouched.

Sex can be an outgrowth of a total relationship and understanding between a man and a woman. This is why the Torah refers to sexual relations as "knowing."[2] For instance, Adam "knew" his wife Eve. A husband and wife should know and understand each other emotionally, intellectually, and spiritually. Only after reaching this level of intimacy should they express it by physically knowing one another. When sex occurs under these circumstances, it can be a vehicle for developing the couple spiritually and emotionally.

When a man and a woman have sex only because their physical desires motivate them to do so, the act of sex is independent of really knowing their partner. Such sex divorces spirituality from the couple's emotional and spiritual facets. Under these circumstances, sexual feelings cannot be harnessed to knowing one's partner. These feelings are misused by one or both people, as they artificially create representations in their minds about who the partner is and how he or she will gratify their needs. When this happens, they merely relate to their fantasies of whom they would like the other to be, not to whom the other really is.

WOMAN'S RITUAL IMPURITY

The Torah tells us that a menstruant woman must separate herself from physical contact with her husband: "When a woman has a flow of blood, where blood flows from her body, she shall be a *niddah* for seven days."[3] The word *niddah* means "separated." Once a woman becomes *niddah*, she remains so unless and until she properly immerses herself in a *mikvah*.

Currently, married Jewish couples must abstain from physical contact from the time that the wife begins her menstrual period until seven days after it ceases. After these twelve or more days have passed, she immerses herself in a *mikvah*, after which the couple may resume their physical relationship.

An unmarried woman is forbidden to have physical intimacy with any man, and vice versa. This is based on the verse, "And to a woman who is *niddah,* you should not approach to uncover her nakedness."[4] (The term *uncovering nakedness* is a euphemism for sexual intercourse.) As long as a woman remains a *niddah* and has not properly immersed in a *mikvah,* it is prohibited for a man to be physically intimate with her. (The rabbis forbade unmarried women to ritually immerse themselves in order to remove their *niddah* status because premarital relations are forbidden.)

THE APPLICABILITY OF RITUAL IMPURITY

When the Temple stood, any Jew who was ritually impure was forbidden to enter it. Becoming ritually impure was permitted as long as one did not need to be in the Temple. Currently, all Jews are ritually impure because of coming into direct or indirect contact with a corpse. This is because the means for removing this specific type of impurity was lost when the Second Temple was destroyed. Everyone today is presumed to have been in a room with a corpse, or to have had contact with someone else who was, thus acquiring a form of ritual impurity.

The sole implication of this for contemporary Jews is that we are all forbidden to enter the area in Jerusalem where the Temple once stood. There is no implication that Jews are sullied or bad because they are ritually impure.

Apart from being prohibited from entering the Temple Mount, Jews have not concerned themselves with various types of ritual impurity since the Temple was destroyed. Contrary to popular belief, when a woman has the status of *niddah,* the prohibition of not being with men has nothing to do with making them unclean or defiled. Women who currently go to the *mikvah* still retain the ritual impurity that disqualifies every Jew from entering the Temple. When women immerse today, they primarily do so to change their status from being sexually forbidden to their husbands, to being sexually permitted.

Since the Second Temple was destroyed over 1,900 years ago, *taharah* (ritual purity) and *tumah* (ritual impurity) became inoperative in daily life. However, a woman who is *niddah* still remains sexually prohibited to any man, since this prohibition derives from the verse, "And to a woman who is *niddah,* you should not approach to uncover her nakedness." The prohibition of physical contact between a woman who is *niddah* and a man is independent of whether such contact could make him ritually impure.

For example, a modern woman who is *niddah* is not prohibited from touching her father, her male children, or other women. If the transfer of *tumah* was what made contact between a *niddah* and her husband prohibited, a woman who is *niddah* could not touch anyone.

From the time that a woman first menstruates (usually as an adolescent), she acquires the status of *niddah*. Until just prior to her wedding, she is not allowed to change this status, because the whole purpose of women's immersions today is so that wives and husbands can be physically intimate.

THE FRAMEWORK FOR SEXUAL EXPRESSION

It has been theorized that the Jewish laws regarding sexuality are more rigorous than laws restricting many other areas of life because sexuality is such a powerful gateway for either holiness or its opposite. Expressing sexual feelings normally affects us. Perhaps Judaism only permits it within the framework of marriage because it is only there that one can truly commit oneself to one's partner. This framework allows sexual relations to be a conduit for the flow of spiritual nourishment into one's body and mind. However, even within this framework, strictures need to be applied to guard these spiritual potentials.

Physical intimacy between a husband and wife is metaphysically understood to parallel the male and female attributes of God. There is an aspect of men that parallels the divine attribute that acts upon the world, and an aspect of women that allows the world to be receptive to God's providence. God gave some part of these attributes to us so that we can imitate Him in our creative capacities. Through sexual intimacy, a husband and wife can create a child with God as their partner.

The Talmud says, "There are three partners in the creation of a child—the father, the mother, and God."[5] The tremendously physical nature of sex has the potential to be nothing more than an animalistic act, or the most spiritual act of which mortals are capable. That pinnacle of spirituality can bring God's holy presence into this world, and in so doing can create a child who is imbued with a divine soul. The more harmonious, loving, and holy is the relationship between a husband and wife, the greater is the spiritual contribution to the child who can be conceived through their union.

In order for sex to be positive and holy, it must involve giving, especially on the man's part, rather than taking. The laws that govern sexual expression reflect God's concern that the body and the soul form an integrated and balanced unit. Thus, when one spouse responds to the partner's desire for sexual intimacy, this act of sensitivity forms the foundation for the sanctification of their subsequent union. In Judaism, sensitivity to one's spouse is a cornerstone for true intimacy.

SEXUAL RELATIONS

Medieval writings discuss how the husband should initiate sexual intimacy with his wife.[6] First, he should speak to her in a manner that will "draw her heart" to him, settle her mind, and make her happy to unite his mind and intentions with hers. Then he is supposed to arouse her with words that will make her feel desire, attachment, love, and passion. It is appropriate for him to draw her emotionally close through words and actions, so that their minds can be united and they can concentrate on the holiness of their union.

Maimonides says that when the man is ready for intimacy, he must make sure that his wife's feelings are similar to his. He should not try to arouse her too quickly. By being patient, he allows her mind to stay at peace. He should try to please her and make sure that she is sexually satisfied before he achieves his satisfaction.

Sexual relations are prohibited when there is disharmony between a husband and wife. If their hearts and minds are not integrated with their actions, the physical aspects of sex stay separate from the spiritual ones.

Jewish wives are entitled to complete sexual satisfaction, and it is the husband's obligation to provide it.[7] The Talmud mentions the special rewards for husbands who make sure that their wives are sexually satisfied.

It is forbidden for a man to have relations with his wife against her will because such relations do not have love and desire.[8] When a couple's minds are not united during sexual intimacy, they cannot draw down the Divine Presence through their act.

When a husband and wife have sexual relations properly, their act expresses the image of God. There are a number of requirements for sexual intimacy to be considered holy for Jews. First, a man and woman must be married according to Jewish law. Second, the woman must be permitted to her husband insofar as she has properly gone to the *mikvah* and has not subsequently had uterine bleeding that would require them to separate. (There are kinds of uterine bleeding that don't require separation.) Third, both husband and wife must be in states of mind where they can lovingly concentrate their attentions on their spouse. This precludes having sex when one or the other is contemplating divorce, is fantasizing about other people, is drunk, or is asleep.[9]

By the same token, the communion of hearts and minds alone does not legitimize two consenting adults having a physical relationship. Certain physical relationships are so distracting (incest, adultery, premarital sex) that they make it impossible for two people to integrate their physical and spiritual selves. No matter how positive a couple's intentions, when their physical union takes precedence over their spiritual, it precludes their finding true fulfillment.

The sexual discipline of Judaism helps preserve the unity between body and soul that God wanted us to have. When sex cannot be sanctified, such relations are forbidden. This applies to unmarried people, as well as to a wife who is *niddah* with her husband.

THE LAWS OF FAMILY PURITY

Whenever a woman experiences nontraumatic bleeding that emanates from her uterus (normally this occurs when she has her menstrual period, but it can also occur as mid-cycle bleeding or as a result of hormonal abnormalities), she is considered to be *niddah.* At that point, she and her husband must refrain from physical contact with each other. They are also prohibited from doing things that might lead to physical contact. Thus, couples sleep in separate beds, do not hand things to each other, and do not sit close enough to each other that their bodies touch.

In addition to these prohibitions, there are also prohibitions against women doing various domestic chores that are "wifely." For example, if she serves him food, she doesn't hand him the plate, nor does she pour water in a glass that is directly in front of him. One outgrowth of this is that the husband appreciates how many kindnesses his wife normally does for him that he might otherwise take for granted.

Ending the Niddah *Status*

A woman becomes *niddah* once her menstrual period begins. She then waits a minimum of five days, or until her period ends, whichever is longer. When she believes that her period has ceased, she determines this conclusively by gently inserting into her vagina a small white piece of cloth wrapped around a finger. This is done during daylight hours, prior to sunset. If the cloth shows no blood when it is withdrawn, her period is considered to have ended. (She may repeat this as many times as necessary in order to obtain a white specimen after insertion.) (The laws regarding the procedures of ending the *niddah* status and going to the *mikvah* are more comprehensive than can be detailed here. See the Suggested Readings for a fuller description.)

It is customary for a woman to leave a small, white cloth inside her until nightfall to ascertain more definitively that her bleeding has ceased. If this is unstained when she removes it that evening, she begins counting seven "preparatory" days. These days are also known as "white" days, because the woman wears white underpants during that week. This is so that if she stains, indicating that her period has not truly ended, the stains will be readily recognizable against a white background.

A woman normally makes an internal examination twice each day during the seven "preparatory" days to determine that no bleeding has occurred. If there are no signs of bleeding during these seven days, she prepares herself to immerse in a *mikvah* at their completion. She should preferably begin these preparations before sunset on the seventh "preparatory" day, and continue them until dark, when she can immerse. (When her night of immersion falls on the Sabbath or a Jewish holiday, this protocol is slightly different.)

In order to prepare for the *mikvah,* she brushes her teeth, shampoos her hair, and combs her hair free of tangles. She removes her nail polish and cuts her fingernails and toenails, making sure that there is no dirt underneath. She removes all of her jewelry and any bandages. She then takes a long bath, cleaning her entire body. She also removes all dirt, any loose pieces of skin, and any secretions in her ears, nose, and eyes.

She may make these preparations at home, or in rooms provided for this purpose at the *mikvah.* When she prepares at home, it is customary to shower at the *mikvah* just prior to immersing to ensure that she is totally clean. After nightfall (approximately 45 minutes after sunset), she is allowed to immerse herself.

Privacy

The *mikvah* itself is generally in an unmarked building, set away from a main street. This is due to the absolute privacy that is supposed to surround a woman's immersion. No one is supposed to know when she does this, let alone when she is *niddah,* with the exception of her husband and the *mikvah* attendant. Therefore, all preparation rooms at the *mikvah* are private, and the immersion itself is not discussed with anyone. If men drive their wives to or from the *mikvah,* they are not allowed to stay near the building, to ensure that they not see any other wives who might be there.

Most *mikvah* buildings have a waiting area for the women, furnished with chairs and reading material. There are usually a series of preparation rooms, each furnished with a bathrobe, towels, disposable slippers, combs, nail clippers, and whatever else might be needed to properly prepare for an immersion. Normally, each room opens directly into a *mikvah* so that no one besides the *mikvah* attendant will be able to see the woman as she prepares to immerse.

A Personal Prayer

Prior to immersing, some women like to take a few moments to contemplate what they are about to do. Some say a prayer, of which the following is an example:

> May it be Your will, Lord our God, that Your Divine Presence rest between my husband and myself. And may Your holy Name be unified through us, and cause a spirit of purity and holiness to enter our hearts. Distance me from all bad thoughts and fantasies, and give my husband and myself a pure and clean soul. Let neither of us cast our eyes on any other person in the world, but let my eyes be on my husband, and let his eyes be on me. And let it seem to me that there is no man in the world who is better, more handsome, and more gracious than my husband. . . . And so should I seem in his eyes, that there is no woman in the world who is more beautiful, gracious, and appropriate for him than I. And all of his thoughts should be directed toward me, and not toward anyone else. . . . As it is said, "Therefore shall a man leave his father and his mother and shall cleave unto his wife."
>
> And may it be Your will, Lord our God, that our union be beautiful, a proper union of love, unity, peace, and friendship; a union that is proper according to the law of Moses and Judaism; a union that has proper fear of Heaven and fear of sin; a union that will result in deserving children who are righteous, perfect, and upright. It should be a union that will result in healthy children, a union full of blessing . . . a union through which will be fulfilled the verse, "Your wife shall be like a fruitful vine in your house, your children like planted olive trees around your table."
>
> Our union should be one in which my husband is happier with me than with all of the good things that he has in the world. . . . Our union should never be one of anger, quarreling, contention, or jeal-

ousy. Rather, it should be one of love, unity, peace, friendship, humility, modesty, and patience. It should be a union of love, righteousness, doing of charitable deeds, and doing good to (God's) creatures; it should result in a healthy and good child, whose body will not be damaged, or lacking, who will have no affliction, plague, sickness, disease, pain, trouble, weakness, or failing, and who will not lack goodness for all the days of his life.

We should form a union that will allow holiness and purity to flow in thought, speech, and action as befits proper Jews, in our souls, our spirits, and our bodies. Our union should be according to the Jewish laws of holiness, with success and blessing, the blessings of heaven above, blessings of the deep below, blessings of the breasts and the womb. A union of holy and pure seed, good and beautiful, sweet and acceptable.

Therefore, for the sake of unifying the Holy One, blessed be He, with His Divine Presence . . . I am prepared and ready to immerse myself according to the law of Moses and Israel. May it be Your will, Lord God, that You purify us, and sanctify us with Your holiness, and cause to flow down to us from You a spirit of purity and holiness. And be pleased with us, and with our deeds, and let us be worthy of doing Your will forever, all the days of our lives. And bless us from Your blessing, because You are the Source of all blessing, forever.

The Immersion

After completing her personal meditations, the woman presses a button in her preparation room, which summons the *mikvah* attendant. The woman enters the *mikvah* area wearing a bathrobe and slippers. She then disrobes so that the attendant can examine her body and make sure there are no loose strands of hair adhering to her skin. The attendant may also ask the woman if she has done all of the appropriate preparations. The woman then leaves her robe and slippers behind and walks down several steps into the *mikvah* itself.

The *mikvah* looks like a small swimming pool, about 5 feet by 8 feet, approximately three-and-a-half or four feet deep, and contains comfortably warm water. The dimensions of *mikvahs* have not changed since the time of Moses, and they are similar in Jewish communities around the world. Even Masada, originally built as a palace on a mountain for King Herod over 1,900 years ago, had *mikvahs* like our current ones. The major difference between such ancient *mikvahs* and ours is that ours are tiled, with heated water, and our water is kept very clean.

The woman stands in the *mikvah* with her feet apart, her arms away from the sides of her body, and her fingers spread. She quickly bends her knees so that she is entirely submerged, as the water briefly covers her whole body. Her eyes and lips are gently closed, and she allows the life-affirming water that symbolizes the pristine waters of the Garden of Eden to touch every part of her. When she stands up, the attendant tells her that her immersion was *kosher* if she did it properly. The woman then covers her head with a dry washcloth or other covering and recites the blessing, "Blessed are You, Lord our God, King of the Universe, who has sanctified us with Your commandments and commanded us concerning the immersion."

She hands the attendant the cloth, and again immerses herself two (or more) times, depending upon her custom. When she walks up the steps and out of the water, the attendant covers her with her robe. The woman then returns to her preparation room, and she gets dressed.

Many couples enjoy meeting each other as soon as the wife leaves the *mikvah* building, at which point they are finally permitted to resume physical contact with each other. When this is done, it must be at some distance from the building so that the husband will not see other women coming or going to their immersions.

EFFECTS OF FAMILY PURITY LAWS

We can never know God's precise reasons for commanding any of the laws of the Torah. Nevertheless, our sages have commented about some of their rationales.

The Talmud asks, "Why did the Torah decree that the impurity of menstruation should continue for seven days? Because (when a husband) is with his wife continuously, he might come to loathe her. Therefore, the Torah said that she should be in a state of *niddah* for seven days, in order that she be as beloved to her husband as the time when she first came into the bridal chamber."[10]

There are other obvious outgrowths of the laws that govern sexual relationships. Even though monetary issues, sexual problems, and in-laws are commonly quoted as the three primary reasons for divorce, many couples' therapists conceptualize marital discord into one overriding category: poor communication. Unless a couple develops goals that transcend the material and physical, and unless the couple can actively communicate their feelings, their relationship is unlikely to remain gratifying.

The 12–14-day period of physical restraint that "family purity" requires provides a monthly framework within which a couple can air out their differences and create meaningful goals that transcend the mundane and the sensual.

The laws that prohibit physical contact help prevent men from viewing their wives as objects to serve them sexually or domestically. During this period of separation, a wife is not allowed to do the usual, personal domestic chores for her husband, thereby underscoring to him how treasured her usual kindnesses are. By the time the 12–14 days pass each month, the couple has been reminded not to take each other for granted.

During this time, wives are forbidden to neglect their appearances. They are required to look attractive, although not attracting. This means that although husbands and wives interact in nonsexual ways, their respective sex drives can also be activated in a low-key manner. As the period of abstinence continues, this creates a certain sexual tension. It is this type of sexual tension that can re-create a sense of having a honeymoon every month when the wife returns from her immersion.

OPPORTUNITIES FOR SPIRITUAL EVALUATION

In Judaism, women have many opportunities for spiritual evaluation. Every Sabbath and holiday, Jewish women light candles, followed by making personal supplications to God, if desired. At these precious moments, Jewish women may feel very close to their Creator. They have a chance to introspect and evaluate what has transpired during the past week, and contemplate what they wish the future to hold in store for them.

When a woman lights the Sabbath candles, she can ask herself, "Am I happy about the way I just spent the previous week? Are there things that I need to improve upon during the coming week? What has God given me that I should be grateful for at this moment?" She humbly requests additional blessings that she wishes God to bestow during the Sabbath and during the week ahead. This is a time for intimate communion with God, an opportunity to evaluate where she just came from and where she is going.

Every time that a woman goes to the *mikvah,* she has a similar opportunity for introspection and evaluation. She can ask herself, "What has transpired between my husband and myself during the past two weeks? Am I satisfied with how we conducted ourselves? Did we make the most of our opportunities together?" She then contemplates what she would like the next two weeks to be like, and begins the process of preparing for it physically, mentally, emotionally, and spiritually. In this way, going to the *mikvah* provides an opportunity for women to objectively view their marriages every month and make sure that they are progressing in the direction that they should.

BONDING THROUGH FAMILY PURITY

Every couple may differ in how they observe various *mitzvot*. For example, a husband may be more stringent than his wife in how he keeps kosher, or she may be more stringent than her husband in how she observes the Sabbath. Their attitudes about keeping the *mitzvot* may also differ. The one area in which a couple must be totally on the same wavelength is in how they keep the laws of family purity. This need to be equal contributes a tremendous opportunity for bonding in their relationship.

The process by which a couple adjusts to an identical commitment to these laws has at least two effects: First, it brings about a true union and parity between a husband and wife. Second, they bring God into their relationship in the most intimate way possible by realizing that whatever feelings they have toward one another, they are both limited by the constraints of Jewish law. When God oversees and is a partner in their relationship, a husband and wife cannot relate to each other in terms of, "What's best for me?" The relationship becomes one of, "What's best for us, in God's eyes?" Learning the self-restraint to be absolutely congruent in this area sets the stage for resolving differences and for mutual respect in all other areas of marriage.

After some years of marriage, many couples complain that life feels mundane, insignificant, and boring. The experience of observing the laws that govern Jewish marriage adds a special significance to life. Every time a married woman returns from the *mikvah,* she and her husband confront the enormous powers that they wield. They literally have the ability to create or to destroy "worlds," both physically and spiritually. They can come as close to being God-like as it is possible for mortals to be. Every month, a fertile couple must decide if they wish to take on the challenge of creating life, or of preventing it.[11]

This idea of creation extends to their relationship as well. Will they use the opportunity for renewed physical bonding as a foundation to create life in their relationship with each other, or will it stunt their growth? Will they become so caught up in the physical pleasures of marriage that they stop appreciating their partner's uniqueness and sensitivities?

When a couple is allowed to be physically intimate, their intimacy can occur on many levels. If the physical relationship occurs without preparation, it is like a check that is drawn on an empty bank account. Its true depth and potential meaning remain unappreciated and untapped.

The process of separation that precedes even holding hands or kissing can be used to make emotional contributions to a couple's relationship. When their physical relationship is backed up by verbal expressions and by shared communication, a much deeper bond cements them, and their subsequent physical relationship has an added dimension.

SIGNIFICANCE OF MENSTRUATION

Biologists and anthropologists typically try to explain away the significance of menstruation and menopause as mere artifacts of evolution. Their ideas have nothing in common with the Jewish perspective about women's physiology.

Judaism teaches that everything in the physical world was designed to reflect how it was meant to be used. By understanding the meanings of physical creations, we can use them as vehicles for drawing down greater spirituality. Women's menstrual cycles were designed to instruct us about the physical world's limitations and the need to strive to elevate it toward spiritual goals.

The timing of a couple's required sexual abstinence coincides with a woman's menstrual period. The menstrual cycle is a divine creation originally given to Eve as a result of her sin in the Garden of Eden. It has been theorized that this cycle was to serve as a means by which she could partially rectify her failure to communicate properly with Adam. It was passed down to her female descendants so that subsequent generations could collectively rectify her initial failures of communication in Paradise.

People often deny that the menstrual cycle was designed to transmit a message, or they misconstrue that message. Many ancient societies misinterpreted it to mean that menstruating women were dirty and taboo, and that they should be shunned. Modern societies tend to deny the message by telling women that they can have intercourse during their periods, that they should not let their periods affect them in any way, and so forth.

Judaism says that when a married woman has her period, she should view this as an opportunity to achieve better communication with her husband. She should use their separation as a time to evaluate how she can spiritually enhance her own life, as well as her marriage.

When a woman menstruates, her egg (potential life) and the lining of her uterus both die and leave her body. This loss of potential life, along with its nurturing environment, reinforces to a woman that physical life is finite. When her body gives her this message, this is exactly the time that the Torah deems it appropriate for her to separate from her husband, and vice versa. Just as she becomes aware that her physical life is limited, so should the couple become aware that their physical relationship should be limited. This is a time when they should develop the spiritual aspects of their relationship, in order to enhance it and make it enduring.

In addition, when a woman is trying to conceive, she typically experiences a sense of loss and sadness when she begins to menstruate. An opportunity to create life has slipped away. The blood itself reminds her of the potentials that have just been lost. Her immersion in a *mikvah* can help her emerge from her mourning and feel hopeful once again. When she does so, she experiences the essence of the Garden of Eden, with its reaffirmation of the immortality of the soul.

MYSTICAL SIGNIFICANCE OF SEVEN CLEAN DAYS

The Torah requires women to count seven preparatory days after their menstrual flow has stopped, and this number has mystical implications. In mystical thought the number *seven* represents perfection in the physical world. This is because the world was created in seven days, with the physical world being created during the first six days. On the seventh day, God created the Sabbath, which transcends the physical world. The creation of the universe was not complete until the physical world culminated in a day of total receptivity to its Creator. The Sabbath is a day when the physical world can be viewed in its proper perspective, integrated with the spiritual. Thus, *seven* symbolizes the integration of what is revealed and physical with what is hidden and spiritual.

The Torah requires certain people who are spiritually blocked, such as those who came into contact with a corpse, acquired *tzaraat,* or were *niddah* to count seven days prior to reinstating a spiritual free flow. This symbolizes that people who are spiritually blocked, that is, who are not fully in touch with what is hidden (spiritual), require seven days to reconnect fully to their spiritual Source. At the end of a full week, they can transcend the physical world and rejoin fully with the spiritual.

HISTORICAL MODIFICATION DUE TO WOMEN

Married women currently count seven preparatory days after their hormonally induced uterine bleeding stops. They may only immerse in a *mikvah* after this entire week passes without their discharging any blood.

In ancient times, it was possible for women to have a flow of blood that did not require waiting an entire week after its cessation before they could immerse. The number of preparatory days they counted after each term of bleeding depended on when in their cycle each flow began. The number of preparatory days ranged from none to seven, depending on particular timing factors too complex to discuss here.

Approximately two millennia ago, due to the complexities in the law, Jewish women became concerned that they might count too few preparatory days. Were this to occur, husbands and wives would be intimate when sex was forbidden, and they would sin.

For this reason, our female ancestors collectively decided that they would always wait one week after their bleeding stopped before immersing in the *mikvah*. (Our rabbinic sages affirmed the women's decision to do this.) These women determined how the law would be practiced by adding their stringencies to what was required. (This is but one example of how Jewish women have affected the complexion of Jewish laws that apply to them. It should be noted that any rabbinic enactment always takes into consideration the needs and limitations of the populace who will be impinged upon by it. Our sages did not render their legal decisions ensconced in ivory towers, far removed from any awareness of the ramifications their decrees would have on people's day-to-day lives. The sages were well aware of how their imposing legal safeguards and stringencies would affect various individuals, and they would never legally alter conduct that would be too onerous for the people to bear.)

SIGNIFICANCE OF THE *MIKVAH*

A woman terminates her seven preparatory days by readying herself for and immersing in a *mikvah*. A *mikvah* is a collection of water emanating from a natural source, such as a spring or rainwater. One reason why a bathtub, Jacuzzi, or swimming pool cannot serve as a *mikvah* is because the water that goes into them is not directly connected to the natural source from which it emanates.

As was previously mentioned, all forms of ritual impurity represent blockages in our ability to connect ourselves fully to our spiritual Source.

When God created the world, Adam and Eve were put into the Garden of Eden, where they were intended to live forever. Anything connected with death represented a severing of ties with God, who is everlasting and immortal. When Adam and Eve sinned and were consequently banished from the Garden, God didn't want them or their descendants to feel incapable of ever reconnecting with Him.

As part of our Creator's tremendous lovingkindness, He put some essence of the Garden of Eden into this world. He delineated places where the shackles of our mortality can be dissolved and where we can regain the pristine spiritual connection with Him that existed in Paradise. One such place is the *mikvah;* another, natural bodies of water.

Any man or woman can go to a *mikvah* and immerse in natural waters. The Torah tells us that when God created the Garden of Eden, four rivers flowed out of it.[12] It is from these waters of Eden that all natural earthly waters are fed. This is why the *mikvah* must contain natural water, not water that is channeled by human effort. Just as the waters in which we immerse are connected to their source, so can we reconnect ourselves to our Source when we immerse in them. Before immersing, we can introspect about the true function of the physical and how we should integrate it with the spiritual. Through this process, we reconnect ourselves to our infinite spiritual Source and totally remove the spiritual blockages that were part of us in our states of ritual impurity.

Even though a Jewish man can immerse himself in a *mikvah,* it is the Jewish woman who has a primary ability to bring the influence of Paradise back into the realm of her womb, her home, and her family.

During Temple times, anyone who experienced *tumah* was reminded of what was lost when Adam and Eve were expelled from the Garden of Eden. A person in a state of *tumah* was barred from entering the Temple, just as Adam and Eve were barred from the Garden of Eden.

A woman's observance of the laws of family purity can create a holy Temple within her body. Just as it was forbidden to enter the Temple in a state of *tumah,* so is it forbidden for a man to enter his wife's body when she is in that state. Once there has been proper contact with the waters of Eden, the state of *tumah* is left behind. In a state of unblocked spirituality, couples can once again aspire to the state of perfection that existed in the Garden of Eden, existed in the Temple, and can exist in a woman's body.

BACK TO THE SOURCE

When a woman goes to the *mikvah* and sanctifies her sexual relationship with her husband, she reconnects herself, her husband, and any resultant children with the Source of all life. She reestablishes her entire family's equilibrium by linking them with the Creator of the Universe.

When women immerse, they are not allowed to have even a speck of dirt on them. This is because whenever we renew our spiritual connections with God and remove our spiritual blockages, nothing can stand between us and the Source of all spiritual blessing.

A *mikvah* must contain a certain amount of water. There must be at least 40 *seah* (about 200 gallons) of water. The number 40 symbolizes the amount of time (in days) that it takes for a fetus to attain human form. It also symbolizes the amount of time (40 days) needed to achieve spiritual and physical creation. The *mikvah* itself represents the womb.[13]

The Hebrew words *mayim* (water) and *mikvah* both contain the letter *mem*. The *mem* is the exact middle letter of the Hebrew alphabet. It symbolizes the transition point between the beginning of life (rebirth) and its end (death). The *mikvah* and its water are vehicles by which we make the journey from tasting death (the state of spiritual blockage) to rebirth and renewal.

The *mikvah* is one of the most important institutions of any Jewish community. Its establishment takes precedence over the construction of a synagogue or *yeshivah* (school for Jewish studies) and the buying of a Torah scroll. This illustrates the central importance that observing the laws of the marital relationship has on Jewish communal and family life.

Immersing in a *mikvah* also teaches us that we can always reestablish our spiritual purity and our links to God by submerging our egos. Since water can always change its form, it represents our ability to change and transform our identities. The laws of *mikvah* symbolize that constructive change and rebirth are always possible. When a woman immerses herself, she symbolically demonstrates that she has no existence independent of God. After submerging under the water, in a position that resembles that of a fetus, she emerges as a newborn. She is unencumbered by any spiritual blockages, reconnects to God, and can potentially connect herself physically and sexually in a holy and spiritual union with her husband. Her relationships with God and her husband are thus renewed on a monthly basis.

IT'S NEVER TOO LATE

Like many other aspects of Judaism, the *mikvah* has to be experienced to be truly appreciated. On the other hand, no one should be deterred from observing the laws of immersion if she cannot feel the emotional and spiritual benefits of doing it. Although the spiritual benefits of doing any *mitzvah* always occur, we may not always be sensitive enough emotionally to appreciate them. This sensitivity is something that we can strive to develop throughout our lives.

If a woman has never properly immersed herself, she retains the status of *niddah* from the time when she first menstruated. This is true even if she can no longer bear children, if she is infertile, or even if she is postmenopausal.

When a woman immerses herself according to Jewish law, she connects herself to Jewish women over the past 3,300 years who have sanctified their home lives and bodies through the laws of family purity.

12

Birth Control

The Torah's first commandment to humanity was the requirement for men to procreate. After the Great Flood, Noah and his family emerged from their ark and discovered that the world's inhabitants had been totally annihilated. Noah and his sons were then commanded by God to "be fruitful, and multiply, and bring forth abundantly in the earth, and multiply in it."[1]

According to one opinion, God had to command human beings to procreate. This was because man was created in His image, from which he might have deduced that he should devote himself only to intellectual and spiritual pursuits, while neglecting the material world. The commandment to reproduce was one way of God's telling man that he needed to preserve the physical world.[2]

The commandment to "be fruitful and multiply" was transferred from the descendants of Noah to the Jews, who chose to fulfill the spiritual potentials God had wanted all of humanity to bring to fruition. The commandment to procreate is fundamental for Jews because it permits the observance of all of the other commandments for future generations.[3] The Talmud goes so far as to say that "he who does not engage in procreation is as if he committed murder."[4]

THE JEW'S OBLIGATION TO PROCREATE

The requirement for a Jewish man to procreate derives from three separate commandments. The biblical command is defined by the *Mishnah*[5]:

"A man shall not abstain from performing the duty of propagating the race unless he already has two children. Bet Shammai ruled (that a man must father) two males and Bet Hillel ruled (that he must father) a male and a female." This is based on the scriptural verse, "male and female created He them," which refers to God's initially having created human beings in both genders.[6]

Beyond fulfilling the minimal biblical commandment to procreate, a Jewish man must fulfill two additional rabbinic commandments with respect to fathering children[7]: The first of these is based on the verse, "For thus says the Lord, Creator of the heavens: He is the God who formed the earth and made it, He established it, He didn't create it void – He formed it to be inhabited."[8] This is interpreted to mean that men are required to reproduce so that the world will be populated.

The Talmud discusses the second rabbinic commandment, which is based on the verse, "In the morning sow your seed, and in the evening don't withhold your hand (from sowing), because you don't know which will prosper, this or that, or if they both will be equally good."[9] Rabbi Joshua uses this verse to support his contention that "if a man had children in his youth, he should also have children in his old age."[10]

The commandment to procreate requires a man to father at least two children who will grow to maturity and who will in turn have children of their own. Since no one ever knows if his children will later reproduce and thereby contribute to the habitation of the world, a man should father more than the minimal number of children to ensure that he has fulfilled his obligation.

Practically speaking, Jewish legal works do not distinguish between the biblical and rabbinic commandments to procreate. Jewish law never assumed that a couple could automatically use contraception once a man fathered two children. In fact, Maimonides wrote, "Although a man has fulfilled the commandment to procreate, he is still commanded by the rabbis not to refrain from procreating as long as he still has strength."[11]

Marriage and Procreation for Women

A woman is neither obligated to marry[12] nor required to procreate. Maimonides says that women should marry so that they will not be suspected of immoral behavior.[13] Since people generally want to express their sexual feelings, if a woman is not married, she might be motivated to find a sexual outlet outside of marriage, or at least be suspected of doing this.

The Talmud says that women are not required to procreate because the commandment to "increase and multiply, and fill the earth, and subdue it" applies only to the one whose nature it is to subdue – i.e., to the man.[14] Another opinion says that women are not required to have children because childbirth can endanger their lives.[15]

A talmudic commentary notes that even though a woman is not personally commanded to procreate, she performs a *mitzvah* by marrying.[16] This is because she thereby permits her husband to fulfill his obligation to be fruitful and multiply. Moreover, when she joins her husband in bearing and raising children, her reward for so doing is greater than his.[17] The Talmud further adds, "The enabler of an act is greater than the one who does (the act)."[18] In other words, even though women are not commanded to marry or have children, their reward for doing so is great.

Mystical Perspectives about Procreation

Beyond the Jewish legal requirements to procreate, the Talmud discusses a mystical perspective that underscores the importance of bearing children.[19] It says that the Messiah will not come until enough people have been born to allow all of the souls that are waiting to come into this world to be placed into bodies. The extent to which Jewish parents prevent themselves from bearing children is the extent to which our ultimate redemption may be delayed.

This same idea plays a role in why couples should have children even when they are not legally required to do so. No couple can predetermine that the children whom they are destined to bear and raise will not make vital contributions to the world. Every person has a unique contribution to make in furthering the goals that God has for humanity. If a soul is prevented from coming into the world, its intended contributions will be delayed.

In ancient times, King Hezekiah was punished with a nearly fatal illness for deliberately not having children.[20] The Talmud says that God told the prophet Isaiah to inform the king that he would die and would have no share in the World-to-Come.[21]

Hezekiah tried to defend his actions by saying, "I did not marry (or have children) because I saw through divine inspiration that my children would not be righteous." (His foreknowledge was also correct.)

Isaiah replied, "Of what concern are God's secrets to you? You should have done what you were commanded to do and let the Holy One, blessed be He, do what pleases Him."

After this reproof, Hezekiah married and had children. He lived fifteen additional healthy years.

CONTEMPORARY ATTITUDES ABOUT CONTRACEPTION

History is replete with pogroms, massacres, and destructions directed against Jewish communities. Nevertheless, observant Jews never used birth control as a means of avoiding bringing children into a hostile or immoral world.

Current rationales for using contraception – to avoid social or economic hardship, and allow greater personal comfort – were rarely used by observant Jews. The primary leniencies for using birth control have been associated with medical considerations of the mother or hazards that more children might present to the health of already existing children.

Many people feel that Jews should do all they can to replenish the millions of Jews who were annihilated during the Holocaust. This would help to replenish the spiritual contributions and the quantity of souls that were eradicated during World War II. Unfortunately, contemporary Jews have one of the lowest birth rates in the world.

Judaism has numerous laws designed to maintain the holiness of marriage and the family. Sexual intimacy between anyone other than husband and wife is strictly forbidden by Jewish law. By contrast, many societies accept that adults have a right to be sexually active in nonmarital, premarital, or extramarital relationships.

For Jews, sex is an extension of a couple's commitment to and knowledge of each other on emotional, intellectual, and spiritual levels. Acting on one's sexual feelings when such relations cannot be sanctified is forbidden. Sexual intimacy cannot be holy unless a couple is in a committed, monogamous relationship that has been sanctified through the Jewish laws of marriage.

One of the beauties of sex is that it enables mortals to "create worlds." Being a partner with God in the act of creation is a tremendous responsibility that we should take seriously. We should not degrade sex by allowing it to be a mere outgrowth of a physical urge or an expression of love as an end in itself.

It is forbidden for Jews to use contraception outside of a marital relationship in order to avoid the complications of pregnancy. Rather, an unmarried couple should abstain from sex. They should sublimate their sexual feelings in a way that fuels their personal and spiritual growth rather than diminishes it.

Proponents of birth control maintain that there are societal and global repercussions of bearing children in an already overpopulated world. They argue that it is immoral to have more than one or two children per family, given the world's limited resources and current global problems with poverty.

Judaism puts a premium on providing for existing life, and it does not insist that people have additional children when those already living cannot be fed. However, when dire circumstances do not exist, God wants us to continually create and populate the world. Our obligation is to "replenish" the world.

The Torah is replete with stories that teach us the importance of giving of ourselves instead of focusing on taking and concerning ourselves only with our personal comfort. People can be so self-absorbed that God has no choice but to destroy the civilizations that they create. Thus, the Great Flood in the days of Noah was brought about in part because people only wanted to take and had no interest in giving.

Today's world has so many problems that certain people believe that if every family had only one or two children, the quality of life would be vastly improved. The truth is that things are not so simple.

This has been comically portrayed in the story of a mother who chides her beleaguered son. "Why don't you eat all of the food on your plate? Don't you know how many children are starving in China?"

The precocious son quips back, "And if I eat all of my vegetables, name three children who will be less hungry!"

When people use birth control, it does not automatically follow that others will benefit from their small family size. The poor still require help from those who are wealthier, more knowledgeable, and more powerful in order to achieve adequate nutrition, shelter, and basic living conditions. Countries like the United States produce enough food to supply its own impoverished citizens, as well as others around the world. A major reason why people in wealthy countries still starve to death is because of the way resources are distributed, not because of overpopulation per se.

If people want to contribute to and preserve the world, they must reduce the way they personally waste resources. Having fewer children, in and of itself, does not necessarily accomplish this. For example, the United States currently has only 5% of the world's population, yet it uses 26% of the world's oil.[22] Reducing population growth per se does not curtail wasting resources and polluting the environment as much as does instilling respect for the value of life and for the sanctity of God's world. People need to internalize a sense of responsibility for preserving the integrity of the world and the value of life that God gave us.

If people were truly concerned about others' welfare, they would give a tenth of what they have to the needy. People contributing their proper share to provide for others not only remedies how resources are allocated, but it also encourages God to provide us with greater abundance. If we ask Him to give us what we need after making appropriate efforts to do our share, He will help us.[23]

Jewish law recommends that every Jew give 10% of his or her income to charity. The verse on which this is based can be homiletically understood to mean, "Give ten percent so that you will become rich." We are promised that the more charity we dispense, the more blessing God will bestow on us, such that we will have greater and greater wealth. If everyone who had more than basic necessities would give 10% of their incomes to the needy, and if they strove to model and encourage moral behavior, poverty would lessen more quickly than if Jews had fewer offspring.

FINANCIAL CONSIDERATIONS

Many rabbinic authorities oppose Jews limiting their family size by marital abstinence or contraception when there is not a justifiable medical reason or extreme financial need.[24] Poverty that threatens a family's physical or spiritual welfare may justify a couple's delaying marriage until their financial situation improves, or it may allow them to use acceptable means of contraception.[25]

Birth control is often permitted when a family subsists at poverty level and having additional children would unbearably strain the family. Nevertheless, a couple who feels that they lack the financial wherewithal to bear and raise children must consult a qualified rabbinical authority before deciding to use contraception.

The definition of "lacking financial wherewithal" is quite subjective. American parents may define it as meaning that they will have to give up their annual European vacations or forego certain materialistic dreams. This is generally not a valid justification for using birth control.

One consequence of marriage is that a couple's life is supposed to change. We are supposed to grow through the process of raising a family. Part of this requires reorienting our assessments of what should be priorities in life and what should be secondary considerations.

There is a poignant story about a man who wished to see heaven and hell. The angels acceded to his request and showed him hell. The man observed numerous people sitting around long banquet tables, all overflowing with delicacies and tempting food of every variety. Unfortunately, the people seated at the tables were all pitifully emaciated and anguished. Their hands were tied in such a way that they could reach the food in front of them but could not bring their hands close enough to their mouths to actually taste it. Thus, they were eternally tortured by tantalizing food that remained within reach, but just out of tasting range.

The angels then took the man to heaven. Much to his surprise, he witnessed the same scene of tables laden with food. They were surrounded by people whose hands were tied in exactly the same way as those poor souls he had just seen in hell. This time, however, the people were all happy and well fed.

The puzzled man asked the angel, "Why is it that in both places, everyone's hands are tied, yet in hell, they are all starving, whereas in heaven, everyone is so happy and well nourished?"

The angel replied, "In hell, everybody is concerned about feeding himself. That is impossible. As long as those people try to put food into their own mouths, they starve.

"In heaven, everyone feeds the person next to him."

When people channel their resources into what's best for them alone, there's never enough time, money, or emotional energy to give to others. When people have the attitude that they want to provide for many children, they often discover creative ways of doing so that might have been unimagineable previously.

CIRCUMSTANCES THAT MAY ALLOW FOR BIRTH CONTROL

According to some authorities, women are permitted to use birth control in order to space having children if domestic peace would otherwise be disrupted, and/or where the parents would be unable to raise several small children at the same time.[26] In general, however, allowances for women to use contraception are given primarily for medical reasons. When pregnancy might endanger a woman's life, contemporary authorities permit her to use birth control. Contraception may also be used to prevent pregnancy in cases where the woman wants to avoid the extreme pain of childbirth, or where pregnancy would cause the mother serious medical problems, such as blindness or psychiatric illness.[27]

Decisions to allow contraception for reasons other than when pregnancy poses a serious health hazard are generally reevaluated every year or two. Moreover, greater leniency to use contraception is given to women who already have a son and a daughter than to those whose husbands have not yet fulfilled their obligation to procreate.[28]

In general, birth control is prohibited for financial or social reasons, for general convenience, or because a child may be born mentally deficient, unless the child's problems will prove a serious detriment to the mother's psychiatric condition.

MARITAL OBLIGATIONS OF HUSBANDS

Under Jewish law, a man is required to marry[29] and to provide for his wife's sexual pleasure.[30] The requirement to provide a wife's conjugal rights is known as *onah*.

The commandments of marriage, *onah,* and procreation are three separate *mitzvot*. Thus, even when biological factors make it impossible for a wife to become pregnant, the man is still required to fulfill his obligation of *onah* with her. Thus, intercourse with a wife who is incapable of childbearing is permitted, as long as the intercourse is in a procreative manner (e.g., excluding coitus interruptus). It is not forbidden for a man to have relations with a wife who is barren or sterile; he is simply unable to fulfill his commandment to procreate with her.[31]

A man is obligated to have intercourse with his wife when she desires it, even if she is incapable of becoming pregnant. When a woman is unable to conceive during marital relations, the husband still fulfills his *mitzvah* of *onah* with her. Part of this *mitzvah* involves giving joy to his wife during marital relations[32] and responding to her desire to have relations with him. This is independent of whether or not she might conceive from such intimacy.

Part of the *mitzvah* of *onah* also requires, according to certain opinions, the complete union of the couple's bodies.[33] Therefore, sex should occur with full contact between the husband and wife. This is derived from the verse, "Therefore shall a man leave his father and his mother and cleave unto his wife, and they shall be one flesh."[34] They can only be "one flesh" if the couple's bodies make unimpeded contact with each other. Moreover, ejaculation is supposed to occur inside the woman's reproductive tract. Anything that intervenes so that it precludes full contact between the two people or prevents ejaculation from occurring in the normal fashion is considered to interfere with proper sexual relations.

FEMALE CONTRACEPTION

Contraception is generally allowed when the mother's health is at risk, or when having additional children will adversely affect the health of the family's children. The rationales for allowing birth control derive from the following talmudic selection[35]:

Three women may (or must) use a contraceptive tampon (*moch*) in their marital intercourse: a minor, a pregnant woman, and a nursing woman. The minor because (otherwise) she might become pregnant and die as a result. A pregnant woman because (otherwise) she might cause her fetus to become a *sandal* (a fishlike fetus that will be aborted). A nursing woman because (otherwise) she might wean her child prematurely, resulting in his death. . . . This is the opinion of Rabbi Meir. But the sages say that the one and the other have marital intercourse in the usual way, and mercy will come from Heaven (to save them from danger), for the Bible says, "The Lord preserves the simple."[36]

The question of whether the above three women *may* or *must* use contraception is a matter of dispute. Rabbenu Tam, a medieval talmudic commentator, understood Rabbi Meir to mean that the above three women *must* use a *moch,* whereas the sages say these women are not required to use a *moch,* but they *may* do so. According to the commentator Rashi, Rabbi Meir means that the above women may use a *moch,* whereas the sages say that they may not. These differences in opinion result in differing views as to when contraception is permitted. For instance, authorities differ as to whether the above-mentioned three women are *paradigmatic* of the types of women who may use contraception, or are the *sole* categories of women who may use birth control. Certain authorities allow any woman whose life might be threatened by pregnancy to use contraception.[37] Other authorities maintain that only the above-mentioned three women are allowed to use contraception.[38]

HIERARCHY OF PREFERENCE FOR FEMALE CONTRACEPTION

Even when women are allowed to use contraception, there is a hierarchy of most-preferred to least-preferred means. This hierarchy is based on understanding what the *moch* is, the degree to which contraception interferes with the woman's *onah,* and what happens to the sperm when various forms of birth control are used.

Judaism strongly prohibits improperly discharging or destroying a man's seed *(hashchatat zera levatalah).* This prohibition includes discharging semen without normal intercourse (for example, by masturbating or by coitus interruptus) and a man's destroying his sperm after it is emitted. Thus, contraception that prevents intercourse from proceeding in a normal manner (which will be defined below) or destroys the man's sperm is often prohibited.

A rabbinic authority, Rabbi Chaim Sofer, said that when contraception impedes total contact between the husband's and wife's bodies, he violates the prohibition against destroying his seed.[39] This is because such intercourse does not occur in the manner through which a man "cleaves" unto his wife and becomes "one flesh" with her. A couple is supposed to have mutual, pleasurable bodily contact during intercourse.

Furthermore, the free flow of the ejaculate within the woman's body adds to her pleasure. Rabbi Sofer did not consider contraceptives such as condoms to be proper intercourse, since they separate flesh. Such relations also result in the man "casting his seed as if on wood and stones."[40] Sexual relations are normally permitted only when there is unimpeded contact between the couple's bodies and when the ejaculate is allowed to run its course within the woman.

Rabbi Sofer adds that when a diaphragm is used, the bodies have unimpeded contact with each other, and the ejaculate follows its normal course "in full physical pleasure" and in the "flaming ardor of passion."[41] Even though the sperm doesn't enter the uterus, the pleasures of the sexual act are not diminished, and so the act is permitted. In general, the more a contraceptive interferes with sexual pleasure, the less acceptable it is.

Thus, even when medical reasons necessitate using birth control, and the *mitzvah* of procreation cannot be fulfilled, the *mitzvah* of *onah* (sexual pleasure) is still important. Even when the procreative function of sex cannot be performed, the pleasures of the act should not be interfered with any more than is necessary. The permissibility of the type of birth control depends upon the degree to which it permits the satisfactions of *onah,* and whether or not the sperm are destroyed once they are emitted.

Many contemporary halachic authorities do not emphasize this differentiation between the *mitzvah* of *onah* and of procreation. According to their positions, having intercourse when a diaphragm is used is considered to be "casting upon wood and stones" and is classified as being in serious violation of the laws that prohibit contraception.[42]

Once intercourse has proceeded in a proper manner, most rabbinic authorities agree that the woman is not forbidden to destroy her husband's sperm when contraception is required.[43] However, the man is forbidden to do this.

Hence, contraception that does not interfere with the viability or passage of sperm in the woman's body is to be preferred. However, there are times when methods most preferred by Jewish law will not be medically acceptable or otherwise feasible for certain women. In such situations, rabbinic experts may recommend that less-preferred types of contraception be used. Couples are not required to abstain from marital relations when pregnancy presents a hazard to the wife.[44]

When contraception is allowed, temporary methods such as birth control pills, hormonal implants, diaphragms, spermicides, and the like are preferable to permanent means, such as tubal ligation and female sterilization. (Female sterilization is problematic due to a separate prohibition against it.) When temporary means of birth control are allowed, the situation should be reappraised annually to determine if the medical (or psychiatric) situations that necessitated their use have changed.[45]

Generally, the most preferred form of contraception is birth control pills (the Pill), although many contemporary authorities prohibit their use due to their medical complications. (Low-dosage hormonal implants may also fall in this category.) Next are spermicides, followed by intrauterine devices (IUDs) (if they are medically safe). As with the Pill, certain rabbinic authorities prohibit women from using IUDs because they often result in medical complications. The cervical cap and diaphragm are next on the hierarchy of preference, followed by condoms. Finally, when permanent birth control is required, tubal ligation (sterilization) is the least preferred method.[46]

Jewish law considers oral contraceptives and hormonal implants to be agents that cause temporary sterility. Since the Pill and hormonal implants do not interfere with normal intercourse and do not destroy sperm, they are the most preferred methods of birth control.

Two objections sometimes raised about their use are the medical side-effects and the problems that arise due to breakthrough bleeding and spotting. Breakthrough bleeding and spotting commonly occur in women who take the Pill, and these may preclude going to the *mikvah* after the usual 12–14-day period of separation. When mid-cycle bleeding happens, it is difficult or impossible for a couple to resume their physical relationship until the hormonal dosage is adjusted so that nonmenstrual bleeding stops.

Intrauterine devices neither interfere with normal intercourse nor destroy sperm. On the other hand, their contraceptive action is due to their inducing spontaneous abortion of fertilized eggs. This is one reason why IUDs are not considered to be a preferred method of birth control by many authorities, although others permit their use. The medical problems they cause, such as perforation of the uterus and infection, are also a reason why they are not preferred, even when they are otherwise acceptable as a means of birth control.

Some authorities prohibit using spermicides because they destroy the sperm as soon as they are discharged.[47] Those who forbid their use do so because men are prohibited from discharging sperm in a way that they cannot have any reproductive potential. Nevertheless, many authorities consider chemical methods of birth control to be more acceptable than mechanical methods.[48]

Some rabbinic authorities object to women using diaphragms because they create a mechanical barrier that keeps sperm from entering the uterus. Nevertheless, other authorities allow them when they are medically indicated.[49]

If the possibility of pregnancy endangers a woman's life, and she cannot use contraceptives, she may undergo surgical sterilization (such as tubal ligation), especially if she and her husband already have had two or more children.[50] Since a woman is not obligated to "be fruitful and multiply," the prohibition against sterilization is substantially different for her than for a man.

There is a specific biblical prohibition against a man sterilizing himself.[51] This does not apply to a woman rendering herself sterile.[52] Even though women are urged to help the world become inhabited, they are not required to "build the world by destroying" themselves.[53] Thus, if pregnancy is life-threatening for them, they are not morally obliged to have children.

MALE CONTRACEPTION

At the present time, there are five primary forms of male contraception: coitus interruptus, condoms, abstinence, the rhythm method, and sterilization.

Coitus interruptus (intercourse that begins normally, but terminates by ejaculating outside of the woman's body) is strictly prohibited by the Torah.[54] It is generally forbidden for a man to ejaculate outside of his wife's body. One exception to this is when fertility testing requires examining the semen, and it cannot be collected from the wife's reproductive tract following intercourse.

Using condoms is forbidden because they result in sperm being destroyed (*hashchatat zera*) and they also prevent the man's flesh from making total contact with his wife. Only when no other method of birth control is available, and the couple's domestic peace will be disrupted, can leniencies be found to allow use of condoms.[55]

Depriving one's spouse of sexual fulfillment in marriage is forbidden. A man is forbidden to "reduce his wife's conjugal rights"[56] unless she agrees not to have sexual relations. Otherwise, not only does abstinence result in the man's seed not being allowed to fulfill its purpose of *onah,* but it cannot fulfill its reproductive potentials either.

The rhythm method, a form of abstinence, can be the most preferred method of birth control when practiced by a couple who mutually agrees to use it. Unfortunately, it is often unreliable. Rhythm works by having couples abstain from sex when the wife is fertile. This can be emotionally and physically trying for observant Jewish couples because they already abstain from physical contact at least the first twelve days of every menstrual cycle. By the time a woman immerses herself in a *mikvah,* it is generally close to the time of her greatest fertility. Rhythm can only work, however, if couples abstain from intercourse at this time. Thus, most observant couples would have to continue abstaining from sex for an additional few days, beyond the requisite 12–14 days. This prolonged cycle of abstinence every month can be difficult for many couples.

Since rhythm can be extremely unreliable, most physicians recommend that more trustworthy contraception be used when pregnancy must be avoided due to medical reasons. When a couple is allowed to use birth control for other than medical reasons, abstinence has occasionally been condoned.[57]

Sterilization, such as vasectomy, is categorically prohibited due to a specific injunction that forbids castration.[58] Furthermore, a man who has been sterilized is even prohibited from having intercourse under certain circumstances.

Thus, male birth control is forbidden when it results in improperly emitting seed and/or it interferes with the normal sex act. It is possible that a male "Pill" could be a preferred method of birth control when such contraception is necessary. However, at the present time such options are not available.

The issue of contraception is so complex, the rabbinic opinions and attitudes expressed here should not be construed as being definitive for any specific individual. They are illustrative of Jewish perspectives about birth control and procreation. Any individual wishing further information about a particular situation is recommended to consult with a competent rabbinic authority.

13

Abortion

A fundamental Jewish belief is that we each have a unique role and mission that only we can achieve. To this end, everyone was created with unique potentials and weaknesses, and God confronts him or her with custom-made challenges throughout the course of their lives. These challenges are intended to encourage each of us to bring our spiritual potentials to fruition by making certain contributions to the world.

The importance of such uniqueness is underscored by God's having created all forms of life *en masse* when He made the world. Insects, birds, fish, animals, trees, and grasses were all created in "swarms." Man and woman were the only creations that were individually brought into being. This teaches us that it was worthwhile for God to create the entire universe for the sake of one person. Moreover, each individual is so important that "one who saves a life is (viewed) as if (he or she) saved an entire world. One who destroys a life is as if (he or she) destroyed an entire world."[1]

SCRIPTURAL SOURCES THAT DISCUSS ABORTION

The Torah says, "Whoever sheds the blood of man in man, his blood shall be shed, for in the image of God He made man."[2] This is one of the seven laws that Gentiles are required to obey. Since these laws were commanded to Noah and his descendants (long before the appearance of the Jewish people), they are known as the seven Noahide laws. The violation of any of them by a Gentile is a capital crime.

The Talmud asks, "Who is man in man?" Rabbi Yishmael interprets this to mean a fetus, since a developing child is a person within a person.[3] The rabbis derived from this verse that a Gentile is prohibited from murdering anyone, including a fetus. Several rabbinic authorities assert that a Gentile who aborts a fetus for purposes other than saving the life of the mother has not technically committed murder, although it is a capital crime. This is because the fetus is not considered to be a person until it is born.[4]

There are additional textual sources that prohibit Jews from causing abortions. The laws that govern intentional abortions by Jews are derived from laws pertaining to accidental abortions. The Torah says, "When men fight, and one of them pushes a pregnant woman and a miscarriage results, but no other misfortune ensues, the one responsible shall be fined as the woman's husband may ask of him, the payment to be based upon the reckoning of the judges."[5]

When an accidental abortion occurs, Jewish law requires the responsible party to pay monetary damages to the parents for the loss of their fetus.

Aborting a Jewish fetus is generally forbidden, yet it is not treated by the court as manslaughter.[6] This is because the fetus is not considered to be a person until it emerges from its mother's body. The Talmud says that the punishment for murder applies to a "man," but not to a fetus.[7]

Even though a Jew's aborting a fetus is not punishable by a human court as is murder, it does not mean that Jews may abort fetuses at will. Only the One who gives life is allowed to reclaim it. Therefore, abortion for or by a Jew is prohibited, unless the mother's life is threatened by the pregnancy.

Judaism requires us to preserve existing life to the best of our ability (unless someone has been judged guilty of a capital crime and has received a death sentence). Euthanasia, suicide, and maiming or mutilating a person's body are normally prohibited because they desecrate the image of God housed in us. Moreover, we are only allowed to use medical interventions such as amputation or therapeutic disfigurement when we have an overriding requirement to heal ourselves from illness or disease.

When continuing a pregnancy threatens the mother's life, Judaism requires us to save the mother rather than a potential life. Under such circumstances, abortion is allowed or even mandated. When abortion is allowed because the pregnancy threatens the mother, the fetus is viewed as a potential murderer. Jewish law allows us to kill someone in self-defense if he plans to kill us. When we have no alternate way of stopping the fetus from threatening its mother's life, we are allowed to kill it.[8]

Authorities who take this perspective accord a fetus the same status as a live person, and we similarly desecrate the Sabbath or Yom Kippur when it is required in order to save the fetus's life.

REASONS WHY ABORTION IS PROHIBITED

Even though Judaism does not view intentionally aborting a Jewish fetus as a crime that warrants capital punishment, unwarranted abortion is prohibited and is viewed as a serious sin. Several reasons for this are:

1. If a man is married to a woman who is capable of conceiving, he is only allowed to emit sperm in a potentially procreative manner. Abortion causes the sperm that fertilized the egg to be destroyed.[9]
2. Even though a fetus is not a "person," it has to be treated as if it is a partial person. This means that its life cannot be ended without serious justification (such as when continuing the pregnancy might threaten the life or health of the mother).[10]
3. According to many authorities, abortion is murder, even though it is not punishable to the same extent by a human court. It may be punished by God to the same extent as is murder.[11]

Other minor considerations are:

1. It is forbidden to intentionally endanger one's life. Since abortion is an operation that involves medical risk, it may not be done unless the medical considerations in preserving the mother's health outweigh the risk of the abortion.[12]
2. Wounding someone for purposes other than healing is forbidden.[13] Abortions that involve dilation and curettage or injecting intrauterine solutions wound the mother. Since abortions cause damage, not healing, such wounding cannot be justified unless its ultimate consequences will benefit her.[14] (Sometimes, abortions can be done without these, for example, by using the morning-after pill.)

WHO HAS ULTIMATE CONTROL OVER
WOMEN'S BODIES?

Many secular people feel that abortions should be allowed at the discretion of a pregnant woman, insofar as only her body is affected by carrying a child. This view reflects a premise that a woman's body belongs to her and that she should therefore have ultimate say over what happens to it.

Judaism takes issue with this premise. The Torah tells us that men and women were created in God's image and we do not "own" our bodies. We are the proprietors of bodies that were given to us in safekeeping until such time as God decides to revoke our lives. As such, we are supposed to take care of them the best way that we can.

Jews do this by observing the laws of the Torah, and Gentiles do this by observing the seven Noahide laws. We should all do whatever we can to preserve and maintain our inner image of God.

This means that no one has an ultimate say about what happens to him or her when what they want violates the Torah. Life does not belong to any individual, nor is it anyone's right to decide when to end it. This is why Judaism prohibits suicide. Life – potential and actual – is a gift that only God can grant, and it is solely up to Him to determine when it should begin and when it should end.

Life is sacrosanct. We are not allowed to forfeit it willingly unless we are forced to transgress one of the cardinal sins of Judaism: murder, idolatry, and incest or adultery. In circumstances other than these three, we must do everything in our power to sustain and protect life.

The *Zohar* says that three types of people chase the Divine Presence out of the world, making it impossible for God to dwell here and making prayers go unanswered. One of these people is someone who performs abortions, because he or she destroys God's handiwork.[15]

Although Judaism puts a premium on preserving life, it also puts a premium on morality. In the United States alone, there are 400,000 teenage abortions a year.[16] Judaism does not view abortion as a solution for people who wish to be sexually active without accepting responsibility for the consequences of their behavior.

People often seek validation of their needs and rights. In Judaism, when people have rights, we also have corresponding obligations. Judaism does not believe that everyone has the right to be sexually active. It does believe that if people are married, they are granted the gift of enjoying sexual pleasure with their spouses. In allowing themselves to partake of this privilege, they accept the obligations that are part and parcel of sexual intimacy. Unless there are valid reasons for a woman to use birth control, one of the responsibilities of sex is the possibility of creating a new life.

THE FETUS'S STATUS

Jewish law recognizes various statuses of the fetus during pregnancy. The unborn child is considered throughout pregnancy to be a limb of its mother and to have potential life.[17] However, there are also subdivisions of the nine months. Until an embryo is 40 days old, it is considered to be "mere water" (*maya d'alma*).[18] This status is derived from technical laws that discuss how long after widowhood from an Israelite a priest's daughter had to wait before she could eat sanctified food (*terumah*) if she were questionably pregnant. From 40 days after conception until birth, a fetus is considered to have more status. This additional status is reflected in a law that applied when the Temple stood. When a fetus was spontaneously aborted 40 or more days after conception, its mother brought an offering to the Temple, just as if she had given birth to a live child.[19] This supports the idea that an unborn child was considered to be a person.

WHEN IS ABORTION PERMITTED?

The rabbinic opinions that allow or prohibit abortions in various circumstances are complex and often differ from each another. The discussion here about the permissibility of abortion is merely illustrative and should not be considered comprehensive or definitive.

Abortion is generally allowed, or even required, when the mother's life is at risk.[20] Whether abortion is allowed when the mother's health is at stake is a matter of contemporary debate.[21] Examples of conditions that threaten a mother's health and could justify an abortion include a worsening of cancer, deafness,[22] and severe pain.[23] Life-threatening mental illness that is induced by pregnancy is also considered a valid reason for abortion.[24]

Abortions that are justified for psychiatric reasons require that mental health experts determine that, due to a woman's pregnancy or giving birth, she would pose a risk to herself or others through suicidal or homicidal behavior or would be likely to have an emotional breakdown. A therapist would take into account the woman's prior psychiatric history when consulting with competent rabbinic authorities in order to make such a determination.

Although it is usually forbidden to abort a fetus that was conceived through rape, some rabbis permit it when the mother's physical or emotional health may be harmed by her shame, anguish, or embarrassment.[25] When conception results from adultery, abortion is usually forbidden.[26] As with rape, however, it is permitted when the mother's mental health would be seriously threatened.[27]

ABORTION FOR FINANCIAL REASONS

Financial considerations are sometimes advanced as a justification for abortion. Jewish law, however, does not consider poverty a sufficient reason to abort a potential human being.

Although bearing a child and giving it up for adoption is not emotionally palatable to certain women, it is spiritually preferable to aborting it. At the time of the writing of this book, one out of six American couples is infertile.[28] Millions of American couples would like to adopt children, many of whom are hampered by the scarcity of available healthy babies. If women would choose to bear their unwanted children rather than abort them, and gave them to infertile couples for adoption, millions of children could be placed in good homes.

In Israel alone, approximately 50,000 Jewish children are intentionally aborted every year. (This represents approximately one out of every three pregnancies there.)[29] This is especially sad considering the low birth rate among Jews and the long waiting list of Israeli couples who would like to adopt but for whom no children are available. In many cases, having additional financial support during pregnancy would be all that these women would need to carry their pregnancies to term instead of opting to abort. EFRAT is an organization in Israel that accepts voluntary contributions to support mothers who wish to continue their pregnancies but who otherwise could not afford to do so. (EFRAT, The Jewish Association for Birth Encouragement, 8 HaMeiri Blvd., P.O.B. 6325, Jerusalem 91062, (02) 828507.)

ABORTING HANDICAPPED FETUSES

Secular society generally condones, indeed even recommends, aborting fetuses when birth defects are detected *in utero*. Many parents who are told that their child is likely to be born physically or intellectually handicapped opt to abort them. In contrast with this, almost all rabbinic authorities forbid aborting abnormal fetuses,[30] although one authority allows it.[31]

In general, abortions are not even permitted when the pregnant mother has contracted rubella[32] or has taken drugs that can cause chromosomal damage.[33] They are likewise prohibited even when the child will be born with physical or intellectual defects.[34] Children who will be mentally retarded, physically deformed, or the like are viewed as God's creations and have a right to live. Since the value of human life is infinite, any fraction of it is still infinite. One is not allowed to abort a fetus solely because it will be born with a physical or mental defect.

The Chazon Ish, a renowned rabbi, used to stand up when a mentally retarded person entered the room. When questioned about his behavior, he explained, "If God saw fit to limit this person's choices so much by creating him mentally defective, he must have such a spiritually great soul that it does not require a great deal of refinement. Therefore, I stand in his presence, just as I would stand in the presence of anyone who is of tremendous spiritual stature."

Judaism's view of abortion reflects its view of the paramount sanctity of potential life, as well as God's faith that we can accept the challenges that He puts into our lives to help us grow. When the Master of Creation determines that life should begin, we have no right to decide that we know better than He about how and when to terminate it.

PREFERRED TIME FRAME FOR ABORTIONS

When an abortion is permitted, it is generally preferable to perform it before the embryo is 40 days old.[35] At this stage, some rabbinic authorities consider the embryo to not yet have the status of an unborn person.

The above discussion about when abortions are permitted or prohibited are not meant to be a guide for women who are actually deciding whether or not to have an abortion. Such questions must be referred to competent rabbinic authorities.

14

Divorce

Judaism prefers adults to be married, and the Talmud extols the virtues of marriage. For example, it says, "Any man who has no wife lives without joy, without blessing, and without goodness . . . without Torah, without a protecting wall . . . and without peace. . . . Any man who has no wife is not a proper man."[1]

A person's first marriage is considered to be especially precious. "A man finds happiness only with his first wife, for it is said, 'Let your fountain be blessed and joy with the wife of your youth.' . . . As soon as a man takes a wife, his sins are buried, for it is said, 'Whoever finds a wife finds a great good and finds favor with God.' "[2]

Despite Judaism's preference that people marry, it recognizes that not every couple will be compatible, mutually loving and respectful of each other. There will also be instances where one spouse refuses to adhere to Jewish law, thereby interfering with the viability of a Jewish marriage. When a husband and wife cannot live together harmoniously, Judaism allows them to get divorced.

Even though divorce is permitted, and at times is even mandated by Jewish law, it is considered to be a tremendous tragedy. The Talmud[3] says, "When a man divorces his first wife, even the altar sheds tears for him, [as it is written[4]:] 'You cover God's altar with tears, and with weeping, and with crying out . . . because the Lord witnessed between you and the wife of your youth, with whom you acted treacherously.' "

MARRIAGE AND DIVORCE AS CONTRACTUAL RELATIONSHIPS

Jewish marriage and divorce are each effected via a contract. Unlike civil contracts, all Jewish contracts are unilaterally executed, although they require the consent of both parties. This means that one person initiates a contract and the other one accepts it. In order for a Jewish marriage to be valid, the man must initiate it, and the woman must accept its terms. (This does not mean that she has no say in most of these terms. She is free to negotiate financial and practical terms as she sees fit, according to the parameters discussed in Chapter 10.) Once the man initiates the marriage contract and the woman accepts it, they are married.

The Talmud says that men initiate marriage contracts because it is they who actively pursue wives, rather than women who actively pursue husbands.[5] One reason that has been theorized for this is that single men feel more incomplete than do single women. This derives from Eve's having been formed from Adam's body, thus causing him to lose a part of himself. Consequently, his male descendants forever feel that some part of them is missing as long as they are without their female "half." In the eyes of Jewish law, men also have a stronger emotional and spiritual need for marriage than do women.[6]

THE DIVORCE PROCESS

Since marriage is a unilateral contract that the husband initiates, so must he be the one to initiate its dissolution. The Torah says, "If a man takes a woman and marries her, and it comes to pass that she is displeasing to him because he finds in her some immodesty on her part, he shall write her a bill of divorce, and place it in her hand, and send her from his house. When she (then) leaves his house, she may go and marry another man."[7]

This scriptural verse is the source for the laws of Jewish divorce. Judaism requires husbands to be the active agents in any divorce proceedings. This means that in order to be valid, a husband must give his wife a bill of divorce, known as a *get.* Although he must give it, he is forbidden to divorce her without her agreeing to accept it. The rabbis instituted this decree approximately a thousand years ago in order to protect women from being divorced at whim. Even though a woman cannot technically initiate a divorce, she may ask her husband to divorce her, or she may ask a Jewish court of law to convince or order her husband to do so.[8]

A divorce must be formalized by the *get,* which is a written document given by a husband, or his agent, to his wife, or her agent. Two bonafide Jewish witnesses must attend the dissolution of the marriage, just as there were two witnesses when the marriage was originally effected. Once a husband gives his wife a *get,* even if they are not civilly divorced, it totally severs their relationship as a married couple and they may no longer live together.

THE DIVORCE DOCUMENT

The text of an Ashkenazic *get* is normally written in Aramaic. In a Sephardic *get,* the text is the same, but the names are written differently. Loosely translated, it reads as follows:

> On the _____ day of the week, the _____ day of the month of _____ in the year _____ from the creation of the world, according to the reckoning of the calendar that we are accustomed to count here, in the city of _____, which is located on the river _____, and situated near wells of water, I, _____, the son of _____, who am present today in the city of _____, which is located on the river _____, and situated near wells of water, do willingly consent, being under no restraint, to release, set free, and put aside, you, my wife _____, daughter of _____, who is today in the city of _____, which is located on the river _____, and situated near wells of water, who has been my wife from before. Thus do I set free, release you, and put you aside, in order that you may have permission and authority over yourself to go and marry any man you desire. No person may hinder you from this day forth, and you are permitted to every man. This shall be for you from me a bill of dismissal, a letter of release, and a document of freedom, in accordance with the laws of Moses and Israel.

Due to the complex requirements of how the *get* must be written, a Jewish divorce must be conducted by people who are expert in such matters. The *get* itself is written on a blank piece of paper by a Jewish scribe, using a quill pen and ink. He writes the text on twelve lines, and the document is then notarized by two valid witnesses.

Prior to actually writing the *get,* the scribe must ascertain the precise Hebrew and English names of the divorcing parties, as well as any nicknames by which they (and their parents) are known. If there is no chance of reconciliation, the husband and wife are also discouraged from speaking to each other from the time the scribe begins to write the *get* until the husband actually gives it to her. This is to ensure that the husband says nothing that invalidates his intentions to divorce his wife before the proceedings are completed.

It is recommended that the writing and giving of the *get* be done under the auspices of three men who constitute a Jewish court of law (*bet din*). After the *get* is written, the husband, or his agent, hands the *get* to his wife, or her agent. When he does this, he recites a formula that states that from that moment on she is no longer his wife and is henceforth free to remarry. She demonstrates her acquisition of the *get* by carrying it with her as she walks several feet away. She then gives the document to the *bet din,* who cut it with a knife or with a scissors. This precludes anyone else with the same names from using it. This is an added precaution against the remote possibility that someone else would use a *get* that was not specifically written for them.

The torn *get* is then filed away. The woman and her ex-husband receive documents a short time later attesting to the fact that they were divorced according to Jewish law. The entire process of obtaining a Jewish divorce can be extremely brief. Whereas an amicable civil divorce can require waiting months before the case is heard by a court, a Jewish couple can decide to initiate and complete a religious divorce the same day. If both parties consent, and there are no unusual circumstances during the divorce proceedings, it requires only an hour or less to properly write and give a *get*.

Once divorced, a man may immediately marry another woman if he so desires. A divorced woman must wait approximately 90 days before she can marry another man. This is to ensure that if she is pregnant at the time of her divorce, her child's paternity will be known with certainty. If a husband and wife wish to remarry each other, they do not have to wait at all.

Once a couple divorces, certain restrictions apply to their remarriage. They may not remarry each other once the woman has subsequently married another husband. In addition, men of priestly descent (*cohanim*) may not marry divorcees (although they may marry widows). Consequently, once *cohanim* divorce their wives, they may never remarry them, even if the ex-wives have not married anyone else in the interim.

CONSEQUENCES OF NOT OBTAINING A *GET*

A secular (civil) divorce has no religious validity in severing a Jewish couple's marital ties. A civilly divorced Jewish couple is still married in the eyes of Jewish law until they obtain a Jewish divorce. This distinction affects the status of a couple's subsequent sexual relations with people other than their spouse. As long as a Jewish woman is married according to Jewish law, sex with a man other than her husband is adulterous for both parties concerned. That is, as long as a woman has not received a proper *get,* any men with whom she is sexually intimate are adulterers, and she is an adulteress. Technically, if a man is married and has not given his wife a *get,* he is prohibited from having sex with any other women. However, if he does so anyway, neither he nor any unmarried women with whom he is intimate violate the prohibition against adultery, although they violate other laws.

As long as a married woman has not received a proper *get,* her status also affects any children that she conceives with men other than her husband. Secular law defines a bastard as a child who is born out-of-wedlock. In contradistinction to this, Jewish law defines a bastard as a child who is born from an incestuous or adulterous relationship. Thus, a child resulting from the sexual union of a woman who is married according to Jewish law with a man other than her husband is illegitimate. Such a child is known as a *mamzer.* A *mamzer* may not marry a Jew who was born from a legitimate marriage or from an out-of-wedlock relationship that would have been permitted had the couple married according to Jewish law.

The laws that define adulterous relationships and *mamzerus* apply even if women have been civilly divorced. Therefore, it is crucial for Jewish couples to obtain proper divorces, for themselves and for the sake of any subsequent children they may have.

POLYGAMY AND POLYANDRY

Biblical law allows a man to be married to more than one wife simultaneously, provided his wives are not sisters and that he can support them. Nevertheless, the same rabbinic authority (Rabbenu Gershom) who forbade divorcing a wife against her will also forbade Ashkenazic men (of Germanic and Eastern European descent) from marrying more than one wife simultaneously. This edict has been in force for more than 1,000 years.

When Rabbenu Gershom formulated his restriction, it included certain provisions allowing married men to marry a second wife if 100 rabbis in three countries permitted them to do so. This might occur if a man's wife were mentally incompetent, in which case the rabbis forbade him to divorce her. He could also marry a second wife when his first wife was adulterous and refused to accept a *get*. This same leniency could be used when a wife repeatedly refused to accept a legitimate *get*.

Whenever a man uses this leniency, he must deposit his first wife's *get* with a *bet din* prior to obtaining rabbinical consent to take a second wife. This ensures that his first wife will be free to remarry whenever she is able or willing to accept the divorce.

Biblical law never allowed women to marry more than one husband, and this law cannot be changed. Once a woman is married, she can only have additional husbands if her original marriage is dissolved through her spouse's death or through his granting her a *get*.

Because married Jewish men and women need a proper divorce in order to remarry, various difficulties ensue when this does not occur. One major problem is women becoming *agunot* (see below). Another is spouses using emotional and financial blackmail against each other.

AGUNAH

Agunah literally means "a chained woman." This status applies to any married woman whose husband does not grant her a *get* after she appeals to an appropriate *bet din* for help. An *agunah* is not free to remarry until her husband either gives her a *get* or dies. Sometimes women become *agunot* for reasons beyond the husband's control, such as the husband being kidnapped in an unknown location, the husband disappearing on a trip, or the husband missing in action during a war. After World War II, many women whose husbands had disappeared during the war had questions about whether or not they were *agunot*. The question was also raised when an Israeli submarine, the Doron, disappeared in the Red Sea and when an El Al plane was shot down over Hungary in the 1950s.

In biblical times, the most common reason why women became *agunot* was because their husbands went to war and did not return. Unless a husband's corpse was found, or eyewitnesses testified that he had indeed died, his wife could not assume that she was a widow. Until his death was proven, she remained an *agunah* and could not remarry.

During the reign of the Davidic dynasty in the First Temple period, women were better protected from becoming *agunot*. This was because any man who went to war gave his wife a specially worded *get* just prior to leaving for battle. These conditional divorces operated only if husbands did not return by a certain date, at which time the wives were free to remarry, even without proof of their spouses' demise. If the husbands did return as planned, their divorces never became operative. (Due to this historical precedent, Rabbi Moshe Feinstein wrote similar conditional divorces for servicemen to give their wives prior to going away during World War II.)

During mishnaic times (approximately 100 C.E.), women sometimes became *agunot* when their husbands went on sea journeys and never returned. At that time, traveling by sea was quite dangerous, and it was not unusual for ship crews and passengers to drown. Nevertheless, in order for a wife to be able to remarry when her husband did not return, definitive proof of his death was still necessary.

RECALCITRANT HUSBANDS

In modern times, certain women have wanted to be divorced, but their husbands have refused to oblige them. Such recalcitrant husbands, who cause their wives to become *agunot,* were rare prior to the French Revolution. Until that time, Jews by and large had their own judicial authority, both in the Diaspora and in Israel. The Jewish courts were empowered to use a variety of means, including physical force, to convince a recalcitrant husband to grant his wife a *get* if she wanted one.

Since wives do not give *gets,* they can sometimes be at their husbands' mercy when they wish to receive one. Some men refuse to grant a *get* in order to achieve certain emotional or financial gains. They may withhold a *get* in order to punish their wives, avoid paying the *ketuvah* money, wield control, and so forth. (It should be noted that women also blackmail their husbands emotionally and financially by temporarily or permanently refusing to accept a *get* from them.)

THE POWER OF THE *BET DIN*

Although it might seem that biblical law puts women at a disadvantage when they want a divorce, their relative lack of power in such situations was offset by the power of the *bet din,* who could aid them. These courts were empowered to use almost any type of psychological or physical "convincing" to encourage a man to give his wife her *get.* The *bet din* had the authority to beat a man until he said, "I want to give it." If the husband died from the beating, his wife became a widow, and she no longer required a *get!*

Since Jewish law requires the husband to give a *get* of his own free will, it seems puzzling that a court can beat a recalcitrant husband until he acquiesces. The reason this is possible is because Judaism assumes that every Jew's deepest desire is to do what is religiously required of him. If a man's wife desires a *get,* Jewish law usually requires him to grant it. If he refuses to do so, even after the *bet din* tells him that he must, he is considered to be confused about what his true will is. He may be afraid, he may be angry, he may feel hurt, he may have many feelings that get in the way of his most basic desire, which is to do God's will. Left to his own devices, he can't see his way clear to do what is right, so the court applies force to help remove his confusing feelings and clarify what his deepest desire really is.

Practically speaking, Jewish courts can only "convince" recalcitrant husbands to divorce their wives in countries where such means can be applied legally. There are no countries today, including Israel, that allow Jewish courts to use such force. Thus, Jewish law empowers its courts to use means that effectively give husbands and wives equal ability to get divorced. Unfortunately, the prevailing laws of secular society and the fragmentation of Jewish legal authority often neutralize the *bet din's* power.

THE FRENCH REVOLUTION

Even though the *bet din* was empowered to make *agunot* a rarity, recent historical developments have diluted their control. Prior to the French Revolution, divorce tended to be considered a religious matter that was handled by the respective religious authorities in Christian and Moslem countries. Jews usually lived in their own communities, where they were geographically, socially, and legally separate from the Gentiles. Due to this separation, the Jewish courts had a great deal of juridical authority over Jews.

The French Revolution resulted in the Jews' gaining civil liberties, which ultimately led to their assimilating into French society at large. This had several ramifications: social intercourse and intermarriage with Gentiles increased, the centralized authority of Jewish courts was diluted, and Jews adjudicated matters in civil courts formerly handled by the *bet din.* This meant that for the first time in history, secular society allowed Jews to obtain civil divorces.

Had all Jews continued to obtain only religious divorces, civil divorce would have been irrelevant to them. However, when secular Jews began obtaining civil divorces, they felt free to remarry, even without a religious divorce. Thus, secular Jews were forbidden to marry according to Jewish law, yet did so anyway in civil ceremonies.

PROPOSALS TO INSURE JEWISH DIVORCE AFTER CIVIL DIVORCE

Secular divorce was introduced in France in 1884. Shortly thereafter, Rabbi Michael Weil of Paris made the first attempt to deal with the problem of recalcitrant husbands making their wives *agunot*. He suggested that when Jewish women obtained civil divorces they should automatically be considered divorced according to Jewish law. This proposal was unanimously rejected by all rabbinic authorities, citing the fact that there was no precedent in Jewish law for such an idea.

Rabbi Weil then made a second proposal. He suggested that all marriages be initiated only on the condition that the husband grant his wife a *get* in the event of civil divorce. Were the *get* not given by a certain time after obtaining a civil divorce, the marriage would be retroactively annulled. This proposal was also rejected by all rabbinic authorities when it was first suggested, and it has been rejected every time that it has resurfaced. Such conditional marriages cannot occur according to Jewish law because a couple marries by absolutely committing themselves to each other, not by doing so conditionally. Jewish sexual intimacy requires a total, unconditional commitment by both spouses.

Sex between two Jews is only permitted when they are legally married to one another. It is presumed that any married couple who has been sexually intimate has demonstrated by their behavior that they waive most conditions that modify the permanence of their marriage. There are rare situations that can retroactively annul a marriage, but only when a man or woman withheld specific information from their intended mates before marriage. The three basic categories that constitute such withheld information include: (1) concealment that one has a terminal illness, (2) known inability to have children, or (3) emotional problems that preclude a man's earning a living, a woman's maintaining a household, or either party's raising children. If a man conceals the fact that he is homosexual or impotent, it also falls within this rubric. Otherwise, unless such conditions occur, once a married couple has sex, their marriage can no longer be retroactively invalidated by either spouse. It can only be dissolved through death or divorce.

ATTEMPTS TO ANNUL MARRIAGE

A proposal by Louis Epstein in 1930 suggested that once a husband married, he appoint his wife as an agent to divorce herself if he later disappeared or refused to give her a *get*. This type of conditional divorce is also untenable according to Jewish law because once a couple has sex, it automatically invalidates any prior divorce proceedings.

The conditional divorce given in biblical times was very different from that proposed by Louis Epstein. Biblical conditional divorces were automatically nullified once the husband returned from his military service and the couple had sex.

Another reason why contemporary proposals for conditional marriage or divorce are untenable is because biblical law allows sexual relations to be one means by which a husband and wife make their marriage legally binding. (For centuries, it has been rabbinically forbidden for a man to wed his wife by means of sexual intercourse, so that it should not resemble fornication. Giving a wedding ring is the generally accepted alternative.)

This has two implications: If a marriage were retroactively annulled, it would mean that every act of sex within marriage would actually have been out of wedlock. Such fornication is forbidden by Jewish law, as would be any contract that created such a situation. Secondly, Jewish law presumes that people do not do forbidden acts if they can do the same things under permissible circumstances. This means that if the same act of intercourse can be considered legitimate, there is no reason to create a situation in which it is outside of marriage. Since the first sexual union after the marriage ceremony can theoretically be one way of effecting a marriage, there is no reason to retroactively nullify it, thereby making all subsequent sexual relations illegitimate.

HOW TO OBTAIN A *GET*

Given the above considerations, there are several things women can do to help avoid becoming *agunot* by recalcitrant husbands. First, any woman who wants a divorce should consult a Jewish court of law. Many *agunot* could have avoided their situations if they had gone to a *bet din* prior to negotiating a civil divorce. Once a civil divorce is granted, the leverage that may be necessary to convince a recalcitrant man to give a *get* is often lost.

Second, property settlement should generally not be concluded until a *get* has been arranged. Unfortunately, many attorneys who are familiar with civil divorce proceedings are unfamiliar with Jewish divorce proceedings and are not skilled in ensuring that a *get* is obtained along with the civil divorce. It is critical for most Jewish women who wish to get a divorce to consult an attorney who is well versed in the details of Jewish divorce.

Third, couples can sign a prenuptial, legally binding civil document that obligates a spouse who is recalcitrant to pay the other a given sum of money every day until a desired *get* is given or received. Some rabbis have texts that they have composed for this purpose, and couples can write their own, but they must ascertain that the documents are worded in a way that is legally binding in civil court. (For instance, these may not be legally binding when they make reference to "penalty clauses.") Once a spouse has asked the other to agree to give or accept a *get,* a recalcitrant mate will normally be persuaded to do so rather quickly, rather than pay $100 a day, or some such sum, to the spouse.

Even when these documents have not been worded in legally binding ways, experience has shown them to be a very effective psychological and sociological tool to guarantee receiving a *get.*

Another way to make prenuptial arrangements that mitigate against later recalcitrance is to translate the financial obligations of the *ketuvah* into legal phraseology that effectively ensures that a *get* will later be granted if requested. (A sample document of this type appears in the chapter on Jewish marital obligations.) For example, the *ketuvah* requires that a husband pay for his wife's basic living expenses, such as food, shelter, clothing, and medical care. As long as they are still married, he must supply her with a house of comparable value to the one in which she had been living, with all of the amenities that she had there. He must similarly continue to buy her comparable clothes and food.

It should be noted that if a secular court forces a man to give his wife a *get,* it is halachically problematic. This means that if a civil court mandates a husband to give his wife a *get,* the resulting *get* may be invalid. This is because if a man gives a *get* under coercion without the Jewish court finding grounds that he must do so, the resulting divorce is problematic. On the other hand, if a Jewish court orders a man to give his wife a *get,* it is valid for the secular courts to enforce the *bet din*'s decision.

Fourth, if a woman has questions about how to obtain a *get,* or needs support or legal advice about the process, it is recommended that she contact either G.E.T. (Getting Equitable Treatment) or Kayama. G.E.T. is a lay organization, consisting mostly of volunteers, whose goal is to help Jewish women obtain equitable treatment in the process of getting divorced. They can also supply inquirers with names of support groups and other resources that are available for *agunot* in various communities. Kayama is a nonprofit corporation that educates the public about Jewish divorce and helps arrange it when requested [Kayama, 1433 Coney Island Ave., Brooklyn, NY 11230, (718) 692–1876].

Fifth, Jewish women who live in New York State are now somewhat protected by a state law that was designed to help Jewish women obtain their *gets*, once they have applied for civil divorces. This civil law is constitutionally and halachically valid. It is known as Domestic Relations Law, Section 253, and it provides for the "removal of barriers to remarriage." It states, in part:

> Any party to a marriage . . . who commences a proceeding to annul the marriage or for a divorce must allege . . . that to the best of his or her knowledge, that he or she has taken, or that he or she will take, prior to the entry of final judgment, all steps solely within his or her power to remove any barrier to the defendant's remarriage following the annulment or divorce. . . .
>
> "Barrier to remarriage" includes, without limitation, any religious or conscientious restraint or inhibition, of which the party required to make the verified statement is aware, that is imposed on a party to a marriage, under the principles held by the clergyman or minister who has solemnized the marriage, by reason of the other party's commission or withholding of any voluntary act. Nothing in this section shall be construed to require any party to consult with any clergyman or minister to determine whether there exists any such religious or conscientious restraint or inhibition. . . . "All steps solely within his or her power" shall not be construed to include application to a marriage tribunal or other similar organization or agency of a religious denomination which has authority to annul or dissolve a marriage under the rules of such denomination.
>
> No final judgment of annulment or divorce shall be entered, notwithstanding the filing of the plaintiff's sworn statement prescribed by this section, if the clergyman or minister who has solemnized the marriage certifies . . . that to his or her knowledge, the plaintiff has failed to take all steps solely within his or her power to remove all barriers to the defendant's remarriage.

This law's relevance for women who are trying to obtain a *get* from recalcitrant husbands is as follows: If a husband refuses to give his wife a *get* when he wants a civil divorce, she may ask the civil court to bring in a mediation panel to investigate why her remarriage is being obstructed. This panel can recommend that the civil divorce be contingent upon his giving her a *get*. The law allows the civil divorce to be withheld until he grants the *get*. Obviously, if a woman impedes her husband's ability to give her a *get,* and she wants a civil divorce, this law would also apply.

It should be noted that this law still allows a significant loophole. If the person who refuses to grant (or accept) the *get* does not want a civil divorce, the partner who wants the *get* has no civil leverage via this law.

Despite its loophole, this law will hopefully decrease the emotional and financial blackmail that is sometimes an ugly component of spouses seeking revenge when a marriage does not work.

The heinous nature of torturing a spouse by withholding a *get* should not be underestimated. At any given time, this emotional and financial blackmail affects thousands of Jews, mostly women. Some formerly observant women have left Judaism because they felt that not enough was done to alleviate their terrible plight.

People being victimized by a recalcitrant spouse should seek help from as many sources as possible if a *bet din* is unable to help sufficiently. Anyone who could possibly influence the recalcitrant spouse, be it an organization, friends, family, or synagogue members, should do whatever they can to assist *agunot* (or blackmailed husbands) in their efforts to get divorced. This includes synagogues barring recalcitrant husbands from praying there or, when this is not possible, ignoring them. Some synagogues make a practice of announcing the names of the men in the community who refuse to grant their wives a *get*. If such men own businesses, are private professionals, or obtain referrals from a community, boycotting them and picketing their places of work can be helpful in encouraging them to give a *get*.

Relatives, friends, and rabbis can all persistently call or visit recalcitrant husbands and try to persuade them to give their wives a *get*. When this cannot be accomplished through positive persuasion, ostracizing or leveling economic and social sanctions against them can be effective. This includes not inviting them to family affairs, be they holiday meals, *bar* and *bat mitzvah* celebrations, weddings, and the like. Similarly, encouraging a place of work not to employ them if they work where employers are sensitive to these matters can be attempted. For instance, a recalcitrant husband who was a teacher was denied employment by every Jewish school in his town, and he was refused entrance by every synagogue. His wife received her *get* several months later.

Feminists level serious contentions against observant Jews because they don't do enough to ameliorate the plight of *agunot*. While many of the solutions they advocate are impossible because they violate Jewish law, not nearly enough is done within Jewish legal and moral parameters to help *agunot* out of their misery. It behooves us all to be more sensitive to their plight, and to do whatever is in our power to persuade or pressure recalcitrant husbands to release their wives from their marriage bonds. When organizations drag their feet in helping such women, grass roots movements can be highly effective in helping them gain their freedom.

IV

Women in Family and Community

15

Sarah's Contribution to the Jewish People

The Jewish nation was begun by seven special individuals. The first Jewish couple was Abraham and Sarah. Their son, Isaac, married Rebekah, who in turn gave birth to Jacob. He married two sisters—Leah and Rachel (and subsequently their two handmaids as well). These men and women were our forefathers and foremothers, each of whom contributed something unique to the collective consciousness of the Jewish people. Their contributions are gifts from which we still benefit today.

Abraham was a renowned intellectual. Because he was so intellectual, God tested him on ten different occasions by asking him to do things that didn't make sense to him. This encouraged Abraham to believe that God, and not his intellect, should be the ultimate master of his life. We can only achieve moral perfection if we master our traits in a way that they serve God, rather than having them master us.

Once Abraham learned to subjugate his understanding to total belief in God, he was able to perfect his intellect. This is why Abraham was able to transmit a clarity of belief in God to all of his Jewish descendants. One of his major contributions to us was that any Jew can now believe in God by using his or her intellect. This means that we can view the world, see its order and complexity, and realize that it must have been brought into existence by a Creator.

SARAH'S PROPHECY

Sarah possessed tremendous divine inspiration *(ruach ha-kodesh),* even as a child.[1] She later married Abraham, who eventually became a great prophet, yet she surpassed him in her level of prophecy.[2] She so excelled in this that she was known as the mother of prophecy.

Prophecy is the highest level of human access to God, and it represents the highest level of human perfection. It could only be attained by people who first perfected themselves spiritually.[3] Both men and women have always had equal opportunities to achieve prophecy, and it was not always limited to a few individuals. For example, the millions of Jews who left Egypt during the Exodus were all granted prophetic visions. There were also many other Jews throughout history who were prophets or who were occasionally granted prophetic visions. Prophecy by both sexes continued until the time of the Second Temple.

We know little about most prophets because their prophecies related primarily to themselves. However, there were forty-eight men and seven women who were specifically charged with transmitting their prophecies to the Jewish people.[4] Their prophecies had to be communicated to others and were relevant for future generations, which is why they were mentioned in the Bible. The seven female prophets were: Sarah,[5] Miriam,[6] Deborah,[7] Huldah,[8] Hannah,[9] Abigail,[10] and Queen Esther.[11]

SARAH'S PURITY

One reason why Sarah reached such prophetic heights was because she purified her body to a point where she used it only to serve God and dedicated every aspect of her life to fulfilling His will. By evaluating every event in her life, she accurately discerned which parts were good and which were bad, and then chose to pursue only what was good.

At a certain point in Abraham's and Sarah's lives there was a terrible famine in the land of Canaan. This led them to temporarily relocate to Egypt, where food was plentiful. No sooner had they arrived there than Sarah was abducted and was brought into the Egyptian monarch's palace.[12]

Pharaoh took Sarah into his palace so that he could use her sexually. Nevertheless, she lost none of her purity while in Egypt because God miraculously protected her from his advances. She deserved such protection because she had purified her body to such a degree that God would not allow anyone to defile her.

Almost anyone else in the same situation would have succumbed to the temptations presented to Sarah. Egypt was considered to be the most cultured country in the world at that time. Pharaoh's palace was a particularly cultured and appealing place, and he was one of the most powerful men in the world. Despite its allure for many women, and the thrill that they might feel at being a First Lady in the lap of luxury, this held no appeal for Sarah. The palace's atmosphere made no positive impression on her because nothing meant anything to her except serving God.

Sarah and our other foremothers spent their lives discriminating between what could be made holy and what could not. To this end, Sarah had many difficult choices to make. When she thought that she would never be able to bear children, she gave her handmaid Hagar to her husband as a concubine.

Hagar quickly became pregnant by Abraham and gave birth to their son Ishmael. It was not until 13 years later that Sarah finally had a child with Abraham. As their son Isaac grew older, Sarah recognized that Ishmael was a bad influence on Isaac and that Isaac's development required that Ishmael's influence not be allowed to continue. For this reason, she advised Abraham to send Ishmael out of their house, and God ratified her advice.[13]

God granted Sarah and the other foremothers supernatural powers of intuition and prophecy because they directed all of their potentials to serving Him. Whenever someone totally recognizes what is good, and fully dedicates himself or herself to actualizing it and rejecting the bad, God may grant them miraculous abilities.

SARAH'S EULOGY

When Sarah died, Abraham eulogized her with the beautiful poem that husbands sing to their wives every Friday night – "A Woman of Valor" ("*Aishet Chayil*"):[14]

> Who can find a virtuous woman? She is worth much more than pearls. Her husband's heart trusts her, and his wealth will not be lacking. She will do him good and not bad all of the days of her life. She will ask for wool and flax, and willingly works with her hands. She is like a merchant's ships, bringing her bread from afar. She rises while it is still night, and she gives food to her household, and a portion to her staff. She considers a field and buys it; from the fruit of her labors she plants a vineyard. She girds herself with strength, and

makes her arms strong. She senses that her merchandise is good; her candle will not go out at night. She stretches out her hand to the spindle, and her palms take hold of the distaff. Her palm is stretched forth to the poor and her hand is given out to the destitute. She is not afraid of snow for her household because her entire house is clothed in scarlet. She makes tapestry coverings for herself; she dresses in silk and purple. Her husband is known in the gates where he sits with the elders of the land. She makes linen and sells it; she supplies the merchant with sashes. She dresses in strength and honor and will rejoice in the future. She opens her mouth with wisdom and the teaching of lovingkindness is on her tongue. She surveys the conduct of her household and doesn't eat the bread of laziness. Her children arise and make her happy; her husband praises her: "Many daughters have done virtuously, but you have risen above them all!" Grace is false and beauty is vain, (but) a woman who fears God is to be praised. Give her from the fruit of her hands and let her deeds praise her in the gates.

Although the words of *Aishet Chayil* are beautiful in and of themselves, they also allude to deeper ideas that reflect many of Sarah's actions. A homiletical interpretation of some of its verses follows.[15]

"Her husband's heart trusts her" alludes to what happened when Sarah and Abraham went into Egypt. He asked her to tell people that she was his sister, rather than admitting that she was his wife. He did this because he was afraid the Egyptians would kill him and abduct her if they knew that he was her husband. Abraham totally trusted that she would comply with his request, and she did.

"She will ask for wool and flax" is homiletically understood to refer to her decision to separate Isaac from Ishmael by sending Ishmael and his mother out of her house. Wool alludes to Isaac, and flax alludes to Ishmael.

"She is like a merchant's ship" alludes to the incident where she was abducted by Pharaoh. Pharaoh paid Abraham 1,000 pieces of silver as part of his apology.

"And she rises while it is still night" alludes to her rising up early with her husband on the morning that Abraham planned to sacrifice Isaac to God.

"She considers a field and buys it" refers to her having discovered the field of Machpelah, where Abraham later buried her. He, their son, their grandson, and their respective wives were all buried there.

"From the fruits of her labors she plants a vineyard" alludes to her being the mother of the entire Jewish nation, which is likened to a vineyard. She created the potential for every Jew to feel close to God.

"She girds herself with strength" alludes to the time when three angels came to visit Abraham, and he told her to help him prepare food for these guests. The angels later told Abraham and Sarah that they would have a child together the following year at their respective ages of 100 and 90.

"She senses that her merchandise is good" alludes to the time when Abraham went to war against four powerful kings and their armies. People told Sarah that her husband would be killed in battle. Nevertheless, her faith didn't falter, and she trusted God's promise that not only would Abraham come home alive, but they would soon have a child together.

"She stretches out her hand to the spindle" alludes to Sarah's giving food to passersby and guests.

"Her palm is stretched forth to the poor" refers to her giving charity and clothes to the destitute.

"She is not afraid of snow for her household" alludes to the idea that her children will never go to hell (*gehinnom*) "because her entire house is clothed in scarlet." The word for scarlet in Hebrew alludes to two commandments that her household kept: Sabbath observance and circumcision of males. Both of these are signs of God's covenant with the Jewish people. Keeping the Sabbath testifies that God created the world, and circumcision testifies that we accept responsibility for observing His commandments.

"She makes tapestries for herself; she dresses in silk and purple" alludes to the fact that Sarah's descendants would wear priestly garments of silk and purple when serving God in the Sanctuary.

"She dresses in strength and honor" alludes to the Divine clouds of glory that surrounded Sarah's tent.

"Her children arise and make her happy" alludes to her joy when she gave birth to Isaac.

At one level of understanding, *Aishet Chayil* indicates Sarah's accomplishments during her lifetime. At a deeper level, it conveys what she contributed to every successive generation of Jews. It is significant that we recite these words on Friday nights. The Sabbath is that time when we are supposed to elevate our bodies to the level of our souls, without allowing the external world to intrude on our spiritual equilibrium. The Sabbath's essence is precisely what Sarah achieved, insofar as she devoted herself to making peace between her body and soul. This is the same process that we hopefully undergo on the Sabbath. *Aishet Chayil* can be interpreted as making references to how Sarah and those who followed in her footsteps overcame the body's desires using the influences of the soul.

SARAH'S THREE ACCOMPLISHMENTS

The *Midrash* says that Sarah lit Sabbath candles every Friday evening and that they burned until the following Sabbath eve.[16] This symbolized that her spiritual enlightenment, which reached its peak on the Sabbath, didn't wane when the Sabbath ended.

Even though most Sabbath-observers feel very inspired by its holiness, the feeling tends to wane and disappear shortly after the Sabbath ends. This was not the case for Sarah. Her sense of spiritual inspiration was no different on the Sabbath than it was on the six weekdays, since every day presented an equal opportunity for her to serve God. "Her candles burned from one Sabbath to the next" implies that the Sabbath's spirituality extended throughout the entire week for her.

The *Midrash* also says that the bread that Sarah baked every Sabbath eve remained fresh from that day until the following Sabbath eve. This symbolized how Sarah created an ongoing spiritual vitality that infused all of her deeds. Nothing she did grew stale.

When most of us initially do a spiritually positive act, we feel excited. As our physical and emotional drives begin to tug at us, we slowly lose our inspiration and enthusiasm. After a short time, our deeds grow stale. They cease to be uplifting or exciting, and we might even do them by rote, or discontinue them altogether.

This did not happen with Sarah. She retained the same feelings of excitement after doing an act day after day as she did when doing it for the first time. She never lost her sense of novelty and joy at doing God's will. Her enthusiasm with serving Him never diminished.

This is an idea that is emphasized in the text of the *Shema* prayer, which we say twice every day. The *Shema* tells us that certain things will happen if we listen to the commandments that God commands us "today." This is interpreted to mean that we should view all of the commandments as if God had just given them to us that very same day, and we should do them with a corresponding sense of novelty and zeal.[17]

The *Midrash* stresses that the cloud of the Divine Presence (*Shechinah*) always hovered over Sarah's tent. This is because her behavior always invited God's holy Presence to attach itself to her. Whenever we dedicate our lives to doing God's will, He may respond by allowing us to experience His immanence.

Thus, Sarah merited three miracles happening on her behalf: Her candles burned throughout the week, her bread stayed fresh, and God's Presence hovered over her tent. These miracles disappeared when she died but were reinstated by her daughter-in-law Rebekah. This is because Rebekah dedicated herself to serving God in the same way as Sarah.[18]

SUBSEQUENT GENERATIONS

Our foremothers' and forefathers' level of spiritual awareness and dedication is considered to be the epitome of accomplishment for Jews. Nachmanides, a medieval Jewish commentator, says that when the Jews left Egypt during the Exodus, and subsequently accepted the Torah, they were still not totally redeemed. This was only fully accomplished when they built God the Sanctuary (*Mishkan*) in the desert. The *Mishkan* was a God-given opportunity for them to demonstrate that they had unified their bodies with their souls.

After they left Egypt, the Israelites expressed to God that they wanted to live in a way that He could dwell among them. In response to their request, He told them how they could exemplify the types of lives that our foremothers and forefathers had.

These guidelines were expressed by how the *Mishkan* was constructed. The Sanctuary contained within it the Western lamp (everlasting light). This symbolically reinstated Sarah's Sabbath candles. Just as she brought spiritual illumination into her tent, and from there into the world, so did the priests in the Sanctuary.

The *Mishkan* also contained showbread, twelve loaves of bread that were baked every Sabbath eve. Like Sarah's bread, it remained fresh from Friday to Friday. This bread was eaten by the priests after it was left out on a special table for the entire week. Not only did it always taste fresh, but one needed to eat only a small piece of it to feel satiated.

Finally, the Divine Presence hovered over the Sanctuary just as it hovered over Sarah's tent. The manifestation of God's Presence over the Sanctuary symbolized that He wished to dwell, as it were, among the Jewish people. He did this most obviously in the place where the Jews demonstrated that their primary concern as a nation was with doing God's will.

SARAH'S DEATH

The Torah reports that Sarah died immediately after the binding of Isaac (the *Akeidah*).[19] In the story of the *Akeidah,* God told Abraham to take his son and bring him up as an offering on a mountain He would show him. Abraham arose early the next morning and journeyed for three days, eventually coming to the mountain where the Temple would later be built. The Torah says:[20]

> And they (Isaac and Abraham) came to the place which God had told him about, and Abraham built the altar there, and he arranged the wood (on it), and he bound Isaac his son and placed him on the altar, on top of the wood.
>
> And Abraham stretched forth his hand, and took the knife to slaughter his son.
>
> And an angel's voice called to him from heaven and said, "Abraham, Abraham," and he said, "Here I am."
>
> And it (the angel) said, "Don't stretch forth your hand against the young man, and don't do anything to him, because now I know that you fear God, and you haven't withheld your son, your only son, from Me."

Once Abraham had demonstrated his willingness to sacrifice his son at God's command, he was told not to kill Isaac. God had only wanted to test Abraham; He did not want Isaac to die.

One commentary explains why Sarah's death is mentioned immediately after this episode.[21] As soon as Sarah was told that Abraham took their son in order to sacrifice him to God, she died. Since Isaac was not killed, her death cannot be assumed to have resulted from the shock of bad news. Rather, when she heard that Isaac was prepared to die for God, she expired. Upon hearing that her only son was ready to give up his life at God's command, she felt that her life's work in raising him had been completed. Her soul was so attached to God that it simply left her body once it fulfilled its last mission on earth.

Another noteworthy aspect of Sarah's death is the Torah's detailed description of her burial.[22] The Five Books of Moses describe many deaths, but they seem to pay the most attention to Sarah's. Normally, the Torah does not focus on burial and death because a person's soul lives on after death, and it is usually much more significant than the body that housed it during its sojourn on earth.

In Sarah's case, however, her body achieved equal holiness with her soul, since her physical existence perfectly served her soul. Therefore, her body deserved having a great deal of attention paid to it at her burial. She required a special place in which to be buried, since she had used her body in a way that unified it with her soul. This is why Abraham had to go to such great lengths to purchase the Cave of Machpelah in Hebron for her burial plot.[23] This cave was eventually where all of our forefathers and three of our foremothers were buried.

The Torah says that at the time of her death, Sarah was "one hundred years, and twenty years, and seven years (old)."[24] The *Midrash* explains this to mean that when Sarah was 100, she was as innocent of sin as she was at age 20.[25] This means that her ability to maintain a perfect integration of her body with her soul did not fluctuate. Once she attained this level of spirituality, she never lost it. The *Midrash* adds that when she was 20, she was as beautiful as she was at age 7. A biblical statement praising a woman's beauty does not mean that she was beautiful only in a physical sense. Her physical beauty emanated from her spiritual wholesomeness and was praised because she used it only as a tool by which she served God.

SARAH'S CONTRIBUTION TO US

Sarah's major contribution was her implanting in each of her female descendants a spark that motivates us to live and teach Godly values.

There was once a national, central sanctuary where spiritual illumination and enthusiasm for doing God's will was rewarded by the revelation of His Divine Presence. This place was originally the Sanctuary, which the Israelites built when they left Egypt and which they used for hundreds of years. Later, the two holy Temples served this purpose.

One of the fundamental places where God reveals His Divine Presence to us individually, regardless of whether or not we have a Temple, is in the Jewish home. Sarah gave us the wherewithal to make our homes sanctuaries for God, to inspire our children and ourselves with the highest spiritual values, and to use everything in the material world to serve our souls. She transmitted to us the intuition to see what is truly meaningful and good and the knowledge of how to achieve it. She also modeled how we can develop the means to transmit this legacy to others.

16

Raising Jewish Children

I t is a tremendous challenge for parents to raise healthy, well-adjusted children in today's world. Fragmentation of families is rampant, children start using alcohol and drugs in elementary school, the average teenager has watched more than 10,000 murders on television, and sexual experimentation, bearing out-of-wedlock children, and premarital sex are considered normal. Many secular schools are breeding grounds for violence, substance abuse, and peer pressure to engage in a variety of illegal and immoral behaviors.

The secular world offers material and sensual enticements that can lead children away from Jewish values and threaten their physical safety and well-being. How can parents maintain family cohesiveness and raise children who espouse morality and have self-esteem when they must compete with these influences?

Even Jews who were raised in observant homes can leave their Judaism behind when they reach adulthood. This can happen when their belief in why they should live as Jews or observe Torah and *mitzvot* was never very strong, or when the Judaism they were taught was neither emotionally fulfilling nor intellectually satisfying.

Jewish parents are responsible for inculcating a feeling that a Torah way of life is emotionally, intellectually, and spiritually satisfying to their children. But it is not enough to do this in the abstract. The best way to build this foundation is through the parents' relationship with their children.

When children feel loved and nurtured by both parents it protects them from harmful influences in the secular world. Parents give their children a sense of self-worth by nurturing them with love and praise and by keeping lines of communication open.

Children extrapolate what they experience at home to the world outside, and their homes are the most critical schools that they ever have. Unlike secular schools, which primarily teach factual knowledge, the Jewish home primarily teaches how to live. The way that parents relate to each other and to their children models how to relate to the world at large and what to expect from it. For example, when children feel loved by their parents, they can love others and expect to be loved in return. When children learn to obey and value the limits that parents put on them, they learn to respect their parents as well as authority. When parents discipline with love, children learn to modify their innate tendencies to want immediate gratification and learn to concern themselves with others' needs and wants. They also learn to modify their behavior by considering its long-term consequences.

Just as parental authority is resented when children do not feel that their parents love them, so are Jewish restrictions resented when they are not perceived as coming from a loving God. It is very difficult for someone who feels unloved by his or her parents to feel loved by God.

Children who have poor relationships with their parents are especially prone to rebel in adolescence or adulthood. These adolescents or adults exchange their childhood pain for the acceptance and love that they get from people and experiences that are antithetical to their parents. They are likely to reject a religious way of life if they associate it with restrictiveness and lack of parental love, especially when the secular world promises freedom and good feelings.

Children rarely use drugs and have sex because of peer pressure only. Just as people assimilate because they are looking for a life that is more satisfying than the one they leave behind, people turn to drugs and illicit sex because they feel an inner void, and these activities temporarily fill it. They join cults for the same reason, and douse their minds with chemicals or their bodies with momentary pleasures in order to anesthetize themselves against psychological pain. This pain is usually due to a sense of abandonment or rejection that they feel from parents, peers, and others.

Children who are raised in an environment where they feel good about themselves and have meaningful lives do not become assimilated, promiscuous, drug abusers, or alcoholics.

Even observant Jewish parents can no longer afford to raise children in an environment where they keep *Shabbos* or keep kosher "just because" it's the right thing to do. Parents have to inculcate a sense of emotional enrichment from keeping *mitzvot,* as well as some intellectual understanding of why we do them, in order for children to appreciate them.

THE IMPORTANCE OF QUESTIONING

Some parents feel that if they do not discuss sensitive issues with their children, they will not pique their children's curiosity about them. Some parents reassure themselves that if their children don't mention the issues, they will never get involved with premarital sex, drugs, alcohol, or the like.

In reality, parents who don't respond appropriately to their children's questions will have little ability to influence their ideas about forbidden or dangerous behavior. Parents should always address their children's questions according to their children's capacity to understand. Otherwise, children will find friends, books, or strangers who will tell them what they want to know, or may experiment as a means of assuaging their curiosity.

If parents are not secure in their own Judaism, if they do not find it emotionally, spiritually, and intellectually the best way of life that exists, they will not be able to convey this to their children. Alternatively, some parents have never questioned the things that their children question. They may feel threatened by their questioning the very foundations of the parents' existence. Rather than trying to get children to stop questioning, it is useful to say, "You are asking some good questions, and I don't know the answers. How about if we find them together?" In this way, children can learn the importance of using their curiosity to achieve spiritual growth.

Every Jew comes to appreciate Judaism from different directions and approaches, and parents should help children find answers by going to appropriate sources and struggling to come to terms with issues. When children learn that questioning does not lead to finding meaningful answers, their Judaism will rest on a very shaky foundation, if it rests on any foundation at all.

MODELING

Parents convey the essence of Judaism to their children by how they live, what they teach their children, and how they answer their children's questions. They also serve as models for their children of what God is like. If parents are harsh and critical, children extrapolate that God must also be harsh and critical. Children who are raised this way may have a Jewish identity when they become adults only because they don't want an authoritarian God to punish them if they go astray. Fear of punishment alone is not a good foundation for Jewish observance, and it also results in some adults realizing that they can let go of their fear of punishment by distancing themselves from God.

When children are raised by loving parents, they can learn that a Torah way of life is delightful. When parents tell their children not to do anything that is harmful, it forms the basis for their viewing God as a Being who similarly tells them to do only what is in their best interests.

Since parents serve as substitutes for God, they must personally exemplify how Jews should live Torah values. Parents can only do this if they identify with God's value system. If children learn that relating to a parent feels good, they will also feel good serving God. They will want to be as beloved in God's sight as they are to their parents.

EFFECTIVE JEWISH PARENTING – INFANCY UNTIL THREE

Parents begin molding a child's character at birth. Parents' primary task in raising infants is to make them feel loved, cared for, and protected. This teaches children that parents are dependable caretakers, which in turn forms the foundation for their feeling secure and trusting people. When babies are hungry, they are fed; when they are cold, they are clothed; when they are wet, they are changed; when they feel discomfort, they are soothed. Parents' unending acts of love set the stage for children to later trust others, and God.

It has been suggested that we have parents upon whom we depend for so long because God wanted us to have tangible relationships that allow us to experience how He relates to us and how we should feel toward Him. Parents are daily models to children of how God relates to them. When parents are loving, giving, and trustworthy, children learn that God is this way, also. If parents are predominantly withholding, arbitrary, and punitive, children will assume that God has the same inadequacies as their parents. By showering young children with love, by being dependable caretakers, and by protecting them from negative influences, parents set the stage for children to be psychologically healthy.

PROVIDING SECURITY AND MODELING AUTHORITY

Some have suggested that Jewish women are absolved from doing certain commandments because their primary mission is to develop a sense of security, trust, and well-being in their children. If mothers were always running off to pray in the synagogue, or abandoning their children in order to perform certain commandments, children would learn that there is always something more important than they are. Although we must eventually learn that the universe does not revolve around us, young children need to feel that the world does exist only for their pleasure and gratification. This promotes their self-esteem and sense of security.

As babies grow older, parents set limits on them for their own welfare. Children can eat, but not foods that make them sick. They can leave the house, but they cannot run into traffic. They can play with toys in the living room, but are forbidden to stick their fingers in the electric sockets. Through these rules, children learn that real love is accompanied by limits that sometimes deprive them of what they think they must have. They simultaneously learn that their actions have consequences, and they must develop self-control as they interact with the world.

Until children are 3 years old, parents are not obligated to educate them about what Judaism requires them to do or not do. A mother's task during these first few years is to nurture her child without creating barriers that prevent the child's absorbing Jewish values. Even though parents aren't required to train such young children to do certain *mitzvot*, it is good to expose even very young children to positive experiences and values.[1] For instance, a child should see that his parents learn Torah, pray, and dress modestly.

Parents should try to ensure that their children, even infants, eat only food that is kosher.[2] "We are what we eat" applies to our spiritual health as well as to our bodies. Feeding children nonkosher food allows negative influences to affect their budding spiritual sensitivities and dulls their ability to properly absorb parental communication.

In addition to raising children in environments where they are exposed to a positive Jewish way of life, they should not be exposed to negative influences. The early years of life have a very powerful and lasting effect on children's sense of security and self-esteem. To this end, healthy marriages play a vital role in raising healthy children. When parents argue or hurt each other in front (or within earshot) of even very young children, they erode their well-being and replace it with a sense of anxiety and helplessness. Fighting parents also destroy children's trust and confidence in their abilities to be in control and to protect them. This interferes with the parents' abilities to transmit religious values to their children.

STAGES OF EDUCATION – AGE THREE

By the time most children are 3, they face the startling realization that the world does not exist only for them. They can feel very helpless when they realize that almost nothing belongs to them and how little power they really have. At this very sensitive time, Judaism gives them an opportunity to assert their ownership and power in a new way. They may not own the world, but they can perform commandments that do affect the world.

Formal Jewish education begins at age 3 because this is when children can first reasonably retain what they are taught. At this age, parents should formally teach their children according to each child's capacity to learn what they should and should not do. This is also the age at which formal disciplining for doing what is wrong begins.[3]

Among other things, children of this age should be taught to say blessings before and after eating food, to ritually wash their hands at appropriate times, to say the *Shema* prayer before they go to sleep at night, and to learn short verses from the Torah. They can often retain these prayers and blessings best when they sing them.

At the very time that a boy might feel that nothing is his, his parents give him his own *yarmulka* (head covering).[4] If boys are able to keep from soiling or wetting themselves, they should wear *tzitzit* (a fringed, four-cornered undershirt) as well. When their fathers make *kiddush* on the Sabbath and holidays, boys should be given their own *kiddush* cup with grape juice or wine, and make a blessing over them, just as their fathers do. This gives them *mitzvot* that adult men have, and they begin to identify with the male role.

In some circles, girls light Sabbath and holiday candles alongside their mothers. Just as a boy's self-image includes wearing a *yarmulka* and *tzitzit,* a girl's self-image should include dressing modestly.[5] This allows her to identify with her female role and do the same *mitzvot* that adult women do. Both boys and girls at this age can be encouraged to put a few coins into a charity box before the mother lights the Sabbath or holiday candles.

At this age, both boys and girls derive a strong sense of importance and power from the many rituals they can now observe. Furthermore, each holiday gives children an opportunity to feel loved, important, and that they are making a contribution to the world. On Passover, they can help clean the house and rid it of any leavened products. They can help prepare and serve the holiday meals and can participate in the *seder* by asking questions.

On the holiday of Succot (Tabernacles), children can help build and decorate the *succah* (a temporary booth). They can carry the *lulav* and *etrog* to the synagogue, and go *succah*-hopping with friends and neighbors. On Simchat Torah, they can sing and dance in the synagogue as they celebrate the annual conclusion of the Torah cycle.

Every Sabbath, children can help prepare and serve the meals, and they can clean the house in honor of the day. The fact that one or both parents need to be closely involved in teaching children what the rituals mean and how to do them reinforces the child's sense of mastery and accomplishment with a bond of love between parent and child.

Just as parents should encourage positive behavior, they should also set limits on their children. For example, children should be limited as to what they eat, how late they can stay up, where and how they can play, and so on. Since children at this age are very concrete, parents should reinforce their good behavior with tangible and concrete rewards.

When children do a *mitzvah,* they can get a hug or kiss as extra reinforcement. If they are not interested in doing a *mitzvah,* such as saying a blessing before they eat food, they can often be induced to do so with the reinforcement of a few raisins or some other treat.

LIMITS AND PUNISHMENT

Children learn that parents set limits on them to protect them physically. Over time, they learn that parents, and by extension, God, only limit them for their own benefit. Thus, in the same way that children learn that eating too many sweets makes them sick, they eventually appreciate that eating nonkosher food makes them spiritually sick. They learn not to cross the street without their parents' permission. They similarly learn not to travel in a car on the Sabbath and holidays. Just as mundane actions have consequences, children learn that their "religious" behavior also has consequences.

As children learn what they can and should do, they also learn what is forbidden. For instance, they cannot watch television or turn lights on and off on the Sabbath, or eat food without first ascertaining if it is kosher. As children assimilate clear rules about their physical safety and welfare, they do the same with rules that affect their spiritual welfare.

As long as parents do not destroy their credibility by setting arbitrary or inconsistent rules, or set rules only in order to assert their power, children will automatically respect limit-setting when it is done with love.

Many parents think that they are supposed to tell their children what to do and that their children should automatically accommodate them. Judaism grants parents authority over children only for the children's benefit. For example, children must be trained to do household chores so that they will learn to be decent, responsible, and helpful adults when they grow up. Parents should not ask their children to do chores only because the parents don't feel like doing them. All parental orders and rules must be geared toward what is necessary for a child's growth, rather than forcing a child to accommodate to his parents' needs.

Children need to accept parental authority so that they can accept social rules and function in society. When children feel that rules are beneficial in their personal world, they will also feel that way about societal rules. Moreover, respecting parental authority is critical because it is the basis for learning to accept God's authority. If children's belief in their parents' fairness or wisdom is destroyed, they will not believe that God is wise or fair, either.

This implies that parents must be discriminating in the limits they set, while simultaneously emphasizing choices that their children have. When parents only stress what is wrong or forbidden, children usually want to flout their authority. Parents must leave children room to assert their individuality and independence. When children are deprived of what is off-limits, without having other choices, their focus shifts to achieving power instead of learning to choose and accept alternatives or, in some cases, disappointment.

It is important for children to learn how to create alternative choices, especially when their desired one is unacceptable or unavailable.

Even the best of children tend to ignore rules and requests more often than not. Instead of shaming or punishing them for not immediately doing as they are told, parents need to be realistic about how children behave. It is helpful to try to make requests more palatable to children, or offer more realistic ways that they can comply.

For example, when children are told to go to bed while they are in the middle of a television program or game, it is unlikely they will. It is generally more effective for parents to give children advance warning about when they should go to bed or let them make choices. For instance, children might be told a half-hour in advance that they will need to go to bed when a show is over, and be reminded again ten minutes before bedtime. Or, they can be allowed to go to bed somewhat late one night if they agree to go to bed earlier the next night (if that is a feasible option).

In general, Judaism discourages parents from shaming anyone, including children, and punishment should be reserved for times when other avenues of education aren't appropriate. The purpose of punishments is to educate children how to behave more appropriately in the future, not to express parents' frustration and anger. Although children need to learn that certain actions have negative consequences, punishments should be appropriate for the misdeed.

The way that parents punish their children teaches them how God punishes people for disobeying Him. If children learn that punishments are meted out in order to help them mature and prosper, they will ultimately view God's punishments in the same way. If punishment is merely a way that parents command power for their own psychological needs, they will view God as similarly malevolent or inadequate.

Children normally want to imitate their parents, but not when their parents are punitive, aloof, or frustrating. In order not to undermine their children's self-esteem or respect for parents, parents should discipline by first emphasizing children's positive points and then noting their shortcomings. When criticism is necessary, it should address a specific behavior, with specific suggestions about how to improve it the next time. In this way children's self-esteem is not eroded, and the parents can continue to be loving yet concerned role models.

MORAL AND SOCIAL DEVELOPMENT

As children grow, parents teach them moral and social values. Children learn to share their toys with others, to play nicely with their peers, and to be concerned about others' feelings. In general, children learn a great deal by observing what their parents do, not only by hearing what they say. For instance, when children see their parents getting pleasure from giving, they are most likely to imitate them, especially when they are reinforced for doing likewise.

In addition to modeling social behavior, parents also model attitudes about two crucial aspects of Jewish living: learning Torah and refraining from gossiping (speaking or listening to *lashon hara*). When parents refrain from listening to or speaking *lashon hara,* which includes gossip, slander, and saying negative things about others even when they are true, children learn the critical importance of appropriately controlling their speech. When parents are careful not to indulge in this most tempting pastime, they set a powerful example of self-control and love of one's fellow Jew to their children. Similarly, when children see their parents learning Torah, they appreciate its fundamental importance. When the cardinal values exemplified by both of these *mitzvot* are lived, not merely given lip service, it helps children internalize these messages.

Parents teach their children to be concerned about others' feelings, and to behave accordingly. If parents model respect for their children's feelings, express appreciation, and give compliments when children do positive things, children will have a sense of how to do the same with others.

A fundamental tenet of Judaism is that we must learn to be appreciative of what other people and God do for us. When parents are appreciative, and express it through complimenting people and praying, children learn this quality. The same occurs when they see their parents extending themselves in order to help others.

When children see their parents helping family and strangers, offering hospitality, visiting the sick, and comforting mourners, doing kind deeds for others becomes part of their consciousness. They are more likely to be helpful within the family, as well as outside of it, when they see their parents modeling these kinds of behaviors.

In many households, children feel that disrupting their lives in order to help others or to obey parental requests is a burden. Judaism teaches us that each time we help another person, or do what a parent requests, we fulfill one of God's commandments. Every time children do a prosocial act, they fulfill the *mitzvah* of fearing or honoring parents, loving a neighbor as oneself, or doing acts of kindness. When parents take this approach, children learn that every time they do a *mitzvah* it is wonderful, and they feel excited about helping. They can please God, their parents, themselves, and the beneficiary of their good deed, all at the same time. Every act of obeying parents, sharing belongings, or helping another person has intrinsic value that adds to their self-image.

Instead of parents ordering children to do household chores, such as taking out the garbage or setting the table, they can ask, "Who wants to do a *mitzvah?*" When chores are approached in this way, children are often more willing to volunteer to do them. Besides, when parents are excited about doing what benefits others, children often feel good about doing the same things.

Once children begin to interact with the world, they want to make their mark on it and need to find appropriate ways to express these feelings.

By the time most children are 6 years old, they have learned that they can gain power by identifying with their same-sex parent. This is because in the eyes of young children, parents are almost as omnipotent as God. By identifying with and imitating parents, children attach themselves to their parents' powers as they are socially rewarded for being more and more like adults.

Imitating parents allows children to adopt the roles and behaviors that help them mature, and Judaism provides many opportunities for this to happen.

SCHOOL AGE

As children grow older and begin attending religious schools, their teachers are not simply intellectual instructors. They are role models who should inspire children to develop according to their capabilities.

Even though many people think that teachers should instill proper values in their students, the fundamental responsibility for raising children now, as always, rests with parents. Judaism has recognized this for millennia, by viewing the home as the backbone of Jewish survival. Its myriad rituals, traditions, and ethical guidelines help insure that parents raise their children in a healthy and wholesome way. Even when parents send their children to *yeshivot* or Jewish schools, they cannot presume that schools will compensate for a lack of Jewish values and adequate parenting at home.

Unless parents maintain their primary responsibility for this fundamental issue, they cannot blame schools for their inadequacies. Teachers should not be viewed as surrogate parents but rather as mentors who reinforce and augment what children learn at home.

Parents model how children should feel about being Jewish. If parents feel that Jewish rituals are chores, or put their Jewishness on a back burner, their children will do likewise. It is not surprising when such children grow up, drop their Jewish identities altogether, and intermarry.

It is commonplace to hear Jewish parents say that they don't want to "impose" their Judaism on their children. They decide to give their children minimal or no Jewish education, and then let the children decide how and if they want to be Jewish when they grow up. It is extraordinarily difficult for children to know what Judaism has to offer if they are not properly exposed to it as children.

To this end, children should be included from the age of 3 in the observance of *mitzvot* in the home, taking into account their interests and abilities. Parents should not view *mitzvot* as burdens from which children should be shielded until they have to observe them. Rather, parents should show the same enthusiasm and desire for including their children in *mitzvot* as they would show for intellectual achievements or for monetary prizes. The more children are "protected" from doing *mitzvot,* and the less enthusiasm parents generate about doing them, the more disenfranchised children will feel about living a Jewish way of life.

Thus, children should be given active roles, according to their abilities, in preparing for the Sabbath, in welcoming guests, in praying, in going to the synagogue, and so on. For a 3-year-old, this might mean carrying a loaf of *challah* (special bread for the Sabbath or holidays) to the table. For a 10-year-old, it might mean baking a batch of cookies for the Sabbath, or making a bed for a guest.

Children generally love to imitate their parents. When a boy sees his father wearing *tzitzit* and a *yarmulka,* going to the synagogue, and making *kiddush,* the little boy wants to do the same. When the father gives his son an opportunity to feel special by doing a *mitzvah,* the father is building a wall of protection for his son that shields him from negative influences.

When a mother makes a Sabbath or holiday meal, delights in taking care of her children, and does kind deeds for others, her daughter will want to do likewise. When the mother encourages her daughter to light Sabbath and holiday candles alongside her, to help with Sabbath preparations, to put money into the charity box, and to tell what she learned about Jewish topics in school, the mother builds a similar protective shield for her daughter.

On Friday nights and holidays, mothers say special prayers for their children's welfare when they light candles, and parents customarily bless their children. The love that pervades these rituals insures that children feel cherished and special at regular intervals, regardless of how many other things might distract their parents during the rest of the week.

These emotional and spiritual connections are some of the many building blocks of children's self-esteem and social values. The best protection that parents can give their children against eventual use of drugs, emotional problems, joining cults, and so forth, is to make them feel loved by both parents, coupled with instilling a sense of individual importance and mission. Every time children do a *mitzvah,* they reinforce to themselves that they have a unique and irreplaceable contribution to make to the world. The structure of Jewish rituals and the cohesiveness of the family give a framework of stability, clarity, and direction. These positive feelings will later protect young adults from the temptations and hazards of the world when they are on their own.

Until children are of school age, they learn primarily through parental modeling. When they start school, teachers become the most salient models for children. Later, their peers strongly influence them.

Ideally, children should have friends who will be positive influences and will not accentuate each other's negative traits. For example, close friends should eat kosher food, observe the Jewish holidays and the Sabbath, and wear similar clothes (i.e., a *yarmulka* and *tzitzit* for boys, modest clothing for girls). They should exemplify traits of compassion, sharing, honesty, and so forth. A child's negative traits can be accentuated when a peer group acquiesces to his aggressiveness or dishonesty without calling it to an adult's attention, or caters to a child's passivity.

ENCOURAGEMENT, NOT PUNISHMENT

Children should be encouraged to do *mitzvot* that are appropriate for their ages. When children don't want to do certain *mitzvot,* they should never be punished or they will learn to associate *mitzvot* with punishment. Rather, they should be positively reinforced for acting appropriately. In this way, children will have good associations with performing *mitzvot.* Similarly, when a child is not interested in learning Torah, parents should try to make it more interesting or enjoyable rather than punishing the child for not learning.

Through all of these early stages, parents help children learn to love and fear God. When parents unreasonably limit, insult, or humiliate their children, they discredit themselves as transmitters of God's will.

Children have strong drives to be like their parents, which is why they will imitate with impunity both their parents' good and bad behaviors. However, they stop modeling their parents if the parents become frustrating and punitive.

When children are humiliated for stumbling over their words when they attempt to say prayers, or perform tasks too slowly or clumsily, or are restless, or if parents are too engrossed in their own activities to be interested in children's accomplishments, such reactions teach children to avoid religious behaviors and to stop imitating their parents. These parental responses encourage children to withdraw. Alternatively, children might comply with the parents' demands only as long as they must. As they grow older, if their parents continue to be unloving and punitive, they will find more gratifying role models elsewhere, and will often rebel.

If only the Sabbath's restrictions are stressed to the child, he may resent having to forfeit playing with his favorite toys, being humiliated when he cannot sit still in the synagogue, and being confined to sitting quietly at a table where the adults talk to each other but ignore him entirely. Even worse, no matter how hard he tries, he can't seem to keep his special Sabbath clothes clean, and this makes his mother angry every week. This type of Sabbath experience does not hold much appeal for any child, no matter how much the parents try to stress its importance or holiness. Parents have to emphasize to a child what is appealing to him, not what is appealing to adults. This usually includes playing with friends on Sabbath afternoons, attending parties and youth groups, and the like.

Mitzvot have to be conveyed in a way that children can appreciate them. Besides stressing what behavior is appropriate for a child, parents should praise children every day for something good that they did, and express that they are loved for simply being who they are.

PARENTAL CONSISTENCY AND HONESTY

In addition to inadvertently associating negative feelings to *mitzvot,* parents often model behavior that they don't want their children to imitate.

Children assimilate what parents truly value, not only what they say they value. It is not enough to simply teach children intellectually how to live and feel; parents must live the messages that are implicit in Jewish rituals and traditions. Since we live in a world where actions count, it is not sufficient for parents to tell children that they must care about others' feelings.

When parents are upset with their children for being selfish, how does it appear if the parents never have time to give when strangers or friends need help, or never have enough money to give to charity? Children learn what their parents live more than what they preach.

Parents must demonstrate sharing by offering hospitality to guests, comforting the bereaved, visiting the sick, and by giving money to charity. When parents show this concern for others, as well as for their children, children see that their parents can give to others, yet still value and love them. When parents involve their children in the rituals of the Sabbath and holidays, children learn that their parents' love for them is not diminished by simultaneously offering hospitality to guests or strangers.

Even when children cannot articulate what they've learned, they are usually acutely aware of the contradictions that exist between what parents want for their children and what they practice for themselves.

A mother who takes a painkiller for her frequent headaches and a Valium for her nerves and a sleeping pill for her restless nights is a model of drug abuse. A father who smokes cigarettes and has a few drinks when he's had a hard day, or pops pills for his arthritis, back pain, and stomach distress is a similar model. Such parents do more to encourage substance abuse among their children than do most other influences.

Similarly, when immoral behavior is a topic of entertainment around the home, children learn that no matter what parents moralize to them, they should be interested in what the parents converse about. For example, when gossip and slander (*lashon hara*) are mainstays of conversation, or when the parents are fascinated by the latest business swindle or tax evasion scheme, children learn that these topics are important and satisfying. Otherwise, why would adults be so intrigued by them?

Also, the effect on children of a parent's emotional absence cannot be understated. Children may find doing *mitzvot* irrelevant when they are preoccupied with feeling that no matter what they do, they cannot get their parents' love and attention. It is terrible for any child to feel that a million other things are more important to parents than spending time with him.

Until perhaps twenty or thirty years ago, it was almost unheard of for Jews to have drinking problems. Now, among secular Jews, alcoholism and drug use have reached the same epidemic proportions as among the population at large. (They have also made inroads into religious communities, but to a much smaller degree.) The Torah teaches us several ideas that mitigate against our resorting to foreign substances as means of solving our problems: we were created in the image of God, our bodies are gifts that He has loaned us, and we are not at liberty to damage them. We are specifically commanded to take good care of ourselves and will be held accountable for abusing ourselves.

Children who are raised in observant homes learn from their earliest years that everything that goes into their bodies is consequential. If they are forbidden to eat food that is spiritually harmful in ways that can't even be observed, how much more is this true of substances whose dangerous effects can be seen?! If parents train children to praise and thank God before and after every meal or snack, they simultaneously learn not to ingest substances that destroy their Creator's handiwork. If God created us with bodies in order to do *mitzvot*, we are required to take care of ourselves so that we will be able to serve our Creator with clear minds and sound bodies. Through doing *mitzvot* and assimilating Jewish values, children learn to respect the importance of always being in control of their minds and bodies.

BUILDING SELF-CONFIDENCE TO CONFRONT LIFE'S CHALLENGES

People frequently feel that life has no particular meaning. Judaism instills self-esteem in us by saying that we are each indispensable to God's plan for the world. The fact that men and women, fathers and mothers, have different roles emphasizes the fact that we each have special contributions to make. The fact that God punishes us for certain acts bespeaks the fact that all of our behaviors are consequential. It is hard to feel unimportant when Judaism tells us that our every action has eternal ramifications. Children learn this message from earliest childhood.

When parents raise children to believe in goals that are worth striving for, and instill in them the knowledge that they have the wherewithal to achieve them, they develop a sense of purpose and emotional well-being. Judaism also fosters children's eventual separation from their parents at an appropriate time by giving them the self-confidence to know that they can, and should, make their mark on the world as adults.

The fact that God has asked us to be partners with Him in bringing the world to fruition bespeaks the fact that we are each indispensable to His master plan and are able to overcome whatever challenges He places in our paths. Parents teach this to their children when they first learn to speak.

One of the earliest memories that Jewish children have is of their mothers greeting them when they wake up in the morning and reciting with them, "I thank you, Living and Existing God, that You returned my soul to me with compassion. Your faith in me is tremendous." As children grow older, they realize that they must be very important for God to have such faith in them that He gives them their souls anew every morning. The first thing that children do every morning is to affirm that they have something unique to accomplish and that God has faith in them that they can do it. By the time such children become adults, they have internalized that message.

Parents' obligations to te...
require their frequent and l...
parents must spend both q...
until they reach maturity. ...

BA...

By the time children ...
rudiments of how to ...
mitzvah teach adoles...
decisions and to be responsi...
the very time when their desire to a...
parents emerges, Judaism gives them a framev...
do so without destroying themselves or the world ...
Jewish rites of passage reinforce to budding adolescents that ...
longer allowed to let their emotions run their lives. They must take in...
account how their behavior will affect not only themselves but the world
as well. This is especially important once their newfound sexual and
rebellious feelings can easily drive them to act in destructive ways.

Unfortunately, the original meaning of these rites of passage has
frequently become obscured by the lavishness of the parties or meals
celebrating them. The real significance of a girl attaining the age of 12
years and a day, or a boy attaining the age of 13 years and a day, is that
they are now obligated to observe the commandments of the Torah. For
centuries in Europe, these events were commemorated by modest meals,
usually at home.

In the United States, *bar* and *bat mitzvah* parties are often gala celebrations whose religious significance is minimal. Instead of lavishing so
much time and money on the parties and meals, people should reconsider
the true meaning of becoming a *bar* or *bat mitzvah*—one's transition into
responsible Jewish adulthood. While boys should acknowledge this by
beginning to put on *tefillin* and by being called up to the Torah, girls can
acknowledge this by preparing a talk about a specific area of Jewish
observance that they can now pursue in earnest. Alternatively, they
might prefer to study some aspect of Judaism that is not being taught in
school, or commit themselves to doing kind acts for others. For example,
some young women start visiting patients in a local hospital or nursing
home on a weekly basis, or help new mothers when they return from the
hospital. Others start saying Psalms on a regular basis, or dedicate themselves to praying more intensively. The possibilities are endless.

242

a *bat mitzvah* is celebrated, it should be remem-
...lebration of a commitment to a life ahead. That life
...ying Torah, doing *mitzvot,* and serving God through
...st as no devoted Jewish parents would aspire for their
...a secular education but one or two days a week until age
...or their vocation until this same age, they should not be
...th their children learning about or practicing Judaism so
...lly. Sending children to Jewish day schools, Sunday school, or
...ious instruction only until *bar* or *bat mitzvah* is simply inadequate to
...them how to live as adult Jews.

THE CENTRALITY OF ONGOING
JEWISH EDUCATION

In order to maintain the continuity of Jewish families for generations to come, children need more than a grade-school education in morality and ethics. Both boys and girls need to learn what it is about being Jewish that makes us unique and how we are different from the rest of the world. Otherwise, simply instilling "nice" values in one's children without anything more is setting them up to intermarry and assimilate with any other people who are "nice."

If parents want their children to get graduate and professional degrees, they should also want them to develop the Jewish tools that will be commensurate with their intellectual and vocational ones.

In former times, mothers used to educate their daughters at home, at least until the daughters got married, and often thereafter as well. Jewish education consisted of full-time learning of all of the details of running a Jewish home, involvement in community affairs, learning biblical lore, Jewish laws and customs, prayer, Jewish history, how to raise a family, and often how to make a living in accordance with Jewish ethics. Judaism was learned in a living laboratory, with mothers augmenting their teaching through a wealth of relationship factors with their daughters. Multigenerational families provided a tangible link to family traditions and previous generations.

Parents need to be secure in their own Judaism if they want to convey the satisfaction of being Jewish to their children. People who are not secure can develop and engage in parent–child projects to help solidify the knowledge of Judaism by both. These projects can be educational, ritual, and/or social. Some examples are model *seders,* in which the parents and children participate; family Shabbatons, in which many families can experience the warmth and excitement of a Sabbath spent together; musical evenings, in which Jewish songs are taught and sung; and classes in Judaism. These and other projects provide opportunities for parents to learn with their children.

Giving Direction

When children have conflicts between the secular and Jewish views of the world, parents should play active roles in helping resolve these conflicts by providing a clear sense of direction when one is needed. Mothers have to model and teach their children the values of self-control, empathy, and ethics. When children see this modeled, and get a clear sense of direction and love from their mothers in a way that feels satisfying, they will not need to turn to drugs, sex, and self-absorption as a means of coping with disappointment and pain. During the early years of life, a clear sense of direction combined with a lot of love helps children feel good about themselves and secure with their roles in life.

When parents raise their children with love, direction, discipline, and Jewish education, they insure that their children will be equipped with the best tools possible to raise their own families in the future.

Sex

When parents demonstrate the physical restraint and self-control that are required by the Jewish laws governing sexual behavior, children can learn that not even married adults can enjoy physical contact whenever they feel like it. They model to their children how to respect and love someone of the opposite sex without having a physical relationship with that person when it is not morally appropriate.

If parents want their children to reserve physical relationships with the opposite sex for marriage, they should ensure that their children feel loved. When adolescents are insecure, males often try to prove their masculinity through sex, and when females feel unloved by one or both parents they often seek substitutes by having physical relationships with males.

Adolescents need to learn to delay gratification, but if their parents cannot wait for what they want, why should the children? When children have a parent who has physical relations with someone of the opposite sex outside of marriage, as is so common with single parents these days, children will have no reason to reserve sex for marriage, either.

CONFRONTING CHALLENGES

The Torah never commanded Jews to ignore the secular world or to sequester ourselves away from anyone whose behavior was not exactly like ours. A Torah way of life is rich enough to teach us how to live in any kind of world. The secular world is not much of a threat if a child's Jewish world is rich, secure, and nurturing. In fact, parents can even use the secular world to illustrate to children what we don't believe, and why.

For example, a child may say that he smells a delicious aroma coming from a nonkosher restaurant, and he would like some of that food. A parent can respond, "Yes, it smells delicious and probably tastes delicious, but God has commanded us not to eat it because nonkosher food isn't good for us."

When children are Torah-observant, they will inevitably confront people whose behavior differs from what they were taught. These situations provide excellent opportunities to explain to a child why he or she has been taught to live in his particular way, and why others act differently. It is important for parents to explain to their children why we follow a Torah way of life, and why other life-styles lack the spiritual, psychological, and sometimes physical benefits of the way we live. It is also important to stress to children not to disparage Jews who do not follow a Torah way of life, especially when they have not been privileged to have had a strong Jewish upbringing.

Parents should help children develop the psychological and moral means to cope with discrepancies between what they have learned and what they see others do. Left to their own devices, children may not be able to resolve these conflicts effectively.

It is much better for parents to provide a Torah perspective about these issues than to trust to luck that a child will obtain positive perspectives from his friends, from strangers, or from books.

It is very important for children to feel that they can talk to their parents. If parents convey that they will talk to their children in a sensitive and accepting manner, children are more likely to come to them with their concerns than to go to the outside world to find answers.

Preserving the holiness of a Jewish way of life requires that Jews live together properly. If we live holy lives in homes that are filled with love of God, love of other Jews, and love of our children, we build walls of protection against the dangers of the outside world. When there is destruction within the home, Jewish children become especially vulnerable to the influences of the outside world.

Parents need to express love for their children and demonstrate that a Jewish way of life is truly gratifying. They should teach their children that God is loving, but has expectations of them, and His good laws are meant to protect them. When parents succeed at this, there is little to fear from the threats of the outside world.

The challenge for parents in today's world is to transmit a Torah way of life to children that is full of vitality. This includes a loving and supportive family network with consistent rules. If children have emotional and spiritual storehouses in their own homes, they won't be tempted to look for cheap substitutes elsewhere. If parents succeed in doing this, they needn't worry about their children, even in times of crisis.

17

Closing Gaps between Women: True Sisterhood

J ewish women throughout the ages have frequently accomplished the impossible. They have raised Jewish children and supported their families economically and emotionally in the worst of times. They have built homes whose hallmarks were charity and hospitality, and they have ensured the continuity of Judaism from one generation to the next. They have created and run organizations whose purposes were to help out those in terrible financial and emotional straits. Through their selflessness, Jewish women have been the cohesive force for our people for thousands of years.

This book earlier described how biblical women raised families and saved the Jewish people in Egypt, even at great risk to their lives. When we look at Sarah, Rebekah, Rachel, Leah, Yocheved, Miriam, Ruth, and others like them, we see they shared many common goals. They were dedicated mothers, did many acts of lovingkindness for others, and risked social ostracism and death to do what was morally right. They put the welfare of others above their own personal comfort.

These women recognized their unique spiritual identities and were not content to let them stagnate. They realized that they, and only they, could accomplish their specific missions in life. By fully utilizing their potentials, they understood that they could change the course of Jewish history forever.

JEWISH FOREMOTHERS

Ensuring the spiritual welfare of the Jewish people was the primary task of our biblical foremothers, and they each strove to do this in different ways. Sarah realized that in order for Isaac to carry on the mission of the Jewish people, he would have to be raised in a home that did not have influences that countered everything that she and Abraham were trying to instill in him.

Rebekah helped her son Jacob understand that once he had developed his spiritual underpinnings, he would have to learn to integrate the spiritual and material worlds. It was not enough for him to simply learn Judaism in theory; he had to also live it in practice, especially when confronted with the challenges of human interactions. Whereas Jacob initially was a simple man who stayed in his tent and studied God's will, he ultimately had challenging encounters with his brother, uncle, nephews, a neighboring nation, and even his own wives and children.

Leah and Rachel further refined the goals of Jewish mothering. Rachel's role was to provide a unifying force so that all of Jacob's diverse children could respect and complement each other. In this way, they could truly be a harmonious nation, unified in love of God and one another.

Leah's contribution to the Jewish nation was her recognition and encouragement of each child's individuality. She recognized that each contributed something critical to the establishment and growth of the Jewish people.

In the Book of Esther, which we read on the holiday of Purim, Mordechai (one of the Jewish leaders) confronted Queen Esther. She was a Jewess who was forcibly married to the Gentile King Achashverosh. After the king gave his viceroy Haman permission to murder all of the Jews, Mordechai told Esther that she must risk her life by going to the king and begging him to spare the lives of their co-religionists. Esther balked at the idea of risking her life, hoping that somehow God would save the Jews through other means. Mordechai told her, "Perhaps it is solely for the purpose of saving the Jews that you have attained royalty. If you don't act on their behalf, don't think that you and your family will be spared. You will be destroyed and the rest of the Jews will be saved through other means."[1]

Esther could have felt that she had no special qualities to use in saving her people. She could have felt that it would be better to save her own skin and hide out in the palace. She could have tried to enlist someone else to save her nation. Nevertheless, she heeded Mordechai's admonishment and risked death in order to save her people. She realized that although she was but a single individual, she had a unique and extraordinary contribution to make to the Jews.

After saving the Jews from annihilation, Esther had a son with King Ahashverosh. He was named Darius, and he allowed the Jews who had been exiled to Persia by the Babylonians to return to Israel and to build the Second Temple. The consequences of her one act illustrate that we can never know the ultimate outcome of even the most seemingly insignificant choices that we make.

IMITATIO DEI

The Bible tells us that God put Adam into the Garden of Eden "to work it and to guard it."[2] From the time of the first person's creation, we were commanded to refrain from taking from the world that which is not ours, and to replenish what we take. God shows us by example that once He created the world, each day offers a new opportunity to renew it and to take what is here and elevate it to a higher spiritual level.

Each day, God makes the sun rise, causes rain to fall in the appropriate places and in just the proper amounts, and makes crops, trees, flowers, and grass grow. He creates new animal and human life and sustains it on a daily basis. He "forever renews with His goodness, on a daily basis, the act of creation of the world."[3] Once God shows us by example that He is not above constantly sustaining the world that He made, He asks us to do the same. We are supposed to make every day meaningful by using our talents to give back some of the goodness that He gives us.

Contemporary Jewish women play many different roles. They have careers, raise families, run homes, and involve themselves in community projects. Unfortunately, there are many women of all ages, from all socioeconomic strata, and from all walks of life who feel no need to give of themselves to people beyond themselves or their families. They feel that they are primarily here to be served or to be left alone.

God could have said to Adam, "Look, I created the world, and now that I've done my part, it's time for you to do yours. You run the world and I'll sit back and enjoy what I made." Luckily for us, God constantly directs and renews life.

When we recite the first prayer of the *Shemoneh Esrai* (the main prayer of each daily service), we say that God is great, mighty, and awesome, and above all worlds. Immediately afterward, we say that He does deeds of lovingkindness. This teaches us that if God is above all worlds, yet gives lovingly of Himself to us, there is no task or role that we can appropriate that will absolve ourselves from imitating God by giving to our fellow Jews.

Once we say to another Jew in distress, "I don't have to help you; your needs don't concern me," we cease to function as part of the Jewish people. Women create gaps among themselves when their goals are self-serving. Anyone who refuses to give removes herself from the community and withdraws into her own personal domain. Women can have no common ground when some say, "You do your thing and I'll do mine."

LIVING UP TO OUR POTENTIALS

Jewish women may be more divided now than ever before, perhaps because people no longer feel as gratified by giving as they once did. An aftermath of the "Me" generation was that people became afraid that by giving away their emotions, money, or time, they would end up being deprived. If they were ethical, they feared not being able to compete with the next person who was not. If they gave of their money to charity, they feared it would diminish their wealth. And, if they gave of themselves, they feared that they would become depleted and drained, instead of nourished and fulfilled. Nowadays, some people's expectations of what is due them are so enormous that despite having greater objective affluence and comfort, they still feel deprived and disappointed.

We all have unique, individual potentials to actualize. But we can simultaneously realize common goals by joining together to serve God communally, and thereby elevate the entire Jewish people to a higher spiritual point. Whether women are young or old, professionals, house-wives, mothers, or retirees, we can all have this same common ground.

There is a well-known story about a righteous man named Reb Zusia. As he lay on his deathbed, his students surrounded him and were shocked to see him sobbing.

"What's the matter, Rebbe?" they asked.

Reb Zusia responded, "I'm terrified of meeting my Maker when my soul leaves this world. When He asks me, 'Zusia, what did you accomplish during your life?' I don't know what to tell Him."

His students hastened to reassure him that he had indeed lived a very holy and productive life, but Reb Zusia would not be consoled.

Instead he countered, "When God asks me, 'Zusia, why didn't you accomplish what your forefather Abraham did?' I'll know what to reply. I'll say, 'I wasn't Abraham.' And when He asks me, 'Zusia, why didn't you accomplish what Moses did?' I'll tell him, 'I wasn't Moses.' But when the Master of the Universe asks me, 'Zusia, why weren't you Zusia?'—for that, I have no answer."

If we want to live meaningful lives, at some point we must ask ourselves, "Why was I put here? What should I be accomplishing with my life? Am I living up to my potentials?"

Whatever the particulars of our responses, we should recognize the unique role that we can each play in the spiritual health of our people. The world cannot come to its ultimate goal unless we each make our personal contributions to this endeavor. As Esther did initially, we can try to convince ourselves that we have done enough, or that it is up to others to take care of communal needs. However, one of the lessons of Purim is that regardless of who we are, if we are Jewish, we will share in the destiny of the entire Jewish people. If we shirk our responsibilities to give of ourselves, then we have no right to share in our people's accomplishments, and we risk being spiritually annihilated in the process.

Perhaps God specifically put us here to give to others and to encourage those around us to do the same. Every day is a new opportunity to make yet another contribution to the spiritual destiny of our people. If we do not contribute to the world's upkeep, we are not entitled to take from it.

THE IMPORTANCE OF GIVING

Our sages suggest that people can be classified according to character types[4]:

> People have four attributes that characterize them. The first type of person says, "What is mine is mine, and what is yours is yours." This person is termed average, but there are those who say, "This is the attribute of the people of Sodom."
>
> The second type says, "What is mine is yours and what is yours is mine." This person is termed an ignoramus.

The third type says, "What is mine is yours and what is yours is yours." This is a pious person whose deeds are characterized by lovingkindness.

The fourth type says, "What is mine is mine and what is yours is mine." This person is termed wicked.

It seems logical that someone who wants everything for himself is wicked and that someone who keeps nothing for himself is pious. It is also reasonable that someone who confuses what is his with what belongs to someone else is a fool. It is perplexing, though, that someone who says, "What's mine is mine and what's yours is yours" is considered to be as wicked as the Sodomites, whom God destroyed.

Perhaps the reason for this is that Jews who feel that they do not have to share what they have are living only in order to serve themselves, not to fulfill the world's purpose by serving God.

Once Jews say, "I don't have to help others," they sever themselves from the Jewish people and from their national purpose. Grabbing what one could and turning a deaf ear to the needy were the hallmarks of Sodom. They believed that every person should go after what he wanted and not concern himself with anyone else.

When women choose their various life paths, they should ask how they can use their individual strengths to contribute to the world. What disrupts the harmony between different groups of women is when the various paths they choose reflect attitudes of, "What is mine is mine and what is yours is yours," or worse, "What is mine is mine and what is yours is mine."

When women model that they are here in order to take from the world rather than finding ways to contribute to it, disunity is likely to result. People are unified by mutual giving and are divided by taking. When we all serve God, we have one purpose in living. When we serve ourselves, we have as many goals as there are people.

Women are likely to have different perspectives about many aspects of life. Nevertheless, as long as we view ourselves as being here in order to make contributions, we can interact harmoniously and respectfully with one another. We will be united by continuing the work that our foremothers began and by forging links with our heritage, which dates back thousands of years.

Sarah played many roles in her life. She was a homemaker, a businesswoman, a dispenser of charity, a teacher, and the like. At the age of 90, she became a mother for the first time. She didn't say to God, "Listen, I'm an old woman. Give me a break. Let somebody else do Your work now." Every day of her life had meaning, whether she was baking bread, providing for her husband, son, and guests, or buying real estate. She viewed her every act as an opportunity to contribute something vital to the world. Everything she did left behind a legacy that would link her with generations of Jewish women who would follow.

BEING MERCIFUL AND COMPASSIONATE

The Talmud says that the hallmarks of a Jew are that we are "compassionate, modest, and do deeds of lovingkindness."[5] We are called "compassionate people who are children of compassionate people." If there is one quality that sets us apart from the rest of the world, it is our desire to emulate our Creator.

How do we do this? Just as God is merciful, we have to be merciful. Just as He is compassionate, we have to be compassionate. And just as He is giving, so do we have to imitate Him by giving. God gave us our good fortunes, talents, and life situations so that we could use them to make the world a better place, a place where He can dwell among us. If we have no place in our hearts for our fellow Jew, if we don't give charity, hospitality, and provide for communal needs, God says that there is no place for Him, either.

Every morning, we recite the following selection in the morning prayers:

> These are the things that one eats the fruits of in this world, but the capital remains to be enjoyed in the World-to-Come, and they are: Honoring parents, doing lovingkind deeds, going to the synagogue morning and evening, giving hospitality to guests, visiting the sick, making weddings for poor brides, burying the dead, praying intensively, and bringing peace between a man and his friend, and between a man and his wife. . . .[6]

There are many ways that we can, and should do these various acts in our personal and professional lives. When Torah-observant women decide to pursue careers, or are full-time mothers or housewives, we can ask ourselves, "How can I serve God and fulfill my role as a member of the Jewish people, given my talents and interests?" We shouldn't ask, "What do I want to do with my life?" and then try to fit God into it in our spare time.

We can always find reasons not to share what we have with others. There are many millionaires who protest, "I don't have enough money to give to charity" or who give in only the most meager ways. Even the poorest Jewish pauper who relies on public donations is required to give something to other poor people, even if he or she is unable to donate the usual ten percent of their income.

In a famous public lecture, Rabbi Moshe Feinstein pointed out that we must tithe our time as well as our money. Those who insist that they don't have time to help others can usually find time to pursue their own interests. Similarly, when a woman wants to give, she will find a way to do so. When she doesn't want to give, she will never have enough time or money to share.

If women want to establish true sisterhood, let us each take stock of our abilities and interests, and join together to make our contributions to the Jewish nation.

Some ways of doing this are by hosting guests on Sabbaths and holidays. On Passover, women can invite *seder* guests that include divorced women with their children, widows and widowers, older single women, and local college students. Women can also prepare and deliver food to poor Jews who would have nothing to eat for the holidays without their efforts.

Apart from women personally doing kind deeds for others, they can encourage others to do the same. Women have started and run many organizations that support needy Jews.

In recent years, women have been actively involved in helping Russian and Iranian refugees who have immigrated to the United States and Israel. We all have the capacity to give of our time, money and energies to others. We don't need lavish homes or superhuman skills in order to help others in a meaningful way. All it takes is our desire to want to help.

In many communities, interested individuals meet at a designated time every week and visit patients in local hospitals on *Shabbat* afternoons. Other groups visit patients during the week, when they can bring them flowers or home-made food to cheer them up.

Other women specifically invite unaffiliated Jews, or those who wish to know more about Judaism, to their homes on *Shabbat* and Jewish holidays. Jews from all walks of life, including beginners to traditional Judaism, join these families and learn about our religion. Guests often decide to become more observant because of the ongoing concern shown to them by such women in various communities.

When a Jew dies, women organize volunteers to cook and bring meals for the mourners. They also arrange for shifts of friends to comfort the mourners every day during the week of *shivah*.

These types of activities are not only for the young. Women devotedly teach hundreds of students, even when they are senior citizens. They work as communal volunteers, organize Torah classes for the community, visit the sick, comfort mourners, and collect money and run projects for the needy.

No matter what form our activities take, we can create a true sisterhood by giving of ourselves to others, and thereby serve God in yet one more way.

18

Making Life Meaningful

One of the most remarkable aspects of Judaism is that it touches every facet of human existence, from the most mundane to the most esoteric. There is no realm of life about which Judaism has no opinion. All of our actions, even those about which we might not give a second thought, have moral and metaphysical consequences.

Our bodies limit us to a physical existence that spans less than a century. In the scheme of universal existence, each of us may seem to be existentially insignificant. Earth is but one of many planets in the solar system, and our solar system is in but one of many galaxies. We may feel miniscule in the context of the entire universe. We weren't here 100 years ago, and we probably won't be here in another hundred. We could easily feel that we are mere drops in a cosmic bucket.

Judaism teaches us how to transcend our mortality so that we do not merely die and wither away. We can each make a mark on the world that will last forever and not disappear once our bodies are gone and our deeds are forgotten by successive generations.

Judaism teaches us how to invest life with infinite meaning, how to take our basest instincts and make them holy and pure, and how to take the trivial and make it Godly. Our every act, thought, and word can elevate our soul and connect us to the Infinite Source.

The Torah teaches us that although our bodies are mortal, finite, and time-limited, we are greater than our physical beings. We each possess not only a body, but a soul, which is a direct extension of God's essence. Therefore, we can transcend our animalistic drives, our sensual desires, our emotional needs, and the limits of our intellects. We can achieve greatness by elevating our physical and emotional drives and by using our free will to serve God.

No aspect of our lives needs to be mundane. How we dress, speak, eat, and even how we engage in sexual relations can be made so holy that we can draw down the Divine Presence. When we follow God's will, we become partners with Him in fulfilling His purpose in creating the world. He started the process, but how much He manifests Himself to the world depends on how fully we recognize His involvement in every aspect of our existence. For this reason, God's purpose in creating and running the world remains incomplete as long as we do not acknowledge His involvement in our daily lives. We allow God's *raison d'être* for the world to be fulfilled, and complete His task of creation every time we do what He asks of us. In this way, our every act, whether it seems major or minor, has cosmic significance. If we do what God wants, we can bring the entire universe one step closer to redemption.

THE MESSIANIC ERA

At some point in the future, one of two situations will occur: either the Jews will live the way that God has asked of them, or they will have failed to do so. At that time, the world will reach its final stage of existence and the Messiah will come. After that happens, all humanity will clearly see God's Presence in all aspects of life.

None of our actions are meaningless or affect only us if we choose to connect them to infinity and holiness – that is, to that which is God's will. We can invest our every act with holiness and cosmic significance, while simultaneously affecting the soul of the entire Jewish people. Or, we can choose to defy God's will and thereby damage the entire world.

Besides having our individual souls, the entire Jewish people shares a common soul. Just as damaging an arm, a leg, or any other limb of our body affects the rest of us, so it is with the Jewish people. It is impossible for us to do any deed that doesn't affect the collective soul and destiny of the entire Jewis nation. Our every deed affects the entire realization (or hampering) of God's plan for the world.

BEING ALL WE CAN BE

Torah-observant Judaism tells us how to make our lives meaningful by perfecting the world. Since we each possess a soul that is holy and immortal, whatever we do to develop our spiritual sensitivities will not be eradicated when we die. Furthermore, we know that whatever we do affects not only ourselves. Our every word and deed, even in private, and even where no one is tangibly affected by it, has positive or negative consequences for the entire Jewish people.

Living fully as a Jew in order to lead a richer, more meaningful life is not always easy. The Ethics of the Fathers says, "The task is a difficult task, and the day is short. . . . You are not obligated to finish the work, but neither are you free to desist from trying."[1]

Our tradition tells us that in every generation, there are righteous women in whose merit the entire Jewish people are worthy of being redeemed. Women need to be intellectually and spiritually honest as they grapple with the challenges of being observant Jews. We can, and should realize our tremendous potentials and grow to greater emotional and spiritual heights in the process. May our actions soon bring our long-awaited redemption of the Jewish people.

Notes

INTRODUCTION

1. Exodus 6:6–7.

CHAPTER 2

1. Genesis 1:27; 2:7; 2:15–25.
2. Genesis 1:27.
3. *Eruvin* 18a.
4. *Berachot* 61a.
5. Genesis 2:7.
6. Genesis 2:15–17.
7. Radak on Genesis 1:26; *Pirkei d'Rabbi Eliezer* 12.
8. S. R. Hirsch on Genesis 1:26.
9. S. R. Hirsch on Genesis 1:26.
10. Sforno on Genesis 2:18.
11. Genesis 2:18.
12. *Torah Temimah* on Genesis 2:18.
13. Genesis 2:19–20.
14. Raavad on Genesis 2:19.

15. Sforno on Genesis 2:19.
16. See Malbim on Genesis 2:18; Rashi on Genesis 2:20.
17. Genesis 2:21.
18. Sforno on Genesis 2:20.
19. Genesis 2:22.
20. *Niddah* 45b.
21. Genesis 2:23–24.
22. Genesis *Rabbah* 17.
23. S. R. Hirsch on Genesis 2:24.
24. Rashi on Genesis 2:24.
25. *Pirkei d'Rabbi Eliezer* 34.
26. S. R. Hirsch on Genesis 2:22.
27. See *Yevamot* 63a.
28. Genesis *Rabbah* 8:10; *Pirkei d'Rabbi Eliezer* 12.
29. For example, see Genesis 49:25.
30. *Pirkei d'Rabbi Eliezer* on Genesis 2:23.
31. Genesis 3:1.
32. Rashi on Genesis 3:1.
33. Genesis 3:4.
34. Genesis *Rabbah* 19.
35. *Ha-Emek Davar* on Genesis 3:4.
36. Genesis 3:5.
37. Genesis *Rabbah* 19.
38. S. R. Hirsch on Genesis 3:4.
39. Genesis 3:6.
40. Rashi on Genesis 3:6.
41. Genesis *Rabbah* 14:4.
42. Genesis *Rabbah* 20:8.
43. Rabbi Dessler on Genesis 3.
44. Rashi on *Sanhedrin* 70b.
45. Genesis *Rabbah* 15:7.
46. Genesis *Rabbah* 15:7.
47. *Shabbat* 55b.
48. Sforno on Genesis 3:6.
49. Genesis *Rabbah* 20.
50. Rashi on Genesis 4:1.
51. Rashi on Genesis 4:1; Genesis *Rabbah* 22:4.
52. Genesis 3:16.
53. *Eruvin* 100b.
54. Nachmanides on Genesis 3:16.

55. Rashi on Genesis 3:16.
56. *Me'am Loez* on Genesis 3:17–19.
57. Rabbi Dovid Cohen on Genesis 3:16.
58. *Ha-Emek Davar* on Genesis 3:20.
59. Malbim on Genesis 3:20.
60. Rabbi Dovid Cohen on Genesis 3:20.
61. Genesis *Rabbah* on Genesis 3:20.
62. Isaiah 34:14.
63. *Eruvin* 100b; *Niddah* 24b; *Bava Batra* 73b; *Shabbat* 151b.

CHAPTER 3

1. S. R. Hirsch on Genesis 1:24.
2. See Genesis *Rabbah* 17 and 18:2.
3. Rashi on *Kiddushin* 35a.
4. Psalm 34:15.
5. *Mishnah Kiddushin* 29a.
6. Genesis 2:22.
7. *Niddah* 45b.
8. Exodus 31:3.
9. The following are some of the 613 biblical commandments that are generally applicable to contemporary women who live in the Diaspora. [For a fuller listing and explanation, please see *The Concise Book of Mitzvot,* compiled by the Chafetz Chaim (New York: Feldheim, 1990)]: To believe that there is one God; to love and fear Him; to sanctify His Name, and do nothing that would desecrate His Name; to walk in His ways; to pray to Him; not to make, own, benefit from, or worship idols in any way; to say grace after meals; to rise before an old person, and to honor a Torah scholar and a cohen (priest); to revere God's sanctuary; to observe the Sabbath by refraining from forbidden creative activity and to sanctify it with words; to rejoice on the festivals, and to refrain from forbidden creative activity on all holy days, including the first and last day of Passover, as well as on Succot, Shavuot, Shemini Atzeret, Rosh Hashanah, and Yom Kippur; to not eat or possess leaven on Passover; to fast on the Day of Atonement; to repent from and confess one's misdeeds before God; to give charity and lend money to the Jewish poor; to honor and fear one's parents, and refrain from cursing or striking them; to love every Jew, especially converts, as oneself, and to refrain from shaming them; to eat meat only if it has been ritually slaughtered and the

thigh-vein removed; to eat only permitted animals, fowl, and fish, and only if the blood of animals and fowl has been removed; not to eat dairy with meat foods; to return what one finds that belongs to a Jew; to remember what Amalek did to us; not to marry Gentiles; not to swear in vain or falsely; not to murder, kidnap, or steal; not to give false testimony; not to covet what belongs to another person; not to oppress the convert, orphan, or widow; to be honest in business; not to loan or borrow money from a Jew with interest.

10. N. Lamm, *A Hedge of Roses* (Jerusalem: Feldheim, 1977), p. 76.
11. Avudraham.
12. Maharal, *Drush Al Ha-Torah.*
13. Chafetz Chaim in *Chomat Ha-Dat.*
14. *Midrash Tanchuma* 2.
15. Numbers 15:17–21.
16. *Shulchan Aruch,* Chapter 242; *Mishnah Berurah, Se'ef Katan* 6.
17. Ezekiel 44:30.

CHAPTER 4

1. *Mei Shiloach.*
2. Paraphrased from Genesis 21:9–12.
3. Rashi on Genesis 21:12.
4. Paraphrased from Genesis 27:1–19.
5. Genesis 29:18–27.
6. *Megillah* 13b.
7. Rashi on Genesis 29:34.
8. Genesis 29:31–30:15.
9. Genesis *Rabbah* 72; see Rashi on Genesis 30:24.
10. *Yoma* 9b.
11. Introduction to *Midrash Rabbah* on Lamentations, paragraph 24.
12. Genesis 22:1–19.
13. *Berachot* 60a.
14. Genesis 34:1–2.
15. Genesis *Rabbah* 76.
16. Genesis 38:12–30.
17. *Iggerot Moshe,* vol. 7, p. 168.
18. Rashi on Exodus 38:8.
19. *Sotah* 11b.
20. Exodus 1:15–19.
21. Exodus 2:2–10.

22. *Shemot Rabbah* 28:2.
23. *Pirkei d'Rabbi Eliezer,* Chapter 44.
24. *Shulchan Aruch* 419:1.
25. Leviticus 22:32.
26. Judges, Chapter 4.
27. *Megillah* 14a.
28. *Yalkut Shimoni.*
29. *Nazir* 23b.
30. *Sanhedrin* 7a.
31. Judges 5:24.
32. Judges 5:7.
33. *Me'am Loez* on Judges 5:7.
34. Abarbanel on Judges 5:7.
35. Metzudat David on Judges 5:7.
36. Rashi on 1 Kings 2:19.
37. *Mishnah Avot* 1:2.

CHAPTER 5

1. Deuteronomy 11:13.
2. *Taanit* 2a.
3. Leviticus *Rabbah* 24:6.
4. Leviticus 19:30.
5. *Megillah* 29a.
6. *Mishnah Avot* 5:5.
7. *Mishnah Sukkah* 51b.
8. *Succah* 51b.
9. Zechariah 12:12.
10. Jerusalem Talmud, *Succah* 5, *halachah* 2.
11. 1 Chronicles 28:10–12, 19.
12. *Mishneh Torah, Hilchot Bet Ha-Bechirah,* Chapter 5, law 9.
13. Commentary on *Mishnah Succah,* Chapter 5, *Mishnah* 2.
14. *Iggerot Moshe, Orech Chaim,* vols. 39 and 42.
15. J. B. Soloveitchik, "On seating and sanctification," *The Sanctity of the Synagogue,* ed. B. Litvin (New York: Ktav, 1987), pp. 115–116.
16. Samuel S. Cohen, "Reform Judaism," in *Jewish Life in America,* ed. Freedman and Gordis, p. 86.

CHAPTER 6

1. S. R. Hirsch, *Horeb,* trans. Dayan Grunfeld (London: Soncino Press, 1981), vol. 2, pp. 472–473.

2. 1 Kings 8:39.
3. Rashi on 1 Kings 8:43.
4. *Berachot* 29b.
5. Chaim Volozhin, *Nefesh Ha-Chaim,* Gate 1.

CHAPTER 7

1. Rashi on Deuteronomy 33:18; Rashi on *Mishnah Zevachim* 2a; *Sotah* 21a.
2. Genesis 49:10.
3. 2 Chronicles 26:16–22; *Sanhedrin* 48b.
4. E.g., Rashi on *Pesachim* 46a and *Chullin* 122b.
5. Nachmanides, *Milchamot Ha-Shem* to *Megillah* 5a.
6. *Mishnah Sanhedrin* 4:5.
7. Rabbi Mordecai Tendler on Tractate *Betzah.*
8. See *Sefer Ha-Chinuch, Mitzvah* 296 and *Minchat Chinuch* there.
9. 1 Samuel 1.
10. Leviticus 9:1–10:3.
11. Biur Halachah on *Shulchan Aruch* 98:3.
12. *Shulchan Aruch* 106:1.
13. Magen Avraham on *Shulchan Aruch* 106:1.
14. See Maimonides, *Hilchot Tefillah* 1:1–3.
15. Mishnah Brurah to *Orech Chaim* 106:1.
16. *Orech Chaim* 70:1.
17. *Tanna D'vei Eliyahu Zuta* 17.

CHAPTER 8

1. *Bava Metzia* 38a.
2. Genesis 3:1.
3. Genesis 3:4.
4. Genesis 3:5.
5. Genesis 3:5.
6. Rashi on Genesis 3:5.

CHAPTER 9

1. Genesis 3:7–11.
2. Micah 6:8.
3. *Shulchan Aruch,* vol. 1, 3:1.

4. See *Avodah Zarah* 47b and *Berachot* 62a.
5. See commandment #22 in the listing of constant commandments in the Preface to the Book of Psalms.
6. Exodus 25:8.
7. Micah 6:8.
8. Proverbs 11:2.
9. Genesis *Rabbah* 17 and 18.
10. *Niddah* 45b.
11. *Shulchan Aruch, Even Ha-Ezer* 21:1; *Mishnah Berurah* 75:7.
12. *Shulchan Aruch, Orech Chaim* 75:1; *Mishnah Berurah* there.
13. *Mishnah Berurah* 75:2.
14. *Ketuvot* 72a; Bet Shmuel, *Even Ha-Ezer* 21:5.
15. Y. Fuchs, *Halichos Bas Yisrael,* Oak Park, MI: Targum Press, 1985, p. 72.
16. Minchat Yitzchak, vol. 2, no. 108.
17. *Shulchan Aruch, Even Ha-Ezer* 21:1, based on *Berachot* 24a.
18. Beer Sheva, *Kuntres Beer Mayim Chaim.*
19. Genesis 2:7.

CHAPTER 10

1. S. R. Hirsch on Exodus 22:16.
2. S. R. Hirsch on Exodus 22:15; *Masechta Kallah Rabati* 3; Rashi, *Midrash Ha-Gadol* on Genesis 49:9.
3. Tosefta, *Ketuvot* 12:1.
4. *Ketuvot* 7a; *Shulchan Aruch, Even Ha-Ezer* 66:1.
5. Rabbi Meir, *Ketuvot* 57a.
6. *Ketuvot* 10a.
7. *Mishneh Torah,* Chapter 12, sections 1–8.
8. *Mishneh Torah,* Chapter 13, sections 1–5, 11.
9. *Mishneh Torah,* Chapter 14, sections 1, 2.
10. Rashi, *Yevamot* 66a.
11. Aryeh Kaplan, *Made in Heaven.* New York: Maznaim Publishing Corp., 1983, pp. 95–122.
12. *Iggerot Moshe, Even Ha-Ezer,* vol. 4, Chapter 91.
13. *Ketuvot* 64b.
14. *Hachalat Shivah* 12:49:3.
15. Courtesy of Rabbi Moshe Tendler.
16. Courtesy of Rabbi Moshe Tendler.

CHAPTER 11

1. *Shabbat* 112b; *Eruvin* 53a; *Yerushalmi, Shekalim* 13b.
2. Genesis 4:1.
3. Leviticus 15:19.
4. Leviticus 18:19.
5. *Kiddushin* 30b.
6. *Iggeret Ha-Kodesh,* quoted by Maimonides, ed. Chavel, 2:336.
7. *Niddah* 71a; Rashi on *Niddah* 31b; *Eruvin* 100b; *Chagigah* 5b.
8. *Nedarim* 20b; *Eruvin* 100b.
9. *Gittin* 90a; Maimonides on *Gerushin* 10:21.
10. *Niddah* 31b.
11. Even if a couple is unable to conceive, the commandment to observe the laws of family purity still applies. This specific aspect, however, is irrelevant.
12. Genesis 2:10–14.
13. A. Kaplan, *Waters of Eden* (New York: Union of Orthodox Jewish Congregations of America, 1982), p. 13.

CHAPTER 12

1. Genesis 9:7; see Rashi on *Ketuvot* 5a.
2. Abarbanel on Genesis 1:28.
3. *Sefer Ha-Chinuch, mitzvah* #1.
4. *Yevamot* 63b.
5. *Yevamot* 6:6.
6. Genesis 1:27.
7. *Yevamot* 62a.
8. Isaiah 45:18.
9. Ecclesiastes 11:6.
10. *Yevamot* 62b.
11. *Mishneh Torah, Hilchot Ishut,* 15, 16.
12. Tosefta on *Yevamot* 8:2.
13. *Isurei Biah* 21:26.
14. *Yevamot* 65b.
15. Meshech Chochmah on Genesis 9:1.
16. *Chidushei Haran* on *Kiddushin* 41a.
17. *Aruch Ha-Shulchan, Yoreh Deah* 246.
18. *Bava Batra* 9a.
19. *Yevamot* 62a.

20. Isaiah 38:1.
21. *Berachot* 10a.
22. *Time* Magazine, Dec. 18, 1989.
23. Psalm 145:16.
24. *Rosh Hashanah* 1:5; *Yevamot* 62b–63b; cf. Rashi ad locum.
25. *Shulchan Aruch, Even Ha-Ezer* 1, 3, and 8; Maimonides, *Hilchot Deot* 5:11.
26. S. C. Aviner, "Family Planning and Contraception," in *Assia* (Jerusalem: Rubin Mass), vol. 4, 1983, pp. 167–181.
27. Weisz, *Responsa Minchat Yitzchak:* vol. 1, #100:3 and 115; vol. 3, #25:5 and 261–263; vol. 4, #120; vol. 5, #100–103; vol. 6, #144. *Iggerot Moshe, Even Ha-Ezer,* vol. 1, Chapter 63; vol. 2, Chapter 12. Waldenberg, *Responsa Tzitz Eliezer,* vol. 10, sec. 25, part 10.
28. I. Jakobovits, "Medicine and Judaism – An Overview," in *Assia* (Jerusalem: Rubin Mass), 1983, pp. 289–310.
29. Maimonides, positive commandment #213.
30. Based on Exodus 21:10.
31. Nimukai Yosef on *Yevamot,* Chapter 5.
32. *Pesachim* 72b.
33. Rabbi Chaim Sofer, *Responsa Mahaneh Chaim* (Pressburg, 1862), #53.
34. Genesis 2:24.
35. *Yevamot* 12b.
36. Psalm 116:6.
37. I. Jakobovits, *Jewish Medical Ethics,* 2nd ed. (New York: Bloch, 1975), p. 389.
38. Luria, *Yam Shel Shlomo, Yevamot* 1:8.
39. Sofer, *Responsa,* no. 53.
40. *Ketuvot* 39a.
41. Song of Songs 8:6.
42. *Iggerot Moshe, Even Ha-Ezer,* vol. 1, Chapters 62 and 65.
43. D. Feldman, *Marital Relations, Birth Control and Abortion in Jewish Law.* (New York: Schocken Books, 1989), p. 128.
44. *Responsa Ezrat Kohen* (Jerusalem: Mossad Rav Kuk, 1969), no. 35, p. 138.
45. Uziel, *Responsa Mishpitei Uziel,* vol. 3, *Choshen Mishpat* #51.
46. Jakobovits, "Medicine and Judaism," pp. 289–310.
47. Waldenberg, *Responsa Tzitz Eliezer,* vol. 9, #51:2–3.
48. See D. Feldman, *Marital Relations, Birth Control and Abortion in Jewish Law* (New York: Schocken Books, 1989), p. 231.
49. *Iggerot Moshe, Even Ha-Ezer,* no. 63.

50. Feinstein, "Women in Whom Pregnancy Is Dangerous to Life," in *Halachah Urefuah,* ed. M. Hershler (Jerusalem: Regensberg Institute, 1980), vol. 1, pp. 328–331.
51. This is based on Leviticus 22:24.
52. Tosefta on *Yevamot,* Chapter 8.
53. *Responsa Chatam Sofer, Even Ha-Ezer,* no. 20.
54. Maimonides, *Mishneh Torah, Hilchot Isurei Biyah* 21:18; *Teshuvot Ha-Rosh* 33:3; Karo, *Shulchan Aruch, Even Ha-Ezer* 23:5.
55. *Iggerot Moshe, Even Ha-Ezer,* loc. cit., p. 162.
56. Exodus 21:10.
57. *Iggerot Moshe, Even Ha-Ezer,* no. 102.
58. *Shabbat* 110b, based on Leviticus 22:24.

CHAPTER 13

1. *Mishnah Sanhedrin,* Chapter 4, *mishnah* 5.
2. Genesis 9:6.
3. *Sanhedrin* 57b.
4. *Responsa Koach Shorr,* vol. 1, no. 20, 1755; *Responsa Maharit,* nos. 97 and 99.
5. Exodus 21:22–23.
6. Mechilta, Exodus 21:12; *Sanhedrin* 84a.
7. *Sanhedrin* 84b.
8. *Iggerot Moshe, Choshen Mishpat,* vol. 2, Chapters 69 and 70.
9. B. T. Frankel, *Responsa Ateret Chachamim, Even Ha-Ezer,* #1; Emden, *She'elat Yaavetz,* pt. 1, #43.
10. J. Rosen, *Responsa Tzafnat Paneach,* pt. 1, #49.
11. Mizrachi on Exodus 21:12.
12. S. Drimmer, *Responsa Bet Shlomo, Choshen Mishpat,* #132.
13. Deuteronomy 25:3.
14. J. Trani, *Responsa Maharit,* pt. 1, #99; Zweig, in *Noam* 7 (1964):36–56.
15. On *Shemot* 3b.
16. *Time* Magazine, July 2, 1990, p. 23.
17. *Arachin* 7a.
18. *Yevamot* 69b.
19. *Keritot* 1:3–6.
20. A. Lifschutz, *Responsa Aryeh Debei Ilay, Yoreh Deah,* no. 19; E. Deutsch, *Responsa Pri Ha-Sadeh,* pt. 4, no. 50.

21. Yosef Chaim ben Eliyahu, *Responsa Rav Paalim, Even Ha-Ezer*, #4.
22. B. Z. Uziel, *Responsa Mishpetet Uziel, Choshen Mishpat*, pt. 3, #46.
23. I. M. Mizrachi, *Pri Ha-Aretz, Yoreh Deah*, #21.
24. N. Z. Friedman, *Responsa Netzer Metaat*, pt. 1, #8; Feinstein, *Iggerot Moshe, Orech Chaim*, pt. 4, #88.
25. Emden, *Responsa She'elat Yaavetz*, pt. 1, #43; *Iggerot Moshe, Choshen Mishpat*, vol. 2, Chapters 69 and 70.
26. M. Y. Kaufmann, *Kunteres Acharon*, #19, p. 58b.
27. Y. Emden, *She'elat Yaavetz*, pt. 1, #30; B. Z. Uziel, *Mishpatei Uziel, Choshen Mishpat*, pt. 3, #46.
28. J. Strangel, *The New Fertility and Conception* (New York: Plume, 1988), p. 1.
29. According to literature published by EFRAT, the Jewish Association for Birth Encouragement.
30. M. Feinstein, *Ha-Pardes*, Nissan 5738.
31. Waldenberg, *Tzitz Eliezer*, pt. 9, p. 237.
32. Unterman, *Noam*, vol. 6, pp. 1–11.
33. M. Y. Zweig, *Noam*, vol. 7, pp. 36–56.
34. I. Jakobovitz, *Journal of a Rabbi* (New York: Living Books, 1966), pp. 262–266.
35. R. J. Rosen, *Tzafnat Paneach*, #59.

CHAPTER 14

1. *Yevamot* 62b.
2. *Yevamot* 63b.
3. *Gittin* 90b.
4. Malachi 2:13–14.
5. *Kiddushin* 2b.
6. Meiselman, *Jewish Woman in Jewish Law* (New York: Ktav, 1978), pp. 98–99.
7. Deuteronomy 24:1–2.
8. *Shulchan Aruch, Even Ha-Ezer* 154.

CHAPTER 15

1. Rashi on Genesis 11:29.
2. Rashi on Genesis 21:12.
3. *Seder Eliyahu Rabbah* 9.
4. *Seder Olam*, Chapter 21.

5. Genesis 11:2.
6. Exodus 15:20.
7. Judges 4:4.
8. 2 Kings 22:14.
9. 1 Samuel 1.
10. 1 Samuel 25.
11. *Megillat Esther.*
12. Genesis 12:14–20.
13. Genesis 21:10, 12.
14. Proverbs 31:10–31.
15. *Midrash Tanchuma* on *Chayei Sarah.*
16. Genesis *Rabbah* 60.
17. Rashi.
18. Genesis *Rabbah* 60.
19. Genesis 23.
20. Genesis 22:9–12.
21. Rashi on Genesis 23:2.
22. Genesis 23.
23. Genesis 23:4–20.
24. Genesis 23:1.
25. Genesis *Rabbah* 58.

CHAPTER 16

1. *Sofrim* 10:6.
2. Remah on *Yoreh Deah* 81:7.
3. *Magen Avraham* 343:1; *Kaf Ha-Chaim* 225:14.
4. *Shulchan Aruch, Orech Chaim* 91:3.
5. *Biur Halachah* 75.

CHAPTER 17

1. Esther 4:13–14.
2. Genesis 3:15.
3. Morning prayer service.
4. *Mishnah Avot* 5:13.
5. *Yevamot* 79a.
6. *Shabbat* 127a.

CHAPTER 18

1. *Mishnah Avot* 2:21.

For Further Reading

Abramov, S., and Touger, M. *The Secret of Jewish Femininity*. Brooklyn: Eishes Chayil Publications, 1988.

Donin, H. *To Pray as a Jew*. New York: Basic Books, 1980.

Epstein, M. *A Woman's Guide to the Get Process*. Jerusalem, 1989.

Feldbrand, S. *From Sarah to Sarah*. Brooklyn: Eishes Chayil Books, 1980.

Feldman, D. *Marital Relations, Birth Control and Abortion in Jewish Law*. New York: Schocken Books, 1989.

Fuchs, Y. *Halichos Bas Yisrael*. Vol. 1. Oak Park, MI: Targum Press, 1985.

Jacobson, B. S. *Meditations on the Siddur*. Tel Aviv: Sinai Publishing, 1966.

Kaplan, A. *Jewish Meditation*. New York: Schocken Books, 1985.

_____ *Made in Heaven*. New York: Maznaim Publishing Corp., 1983.

_____ *Waters of Eden*. New York: Union of Orthodox Jewish Congregations of America, 1982.

Kirzner, Y., and Aiken, L. *The Art of Jewish Prayer*. Northvale, NJ: Jason Aronson Inc., 1991.

Lamm, N. *A Hedge of Roses*. Jerusalem: Feldheim, 1977.

Litvin, B. *The Sanctity of the Synagogue*. New York: Ktav, 1987.

Meiselman, M. *Jewish Woman in Jewish Law*. New York: Ktav, 1978.

Munk, E. *The World of Prayer*. Jerusalem: Feldheim, 1963.

Rosner, F. *Modern Medicine and Jewish Ethics.* New York: Yeshiva University Press, 1986.

Rosner, F., and Bleich, J. *Jewish Bioethics.* New York: Sanhedrin Press, 1979.

Tendler, M. *Pardes Rimonim.* Hoboken, NJ: Ktav, 1988.

Index

ABOUT THE AUTHOR

Lisa Aiken received her Ph.D in clinical psychology from Loyola University in Chicago. A psychologist in private practice, she is the co-author of *The Art of Jewish Prayer* with Yitzchok Kirzner, as well as a public speaker and writer on topics of Jewish interest.

Temple Israel

Minneapolis, Minnesota

IN MEMORY OF
DAVID HINITZ
WILLIAM & GOLDIE SCHNITZER
FROM
MARCIA HINITZ